The Rediscovered Writings of Veza Canetti

Studies in German Literature, Linguistics, and Culture

The Rediscovered Writings of Veza Canetti

Out of the Shadows of a Husband

Julian Preece

CAMDEN HOUSE
Rochester, New York

First published 2007
by Camden House

Camden House is an imprint of Boydell & Brewer Inc.
668 Mt. Hope Avenue, Rochester, NY 14620, USA
www.camden-house.com
and of Boydell & Brewer Limited
PO Box 9, Woodbridge, Suffolk IP12 3DF, UK
www.boydellandbrewer.com

ISBN-13: 978–1–57113–353–3
ISBN-10: 1–57113–353–4

Library of Congress Cataloging-in-Publication Data

Preece, Julian.
    The rediscovered writings of Veza Canetti: out of the shadows of a
husband / Julian Preece
    p. cm. — (Studies in German literature, linguistics, and culture)
Includes bibliographical references and index.
ISBN-13: 978–1–57113–353–3 (hardcover: alk. paper)
ISBN-10: 1–57113–353–4 (hardcover: alk. paper)
    1. Canetti, Veza, 1897–1963.   2. Authors, Austrian—20th century—
Biography. I. Title. II. Series.
PT2605.A588Z8 2007
833′.912–dc22
[B]   2006034120

A catalogue record for this title is available from the British Library.

This publication is printed on acid-free paper.
Printed in the United States of America.

For Pippa
who writes books too

Contents

Acknowledgments

M ANY COLLEAGUES AND FRIENDS have contributed with advice, information, and encouragement. My thanks go to Ritchie Robertson for
recommending I embark on the project; to Peter Conradi, Sven
Hanuschek, and Angelika Schedel for generously sharing their knowledge;
to Eckart Früh at the Stadt- und Landesbibliothek in Vienna; to Jeremy
Adler, Elaine Morley, Jonny Redding, Hamish Ritchie, and the librarians
at the much missed Institute of Germanic Studies. Renate Carey, Milein
Cosman, Rosemary Knight (née Scheuer), the late Rudi Nassauer, and
Derek and Suse Underwood all shared their memories of the Canettis with
me. My research in Vienna, at the Deutsches Literaturarchiv in Marbach,
and at the Zurich Zentralbibliothek was funded by a travel grant from the
British Academy. George Stern kindly read my finished manuscript and
made many useful suggestions.

J. P.
September 2006

A Note on Names

VEZA CANETTI PUBLISHED UNDER a variety of pseudonyms, Veza Magd (meaning maid) being her clear favorite, but her real name was Venetiana or Venezia Taubner-Calderon when her stories began to be published in 1932. She became Veza Canetti on marrying Elias in February 1934, but everyone always called her Veza. Elias Canetti, on the other hand, could not abide his first name and insisted that he be called by his second. For these reasons and for the sake of clarity, I refer to them throughout as Veza and Canetti.

Abbreviations and Translations

I HAVE TRANSLATED ALL THE GERMAN quotations myself, sometimes building on the published English versions. With the exceptions of some of his late "jottings" (Aufzeichnungen), all Elias Canetti's books are available in English. Veza's *Yellow Street* and *The Tortoises* have been translated by Ian Mitchell and are published by New Directions, New York (1991 and 2001 respectively). *The Ogre* is translated by Richard Dixon in *Anthology of Austrian Folk Plays* (Riverside, CA: Ariadne, 1993). I have translated the other stories she published in her lifetime for the Ariadne Press as *The Viennese Short Stories* (forthcoming).

ZB   = Zentralbibliothek (Zurich), followed by a number, refers to the box in which the papers are held in the Canetti Archive.
DLA   = Deutsches Literaturarchiv (Marbach).

Veza and Canetti

BG   *Briefe an Georges.* Edited by Karen Lauer and Kristian Wachinger. Munich: Hanser, 2006.

Veza

WK   Introduction to *Welt im Kopf.* Vienna: Stiasny, 1962.
GS   *Die gelbe Strasse.* Munich: Hanser, 1990. (*Yellow Street*, 1991).
DO   *Der Oger.* Munich: Hanser, 1991. (*The Ogre*, 1993).
GbR   *Geduld bringt Rosen.* Munich: Hanser, 1992. (Patience Brings Roses).
SK   *Die Schildkröten.* Munich: Hanser, 1999. (*The Tortoises*, 2001).
DF   *Der Fund.* Munich: Hanser, 2001. (*The Find*).
TK   "Schweigegeld" (Hush Money) and "Geld — Geld — Geld" (Money — Money — Money), in *Text und Kritik* 156 (Veza Canetti issue) (2002).

Canetti

I refer to the complete edition of his works published by Hanser (1992–2005). Volume and page numbers follow each quotation.

I: *Die Blendung* (*Auto-da-Fé.* Trans. C. V. Wedgwood. New York: Stein and Day, 1946).

II:	*Hochzeit* (*Wedding*), *Komödie der Eitelkeit* (*Comedy of Vanity.* Trans. Gitta Honegger. New York: Performing Arts Journal Publications, 1983), *Die Befristeten* (*The Numbered.* Trans. Carol Stewart. London: Martin Boyars, 1984), *Der Ohrenzeuge* (*The Ear-Witness.* Trans. Joachim Neugroschel. London: Deutsch, 1979).
III:	*Masse und Macht* (*Crowds and Power.* Trans. Carol Stewart. London: Victor Gollancz, 1962).
VI:	*Die Stimmen von Marrakesch: Aufzeichnungen nach einer Reise* (*The Voices of Marrakesh: a Record of a Visit.* Trans. J. A. Underwood. London: M. Boyar, 1978), *Das Gewissen der Worte: Essays* (*The Conscience of Words. Essays.* Trans. Joachim Neugroschel. New York: Seabury, 1979).
VII:	*Die gerettete Zunge* (*The Tongue Set Free: Remembrance of a European Childhood.* Trans. Joachim Neugroschel. New York: Seabury, 1979).
VIII:	*Die Fackel im Ohr* (*The Torch in My Ear.* Trans. Joachim Neugroschel. New York: Farrar, Straus, and Giroux, 1982).
IX:	*Das Augenspiel* (*The Play of the Eyes.* Trans. Ralph Manheim. New York: Farrar, Straus, Giroux, 1986).
X:	*Aufsätze, Reden und Gespräche* (*Essays, Speeches and Interviews*).

Also

Aufzeichnungen 1992–1993 (Frankfurt am Main: Fischer, 1996). (*Jottings 1992–1993*).

Party im Blitz (Munich: Hanser, 2003). (*Party in the Blitz: The English Years.* Trans. Michael Hofman. New York: New Directions, 2005).

Introduction

I FIRST CAME ACROSS Elias Canetti's autobiography fifteen years ago when working on a paper about German writers whose lives were turned upside down by the events of the last century. I still find *The Tongue set Free* and the two volumes that followed to be the most exciting of his big books. His account of a childhood among Spanish-speaking Jews in pre-1914 Bulgaria, of his family's moves, first to Manchester in defiance of his paternal grandfather, to Vienna after the sudden death of his young father, from there to the haven of Switzerland, and then to Frankfurt during the great inflation add powerful historical details to this essentially lyrical book. Canetti's early life is his legend and it belongs to a world that has been obliterated by the wars and exterminations of the twentieth century. He practiced telling it long before he wrote it down. But the real focus of this strangely secretive confession is his battle with a very powerful woman — his mother — who, despite her love of literature, set her heart on thwarting his ambition to become a writer, that is a *Dichter*, who would take his own place in the European tradition that she had taught him to love. After her literary romance with his father ended with Jacques Canetti's unexpected death, she made their eldest son into her precociously bookish confidante and he decided to become a writer just to please her. She turned against him, perhaps in horror at her own creation. The conflict both made and broke him: the wounds she inflicted never healed.

The fourteen-year-old Canetti dedicated a play to his mother on her birthday, which is set in ancient Rome and treats his own Oedipal admiration. He signed it *in spe poeta clarus* ("hoping the poet's meaning is clear," *VII*:240), but, like Kafka's father, who left his son's written offering on a bedside table with the promise to look at it later, she did not comment. It was only on her deathbed that Mathilde gave her blessing to his woman-hating novel, *Auto-da-Fé*, and predicted correctly that he would have success with the opposite sex on account of the misogyny contained in it. Other literary and artistic women played important roles in Canetti's private life once he settled in Vienna, the city where his parents' love blossomed. In 1925, as he turned twenty, Veza Taubner-Calderon, a part-time English teacher and translator, took on his mother's role of teacher, muse, and partner in discussion. She was already twenty-eight, only twelve years younger than Mathilde, whose friend she had at first been. The two women had much in common, particularly their contempt for their fellow Sepharadim, Jews of Spanish origin who now congregated in Vienna's second district, the Leopoldstadt. For both women, these immigrants were uncouth and lacked appreciation of European literature. But their brief friendship could not survive Veza's affair with Mathilde's son and they never spoke to each other again.

By 1992 it was impossible not to notice that there was another author who shared Elias Canetti's surname. Her novel, *Yellow Street*, her play, *The Ogre*, and a collection of short stories, *Patience Brings Roses*, which were all written before the Second World War, had been published — or republished in some cases, since she had written many of the stories for Viennese newspapers before fleeing the Nazis in the late autumn of 1938. The name Veza Canetti was printed on their spine, the same Veza from volumes two and three of Canetti's autobiography, in which her husband of twenty-nine years makes no mention of her writing. The difference in scale and size between the oeuvres of husband and wife could easily be assumed to reflect their relative merit. After picking up one of her books and turning it over, I thought I would discover what Canetti himself had feared, that it only got into print because of the connection with his Nobel Prize-winning name. The truth turned out to be more complicated. Veza Magd, as she preferred to be known, had published before her boyfriend and her stories never appeared under her married name while she was alive. Her episodic novel about life on a Leopoldstadt street, where the different social classes lived cheek to cheek and where she grew up with her mother and stepfather, is a minor masterpiece of modernist urban literature. She wrote it partly in reaction to *Auto-da-Fé*, but her style is very different from Canetti's. It is less allusive and more directly political: she writes explicitly about authoritarian social structures in pre-Nazi Austria. Her subjects are housemaids and orphans, middle-class women in violent marriages and lonely lesbian baronesses, as well as vindictive psychotics and leering sexual predators. The exercise of power and the corroding influence of money are two of her guiding themes (as they are also his), but she looked into her characters' minds to show how their belief in the rightfulness of their subservience contributed to their predicament.

When put together with Canetti's account of her from his autobiography, the sparse details of Veza's publication record hint at another fascinating life story that was inevitably bound up both with his own and with mid-twentieth century European history. When Austria tottered on the brink of Fascism, she was briefly feted in the socialist *Arbeiter-Zeitung*. Thereafter, apart from her translation of a novel by Graham Greene, nothing was heard of her for more than half a century. Then Canetti, who had meanwhile become very famous, allowed these three books to be published.

Veza's biography had a grim topicality at the beginning of the 1990s because she came from a world that was lost to the West during the Cold War but now was being rediscovered and bitterly contested. Her mother's family were from Belgrade and Sarajevo, their ancestors having been welcomed by the ruling Turks four centuries ago. Whether exiled in North Africa or southeastern Europe, these Jews often continued to speak a language based on fifteenth-century Spanish though with substantial Hebrew, Aramaic, and other more local additions, and often written in Hebrew characters. It was variously called Judeo-Spanish, Judezmo, or Ladino; Canetti refers to it as "spaniolisch." In Vienna and London, it was the language of everyday communication for him and Veza, a "secret language" that underscored their exclusive relationship as they used it, even in the presence of others.[1] Most of Bosnia's ancient Jewish community was killed in the Holocaust, including some of Veza's family, while the German-speakers, or "Swabes" as she calls them in one of her stories, who had settled there in the 1700s, fled in 1945. In 1992 Sarajevo was besieged by Serbian militias who wanted to drive out the Muslims and the Catholics too. They failed, but the four hundred remaining Sephardim packed their bags for Israel that same year.

I delivered another paper, this time to a mainly female audience entitled "On the Psychology of Subservience." They greeted my view that it was due to the forces of history and not a male conspiracy orchestrated by her husband that prevented the world from knowing Veza's writings with polite silence. There was no evidence then — and there is none now — that Canetti either prevented her from writing or stopped what she had written from finding readers, on the contrary. When more of Veza's writings were published after his death in August 1994, his defenders were at least partially vindicated: she had after all continued to write after her marriage, contrary to claims made by some of his fiercer critics that becoming his wife entailed the ending of her career. This controversy, which continued for more than a decade, is the subject of chapter 2.

Rudi Nassauer, a Frankfurt-born friend of both Veza and Canetti, began to write poetry in English in the late 1940s and enjoyed some success. George Steiner compared his first novel, *The Hooligan* (1960), which Canetti had helped him write, favorably with Günter Grass's *Dog Years.*[2] A short roman-à-clef entitled *The Cuckoo* (1962) followed where Canetti is depicted as a character called Klein. On a morning in his Hampstead flat in June 1994, he told me how they had been in Switzerland together when the news came over the radio that Canetti had won the Nobel Prize and the new laureate spat out his breakfast in choked surprise.[3] He also recalled Veza's thick German accent, which she could ham up for comic effect, and that she preferred serious jokes, on subjects such as their favorite Russian novelists.

Veza: Why don't you cut Dostoyevsky? He'd be much better cut.
Canetti: Well, I'd start with Tolstoy.
Veza: Nein, nein, you're not allowed to touch him.

One idiosyncrasy of the Canettis' literary relationship was that they never liked the same books: if Veza was for Tolstoy or Flaubert, Canetti was for Gogol or Stendhal; if he was for Kafka, she was for Thomas Mann. He originally entitled the section of *The Torch in the Ear* in which Veza makes her entrance, "Tolstoy or Gogol," which underlined this enduring but productive conflict. According to him, she admired the great nineteenth-century realists who depicted women with insight and feeling in novels like *Anna Karenina, Buddenbrooks, Madame Bovary,* and *Vanity Fair.* But her favorite author was the nineteenth-century Austrian, Adalbert Stifter, a writer of renunciation who is revered for his depiction of children and who committed suicide in his mid-sixties. In her letters to Georg she mentions *La Princesse de Cleves* by Madame de La Fayette and Maupassant's short story, "La Parure." She tells him that she must have written La Fayette's seventeenth-century novel of passion "in an earlier existence" (18 October 1937; *BG*:88) and, after war has broken out and she has moved to England, that she "is Madame Loisel *at the end of her life*" (18 May 1940; *BG*:116, her italics). Her identification with past authors or their literary characters is naive but profound and mirrors her practice of turning people she knew into literary figures.

Nassauer called Veza a "Mütterchen," meaning a homemaker who was always there for her unfaithful, younger husband, who was her protégé, whom she guarded and mothered, cooked and shopped for. Sometimes he "entertained elsewhere" ("Klein has several homes," explains the narrator of *The Cuckoo*)[4] and Veza never — or hardly ever — accompanied him to the parties that were the subject of his posthumously published English memoir. She didn't like going out because she was embarrassed by her missing left arm, which caused problems in company. How should she cut her food or hold her drink without people noticing? Out of respect for her feelings, no one mentioned her handicap, which was how she wanted it.

Canetti had affairs. I already knew his name had been "linked" with Iris Murdoch's and had been told of Friedl Benedikt, who had died tragically in her mid-thirties in 1953 after publishing three novels with Jonathan Cape under the name Anna Sebastian. Nassauer said she was his "great love" and that Murdoch's novels "came from the circle" around her and Canetti. In *The Cuckoo,* the narrator says of E. that she "was a very gifted writer, and she was Klein's mistress" even though Klein does not appear to be married. "Rumour had it that Klein was a demon, that he was terribly strict with her, that she feared him."[5] Nassauer also mentioned the emigrée painter, Marie-Louise Motesiczky, who provided Canetti and Veza with money and accommodation after their move to England. In his view, Canetti had been kind to Veza, though he acknowledged wearily that women may take a different view, like his own ex-wife, the novelist Bernice Reubens. Canetti may have done what he wanted without regard to his wife but he never spoke of her disrespectfully. Like Jean Paul Sartre and

Simone de Beauvoir, they addressed each other formally, always "per Sie," as Canetti also spoke to Motesiczky, though not to the younger Benedikt. Yes, Veza would have believed in justice, he agreed when I raised the subject of her politics (his own seemed to have become right wing), but lots of people back then believed in that. Yes, it was known that she had written stories for the *Arbeiter-Zeitung*, that was not kept secret, and everyone knew about her. He mentioned some names, but they were all either dead or too frail for an interview. She had not had many friends. I had come too late. Veza would have been ninety-six if she had still been alive.

The mid-1990s was not the right time to write a book about Veza Canetti. Her widower did not want to release the manuscripts in his possession until she had "established her reputation," as he wrote in a letter to me the year before he died.[6] After his death, it was assumed her papers would stay under lock and key for thirty years like his own private diaries and letters. I contented myself with publishing the second paper, which this time kept on getting cited and contradicted.

Over the next decade Veza would not go away. In 1999 *The Tortoises*, one of the texts Canetti had withheld, saw the light of day for the first time. Recounting the Canettis' own story of Nazi persecution in Vienna, it is a very different and more personal novel than *Yellow Street*. She wrote it after arriving in London in January 1939 and it was accepted by a publisher in July, but the outbreak of war had caused the contract to be revoked. In 2001 what were taken to be her last remaining stories, novellas, and plays were published as *Der Fund*, but then two more stories appeared the following year in a special issue of *Text und Kritik*. The Viennese archivist, Eckart Früh, had found them in newspapers from 1937, three years after the closure of the *Arbeiter-Zeitung*, which was assumed to have ended of her career. Although Canetti claimed Veza destroyed much material in a fit of melancholy after receiving another rejection slip seven years before she died, her writings now looked more substantial. Her correspondence with her husband's younger brother, Georg, from the 1930s and 1940s, which had been kept in a trunk for more than thirty years in a damp cellar in France, shows her also to be a consummately witty letter writer with a line in bittersweet self-deprecation.

Critical accounts of Veza's work also started to appear and Canetti did not usually emerge from these with much credit. Some of Veza's reviewers, several of whom were novelists, had criticized him with a passion. For them, he was the author of an intellectually challenging novel from six decades ago whose female characters are portrayed according to the precepts laid out in Otto Weininger's misogynist tract, *Sex and Character*, which had been one reason that Veza herself had rejected it.[7] In his autobiography, he brought to life the male-dominated literary world of Vienna in the decades between the world wars. Two years before the publication of *Yellow Street*, Frederike Eigler found the presentation of a number of women, including another of his artistic lovers, the sculptress Anna Mahler, sexist.[8] To learn that the woman who had been married to this apparent *Frauenfeind* for twenty-nine years had been a writer too, to find out on reading her texts that she had greater talent and a more astute eye for gender questions than the handful of other female Austrian writers from the period, then to realize that she had been posthumously portrayed in *The Torch in the Ear* and *The Play of the Eyes*, where he had said nothing about her having written at all, led them to conclude that possibly the best female voice of the 1930s in German had been silenced by her jealous, self-centered husband. Concomitant with the formulation of these suppositions, an English novelist explored the critical mindset that led them to make them in the first place. It was perhaps no coincidence that *Possession*, A. S. Byatt's satirical campus novel on overenthusiastic feminist reclamations of lost women writers, won the Booker Prize in the UK in 1990, the same year that *Yellow Street* was published in Germany.

Among English readers Elias Canetti gained noteriety for his role in Murdoch's equally busy love life. Although he does not appear in Richard Eyre's film *Iris*, John Bayley, who married Murdoch once her affair with Canetti had ended, revealed that the last name she could recognize before Alzheimer's engulfed her mind belonged to the man he dubbed the "Hampstead monster."[9] Peter Conradi devotes a whole chapter to him in his authorized biography and identifies him as the model for the series of malign enchanter figures who stand at the heart of such major novels as *A Fairly Honourable Defeat*, *The Black Prince*, and *The Sea, the Sea*.[10] The picture he paints of this cruel, controlling figure could not have contrasted more with my own image of the author of the three books of autobiography. Bayley himself had first written an appreciative essay that showed a lively and informed understanding of the writings of his wife's former lover and appeared in the *London Review of Books* on the occasion of his winning the Nobel.[11]

According to Bayley, Murdoch was not the first of Canetti's "disciples" to write a novel on the subject of such monsters. Benedikt's partly autobiographical eponymous prototype (*The Monster*) was dedicated to her "master and teacher," as Murdoch's *The Flight to the Enchanter* was dedicated to him too. Conradi argued that Benedikt's novel was inspired also by another Central European with a professional interest in power, who had made an even more profound impact on the course of the author's life, Adolf Hitler. Not for the first or the last time, Canetti the author is conflated with his subject of his second major work, *Crowds and Power*. Conradi also blames him for Benedikt's fatal illness.[12]

Elias Canetti was by all accounts an awkward man, who gave and took offense easily, a self-professed genius who claimed that he wrote for posterity rather than material reward and whose literary vanity stood for many years after emigration in inverse proportion to his public success. He enjoyed toying with people in order to observe their behavior in challenging situations and conveyed the impression that he took his own intellectual superiority as a given.[13] He scorned domestic and marital convention, much like Sartre and de Beauvoir, or another polygamous contemporary, whose methods of literary production were also entangled with his erotic interests, Bertolt Brecht. Anyone who crossed Canetti remembered the experience of his bad behavior for the rest of their lives, but they were usually not aware of his own brittle self-confidence. Even his most embittered enemies, who were legion in 1950s Hampstead, agree that he was exciting to be with because what he had to say was never dull. For Milein Cosman, an important source for Conradi, Canetti was a dreadful betrayer of confidences who had no sense of common decency or simple humanity. Yet, as Cosman proclaimed to me, if he returned from Hell (where she assumed he had been consigned) and appeared at her front door, she would welcome him into her house just to hear what he had to say for himself.[14] Canetti had a reputation for secretiveness and used to boast that his diaries were written in code (in fact a modified form of the shorthand he had learnt at school in Switzerland). London friends remember how he would pretend to be a Chinese cook or an upper-class Englishwoman when answering the phone.[15] Intimates knew they had to ring a certain number of times, replace the receiver, and phone again for him to answer as himself. His moralism could appear eccentric but it was absolute: he refused any form of work as long as the war lasted in case his efforts contributed in any way to the killing, which he deplored in the way that his mother deplored the slaughter of the First World War. Yet he was careful to keep this high-mindedness to himself, pretending to a young Viennese refugee, whom he met at the Student Movement House in Gower Street in 1940, that he did have a job at the nearby University College Hospital.[16]

Canetti ultimately created an oeuvre that is more individualist, more eccentric perhaps, in some ways more original, than that of any of the other great twentieth-century modernists from Central Europe. There is one novel (*Die Blendung* or "The Blinding" rather than *Auto-da-Fé* in the published English translation) written in his mid-twenties in pre-Hitler Vienna. It is a monstrous but brutally funny book that holds up the mirror to the hateful set of mentalities that bred Nazism and does so with a ruthless single-mindedness some find difficult to bear. Bayley recalls how its author, rarely given to false modesty, compared its effect on readers to that of *King Lear*.[17] The novel's hatefulness was not within him, as readers have often assumed, but in the world whose folly he diagnosed. Thereafter, instead of following a Joyce, a Musil, or a Mann and stretching the novel form to capture the hollowed-out contradictions of his terrible age, he turned to other genres. First plays (*Wedding* and *Comedy of Vanity* in the early 1930s; *The Numbered*, premiered at the Oxford Playhouse in 1956), then a travelogue (*Voices from Marrakesh*), books of aphorisms and reflections (he termed them "Aufzeichnungen," which means "jottings" or "notes"), and a book of "Characters" (*Ear-Witness*), modeled on Theophrastus and La Bruyère.

Once in England, no matter how great his own poverty, as an author of a still unsung prewar masterpiece, he held that writing to order was anathema because it compromised his commitment to truth. He was inclined to look down on anyone who did so. After *Auto-da-Fé* came out in English in 1946 he was offered a job reviewing for the *New Statesman*, the sort of opportunity any other writer wanting to make his mark would grab.[18] Canetti turned it down. He also claims to have vowed not to publish a word until he completed *Crowds and Power*, which was his reckoning with the forces that drove him from the Continent. Thanks to Veza's determined nagging and coaxing, this "big book about everything" (*SK*:102), as the narrator calls Andreas Kain's current project in *The Tortoises*, was finally finished in 1959. Benedikt and Murdoch contributed to *Crowds and Power* in various ways too, just as it left its mark on what they wrote. After her death, Canetti counted Veza as his co-author.

One reason that Canetti lived in obscurity even after the success of his novel in translation was that he wanted his work to last. Another was that he was lazy and, according to his wife, wasted his time helping his "disciples" (or "parasites," as she also calls them) with their writing (Veza to Georg, 28 March 1948; *BG*:323, and passim). There was initially one very obvious drawback to his purist approach to the written word: nobody in the London literary circles, which he penetrated with astounding ease, knew who he was. The only Englishman who had read his novel was the China expert, Arthur Waley, who was drawn to it after hearing its hero was a doctor of Sinology: "Imagine what it means in a large country, which for me was the country of Shakespeare and Dickens, to have *one single* reader," he wrote in *Party in the Blitz* (*PiB*:108). Few émigrés had it much better, of course — and there were many with higher reputations.

My intention is not to present the case for his defense when it comes to the woman who shared his life — that task has largely been accomplished by his German biographer, Sven Hanuschek — but to explore their literary relationship through what they both wrote in stories, novels, plays, memoirs, and essays. According to the current orthodox understanding of "literary marriages," the female partner subordinates herself when she teams up with the more powerful male. Her work is then either subsumed into his or sacrificed to it. This assumption underpinned the attacks made by feminists, if not Murdoch's biographers, which I discuss in chapter 2. This sympathy for the women does not necessarily do their memory any favors: it belittles their achievement and denies them a sense of self that all writers need. The writers among Canetti's women all loved literature just as much as he did, they practiced it, and their contribution to his literary career proved often no less tumultuous than Mathilde Canetti's had been in his adolescence. They argued with him, crossed him, threw his own words back in his face, wrote about him, but carried on loving him. The most enduring of these partnerships was that with his wife. It lasted for thirty-eight years and the literary art that out of it grew is the subject of this book.

Veza was at first a teacherly girlfriend, then she became a stay-at-home wife who gave him some precious stability while remaining, on her own insistence, excluded from his love life. She was dependable but made her own demands, sometimes becoming jealous of his other women friends (her hatred and resentment of Benedikt became all-consuming, as her letters show), but sometimes encouraging them — as long as they did not make demands on him that impeded his work or threatened her own position. She was more experienced and better read than he was when he began to write his novel in 1930; she then wrote alongside him in the 1930s and then with him on *his* book in the 1950s. Canetti assured the Göttingen Germanist, Helmut Göbel, who is credited with rediscovering Veza's fiction, that they did not work together in an "Arbeitsgemeinschaft," that is in direct collaboration with one another on the same texts.[19] My proposition is that they worked in parallel in full knowledge of what the other had written. This book tells the story of this literary collaboration and the conflict, hurt, revenge, reconciliation, renewed partnership, and, finally, shared obscurity in exile. It is a private drama played out against the backdrop of European history and cultural politics, first in interwar "Red Vienna" and the clerical-fascist "corporate state" that governed Austria prior to the Nazi takeover, then in Britain during the years of austerity. The twists and turns of their story help us understand their literary achievements, *Yellow Street* and *Auto-da-Fé*, *The Ogre* and *Comedy of Vanity*, *The Tortoises* and *Crowds and Power*. Canetti's literary partnerships, especially with Murdoch and Benedikt, are also much richer and more varied than some of his critics have allowed. Although his dealings with each followed their own distinctive course, his attitude to his literary wife is illuminated through his treatment of his literary pupils and mistresses and that is why I make occasional reference to these parallel stories.

Notes

[1] Jeremy Adler, "Nachwort," *PiB*, 211–28; here: 225.

[2] George Steiner, "A Note on Günter Grass" (1964), *Language and Silence. Essays 1958–1966* (London: Faber and Faber, 1967), 133–40; here: 137.

[3] Sven Hanuschek confirms the choking, but identifies the meal as lunch and the location as the house of Elias's new parents-in-law in Munich. Sven Hanuschek, *Elias Canetti: Eine Biographie* (Munich: Hanser, 2005), 609.

[4] Rudolf Nassauer, *The Cuckoo* (London: Peter Owen, 1962), 14.

[5] Ibid., 16.

[6] Letter to me from Elias Canetti, 18 July 1993.

[7] See, for example, Kristie A. Foell, *Blind Reflections: Gender in Elias Canetti's Die Blendung* (Riverside, CA: Ariadne, 1994).

[8] Frederike Eigler, *Das autobiographische Werk Elias Canettis: Verwandlung, Identität, Machtausübung* (Tübingen: Stauffenberg, 1988), 175–84.

[9] John Bayley, *Elegy for Iris* (New York: St. Martin's Press, 1999), 164. Published in the UK as *Iris: A Memoir of Iris Murdoch*.

[10] Peter J. Conradi, *Iris Murdoch: A Life* (London: HarperCollins, 2001), 345–74 ("Conversations with a Prince 1952–1956").

[11] John Bayley, "Canetti and Power," *Essays in Honour of Elias Canetti* (London: André Deutsch, 1987), 129–45.

[12] Conradi, *Iris Murdoch*, 365.

[13] Bayley, "Canetti and Power," 129.

[14] Milein Cosman, conversation with author, 11 November 2005.

[15] Dannie Abse, *Goodbye, Twentieth Century: An Autobiography* (London: Pimlico, 2001), 224.

[16] Rosemary Knight (née Scheuer), conversation with author, 17 November 2005.

[17] Bayley, *Elegy for Iris*, 164–66.

[18] As related to Conradi by Janet Adam Smith. E-mail to author from Conradi, 28 January 2004.

[19] Helmut Göbel, "Zur Wiederentdeckung Veza Canettis als Schriftstellerin. Einige persönliche Bemerkungen," *Text und Kritik* 156 (Veza Canetti issue) (2002), 3–10; here: 3.

1: A Lost Literary Life Recovered: Veza Canetti

V EZA CANETTI LEFT NO DIARY and her surviving letters rarely mention her own writing. There are no contemporary reviews of the fifteen stories she published in newspapers during her lifetime because they never appeared in book form. Her husband's friend, the Czech-born poet and chronicler of Theresienstadt, H. G. Adler, is the only contemporary to comment on anything she wrote. He did so in a private letter about one of her three plays sixteen years after it was written, seemingly unaware that she was also the author of novels and stories, for which she is now more famous.[1] We know little about what Veza read prior to arriving in London because she left nearly all her books in Vienna when she and Canetti fled in the wake of the Kristallnacht in November 1938. According to Canetti, she destroyed all the unpublished work she could lay her hands on in 1956 in despair at not finding publishers in either Britain or Germany. Shortly before his own death but after the outside world had finally shown interest in his first wife, he burnt the letters they had written to each other. He did not, however, dispose of his own notebooks, in which he expresses his affection and, in the year of her death, his overwhelming grief at her passing. He also kept draft chapters for the second two installments of his autobiography, *The Torch in the Ear* and *The Play of the Eyes*, where he explores her character and their relationship far more candidly than in the denuded versions he presented for publication.

While her life after meeting Canetti has already occupied books, what we know about her childhood, adolescence, and early adult years can fill a single paragraph. Legends have grown up to fill the gaps. We know that she only had the use of one arm, but whether she was born with this handicap or it was the result of an accident in infancy, whether a hand was attached to her elbow or she had no arm at all, we do not know. The question is important because disability is a theme for both her and Canetti and social embarrassment has been cited as a reason for her choosing a retiring role. Why did she remain childless when she wrote about children with such empathy and feeling and showered her love on a multitude of substitute children, among whom we perhaps should count her husband? His critics have readily accepted Bernice Rubens's claim that he made her have abortions;[2] documentary evidence in the shape of a letter in her hand in Canetti's notebooks suggests that the loss of an unborn child in the spring of 1932 can be put down to natural causes.[3] Then there is the entirely bizarre nature of her marriage, which appears to have been nothing of the sort by conventional standards since the couple had ceased having physical relations before they presented themselves to the Sephardic synagogue in Leopoldstadt's Zirkusgasse. Even the date of their marriage, which is given by their biographers as 29 February 1934, is mysterious: 1934 was not a leap year, which means February had a mere twenty-eight days.[4] It was rumored too that Veza was "in love" with Canetti's younger brother, who moved to Paris in 1924 with their mother.[5] Veza was indeed intensely fond of him, as Georg was of her, and she termed her correspondence with him "love letters," but her concern was more motherly than amorous. Georg's erotic interests generally lay elsewhere: he was for many years the lover of the structuralist critic, Roland Barthes.

Perhaps the most potent legend of all is that of Veza's "lost work," the two novels mentioned by Wieland Herzfelde in 1932 and the unknown quantity of material Canetti recalls her destroying when she gave up writing nearly a quarter of a century later. If both men are to be believed those of Veza's writings that have been published represent little more than the tip of an iceberg: anything up to three-quarters of her output may have been lost. Yet Hanuschek wonders whether the story of her destruction was not one of her husband's little legends.[6] Perhaps it gave her perverse pleasure to be a forgotten writer, as she did not always make the most of what opportunities she did have after 1945 to re-establish herself in Austria. She occasionally refers to her own writing projects to Georg but as her tone is whimsical, she does not give titles, and her fictional or dramatic accounts of people are often her way of telling him about them, even her own comments must be treated with caution (e.g. 21 September 1945; *BG*:146). Critics agree that the tone of sarcastic bravado in Herzfelde's mini-biographies in *Thirty New Writers of the New Germany* invites us to treat his information skeptically. Canetti's own testimony on Veza, especially in the last years of his life, is riven with inconsistencies. He wrote to Armin Ayren, for instance, in October 1990 that she destroyed "many of her manuscripts" "in the years after the war," but in another letter five months later he specifies the date as 1956 and refers only to a novel, which was returned from a publisher, and "a few earlier manuscripts."[7] Elsewhere he claims that the only material that she did not destroy survived because he was looking after it. Yet he had forgotten about a number of published stories, including three that she succeeded in publishing in 1937 under the "corporate state" ("Clairvoyants," "Hush Money," "Money — Money — Money"). His omission gave feminists (such as Elfriede Czurda) grounds for arguing that marriage caused Veza to cease writing, which, the evidence now shows, is simply not true. Veza also died in circumstances that are unlikely to be clarified. Did she end her life voluntarily, as she had so many times threatened to do, once her life's work was complete with the publication of Canetti's *Crowds and Power*, or did she die naturally, as stated on her death certificate? All these details matter because they have been used in the battle for her memory.

Even after the publication of her letters to Georg, most of what we know about Veza comes directly or indirectly from Canetti, who outlived her by more than three decades. He writes about her at greatest length in his autobiography, but as it is a work of poetic truth rather than historical accuracy, we cannot rely on what he says. Veza's own comments on his mother are all positive and admiring, giving no sense that there was a rift between the two women over Canetti; Georg states that the conflict only concerned mother and son and did not regard Veza at all (to Veza, 10 June 1933; *BG*:9). Canetti not only leaves out most of the material he had considered including in his autobiography, he changes key details; he is in fact the first to invent legends about his first wife. In an interview on Swiss radio in 1968, he claimed that she had taken him to his first performance by the satirist Karl Kraus (*X*:217), whereas in *The Torch in the Ear* it is of great significance that he met her for the first time at that performance (*X*:217). It makes a difference which version is correct: if he owed her his introduction to Kraus, he was even more in her intellectual debt than he has admitted.

Memoirs of the couple invariably give Canetti pride of place, and many of his London circle met Veza rarely, if at all. Some were surprised to discover in 1990 that he had been married to a writer. His pre-eminence in her affairs continued after she died: he looked after the manuscripts that escaped her destructive frenzy, inscribed on them "Copyright Elias Canetti" and released only some for publication in the 1990s. His destruction of their correspondence makes it unlikely that his own private papers, which cannot be read until 2024, contain any new material from her pen. His diaries, one must assume, will give a fuller account of their thirty-eight-year relationship than the jottings contained in his notebooks or even the unpublished autobiographical chapters.

For the period after 1939 when they were both in and around London, though often not at the same address, there are letters to and from Veza scattered among the papers of her male correspondents. Her friendship with H. G. Adler, as with fellow Jewish exiles, Erich Fried, whose political poems became required reading for student militants in the late 1960s, the novelist, Hermann Broch, and the poet and anthropologist, Franz Baermann Steiner, was independent of her husband. She knew the younger Fried better than he did. The letters she wrote in the 1930s and 1940s to Georg Canetti, who survived the war as a doctor in Nazi-occupied Paris, comprise the greatest corpus of correspondence. Canetti and Veza wrote to Georg independently of one another, just as they wrote prose and plays independently of one another, but the collection of letters reads like a shared project and is the only book to have both their names as authors on its spine. They drew strength from the same source, whom they had different but closely connected reasons for loving. Canetti had encouraged fourteen-year-old Georg's affection for Veza by sharing his own enthusiasm for his well-read older girlfriend; he claimed that he nurtured Veza's for Georg by telling her about Georg's concern for her welfare in the face of their mother's implacable hostility. In Canetti's account that he decided not to include in *The Play of the Eyes* Georg shared their passion for Kraus. Two years later he pacified their mother by pretending he had left Veza, inventing new girlfriends, " 'Maria' in Salzburg and 'Erika,' a violinist who lived in Rodaun" (*VIII*:212), to prove he had extracted himself as Mathilde wished. His first subterfuge involved invented conversations with a certain Eva Reichman, a student in his chemistry lab. He claimed their subject was Dostoyevsky, who, coincidentally, was the nineteen-year-old Friedl Benedickt's great passion when they met in 1935. This fake literary romance among test tubes and Bunsen burners apparently satisfied his mother and kept her off Veza's scent for a while. According to Canetti in this unpublished chapter, Georg could not be let in on the deceit and took Veza's side against what he believed to be his brother's perfidy; he chided Canetti for his faithlessness. He began writing Veza letters, and secretly hatched a plan to marry her himself, though he doubted she would ever overcome the loss of his eldest brother, so great was his own reverence for him. Veza reciprocated his concern: her thoughts were all for Georg when Mathilde died at age fifty in June 1937.[8] Elias Canetti's now well-known facility for emotional secretiveness was surely born in his early twenties at this complicated moment when he was caught between mother and girlfriend and forced to deceive one of the handful of other people he ever confessed to loving in his life.

Anyone interested in Veza's biography and the relationship that defined her life must also scour her writings for indications of self-revelation: her depiction of housemaids is one place to start since she published mostly under the pseudonym Veza Magd. Her self-effacing pen name that invokes the invisible family servant present in every middle-class household tells its own story. When she writes about other writers, they are always men. In *The Tortoises* and "Toogoods or the Light," her fictional alter egos are not writers in contrast to their much admired husbands. A part of Veza surely went into the invention of Anna Seidler, who is crushed by her employer in Veza's very first published story, "The Victor." Anna taught herself to type so that she could be more useful in the textile factory where she works, but her male employer refuses to recognize her skill and drives her to suicide. Another Anna, who also works as a typist, is one of the three women in "Three Quarters," who altogether cannot make a whole to match Bent, the name Veza gives to the male artist all three women adore.

Canetti's published literary writings — not only the three volumes of autobiography, but *Auto-da-Fé*, two of his three plays, and his critical essay on Kafka's letters to Felice Bauer, *Kafka's Other Trial*, his first major project after Veza's death — also provide glimpses into their enduring but uneasy relationship. The surviving evidence indicates that her creative involvement with him lasted for at least a decade after her first *Arbeiter-Zeitung* story in 1932. Her presence in his work stretches over the full sixty years of his creative life.

The world of Veza's fiction was lost by the time she was reintroduced to a reading public. The Vienna in her writing was radically transformed by the destruction and demographic upheavals that she escaped. Picturing how Leopoldstadt, where she lived for twenty-five years, appeared to her requires an effort of mental reconstruction. One problem, as an historian of the district recognized twenty years ago, is that today's streets "offer the imagination no stimulus to picture that this district used to be almost half Jewish."[9] The numerous plaques commemorate only the postwar rebuilding program, not the former residents of the buildings. Yet Vienna's physical layout is largely unaltered, unlike parts of Berlin. All the streets Canetti mentions, such as the Radetzkystraße, where his family lived in 1924, the Novaragasse, where he attended Jewish school before the First World War, or the Haidgasse, where he took lodgings as he was courting Veza after his mother and brothers had moved to Paris, all still have the same names. One can trace the route the twenty-year-old chemistry student took to visit his new girlfriend at 29 Ferdinandstraße, where she shared an apartment with her mother and stepfather. The 38-tram still connects the city center with Grinzing, where the newly married couple moved in September 1935, and the walk up-hill to 30 Himmelsgasse is as strenuous as he recalls in *The Play of the Eyes* and she describes the trek up to the Kains' villa in *The Tortoises*. 29 Ferdinandstraße still stands, though no longer belongs to the family of Ludwig Wittgenstein as it did then. You can still glimpse the Stephansdom, "our most beautiful church" (*GbR*:68), in front of which Seidler in "New Boy" struggled to sell his "pinko" newspapers during the worst periods of the economic Depression and extremist agitation. The Prater Amusement Park that marks the district's northeastern border no longer boasts the wax works in the Panoptikum that so fascinated Herr Vlk from *Yellow Street*, not to mention the young Canetti in 1913, but the rides still look every bit as dangerous as Georgie Burger's father described them in Veza's "The Criminal."

One building that no longer stands housed the Sephardic synagogue that had been built in the Zirkusgasse by Veza's maternal grandfather. In that synagogue, after some arm-twisting and promises that their marriage would not conform to bourgeois convention, she became Frau Canetti — a week after the bloody street-fighting of 12–14 February 1934 between the police and workers that crushed Red Vienna's organized working classes, an event known as the "workers' revolt" or the "civil war" and that resulted in more than 300 deaths. They decided to marry in a religious ceremony, partly to please Veza's mother who was seriously ill, and partly because they were in a hurry and the Jewish authorities were not as strict as those at the *Standesamt* or civil registry office. In a moment of uncharacteristic romantic nostalgia, Canetti reveals that they could not have chosen a more suitable place, but he immediately negates the sentiment with the grim historical contextualization:

> To the right of the entrance two large plaques were set into the wall which bore the names of the founder and his wife. Veza's grandmother, whom she had been named after, was called Veneziana. Her surname was Elias. Thus on the plaque in large letters one could read VENEZIANA ELIAS. Since the building of the Temple — I imagine, a little before the turn of the century — our names had been set next to each other.
>
> (They are no longer there today. In November 1938 this Temple, like all others in the Leopoldstadt, was set on fire and the plaques wrenched out.)[10]

These comments are from the corpus of material on Veza that he decided not to include in the autobiography. It seems she was too difficult, "too close," and too sad a subject for him to do justice to. In the published "jottings," he leaves the year when she died blank without offering a reason or drawing attention to the gap. In the unpublished notebooks, in contrast, he pours out his feelings page after page.

Veza's case is unique among writers persecuted by the Nazis only insofar as she had a famous husband. Many of her contemporaries died leaving no carefully collated *Nachlaß* (literary remains) after fleeing their homes — their possessions and papers were either lost or scattered across the world. Everything the novelist Robert Musil left behind on decamping from Vienna to Zurich was destroyed by a bomb in 1942. For those who survived, not finding publishers after 1945, either in a German-speaking European country or their newly adopted land, was the rule rather than the exception, as H. G. Adler, Fried, Steiner, and Nassauer could all have testified. Other writers, both male and female, needed decades to re-establish their reputation with German readers or, like Veza, be "rediscovered" and republished, regardless of whether they went into exile or not. Ödön von Horváth was barely known until the 1960s and Jura Soyfer until a decade later. Contemporary women writers, such as Marieluise Fleißer and Irmgard Keun, lived in obscurity until their books were printed and read again shortly before they died. Upheaval of this magnitude leaves jagged edges and unfinished chapters in the lives of those it strikes.

More texts by Veza Canetti may still come to light. Like Joseph Roth's journalism that is still being found in newspapers, it is possible that not all of her writings have been located. Herzfelde after all claimed that she had published a novel called *The Enjoyers* in the "Austrian and German workers' press" and this may not have been an empty boast. Eckart Früh's discovery of material from 1937 proves that she succeeded in placing other material after February 1934, when the *Arbeiter-Zeitung* was closed.

The pattern of her publication history looks rather odd. In November 1933 her last two stories ("The Canal" and "New Boy") appeared in the *Arbeiter-Zeitung* that was already being censored. Then, under a different nom de plume, in July 1934, the month the Christian Social Chancellor Engelbert Dollfuß was assassinated in an attempted Nazi coup, she published "Three Heroes and a Woman" in Herzfelde's Prague-based *Neue Deutsche Blätter*. This tale of a cool-headed cleaning woman at the time of the workers' revolt in February 1934 is her only known involvement with exiled anti-Nazis. July 1934 also saw a reprint of "The Poet" in *Deutsche Freiheit*, the last independent German newspaper published on the edge of the Reich in the semi-independent Saarland, which was still under the jurisdiction of the League of Nations. *Neue Deutsche Blätter* continued to appear until August 1935 and would surely have taken more texts by Veza had she supplied the sort of material Herzfelde wanted. The Saarland did not revert to Germany for another year. "Three Heroes and a Woman" was printed next to poems and short stories by Stefan Heym and Anna Seghers, who became pillars of the literary establishment in Communist East Germany. There was also a review by Kafka's executor, Max Brod, who settled in Palestine, and a poem by Brecht. The company Veza kept at the *Arbeiter-Zeitung* and in Herzfelde's anthology was hardly less militant or less distinguished.

After more than two-and-a-half years, three more stories were published in quick succession between March and May 1937. After that there is nothing. It is testimony to Veza's stylistic subtlety that she managed to have these last stories published at all in the "corporate state" which Dollfuß used to dismantle Austrian democracy and smash the organized Left in response to Hitler's rise in Germany. Her subjects appear anodyne at first when compared with the gritty but lyrical realism of the *Arbeiter-Zeitung* stories: a sexual farce, the macabre unmasking of a charlatan medium, or a tale of a maid's revenge on her employer. More careful reading reveals that all three are coded critiques of contemporary Austrian politics. By January 1939, she began *The Tortoises*. It must have seemed to her that the Nazis once again prevented her second novel from being published with the outbreak of war, just as the "corporate state" denied *Yellow Street* readers in 1934. In England, she wrote "Toogoods or the Light," "Last Will," and "Air Raid," which is her only story that exists in an English version. Like Friedl Benedikt, she was prepared to switch languages in order to reach readers or make some money. She mentions other projects in English to Georg which must now count as lost (9 January 1945; *BG*:118 and 22 July 1945; *BG*:131). Her third play and last surviving piece of writing, *The Palanquin*, is set in 1952. None of these were published until 2001, thirty-eight years after she died.

The most intriguing gap in her publishing history is between July 1934 and March 1937. We know that the Canettis were unsure how long they were staying in Vienna and Veza had reason to fear becoming involved with exiled literary circles, which must be why she had changed her pseudonym from the well-known Veza Magd to Veronika Knecht for "Three Heroes and a Woman." In January 1934, she was threatened with deportation because of her work for the *Arbeiter-Zeitung* and her Yugoslavian passport that she held since 1919 despite being born-and-bred Viennese. In April 1934, Canetti, who was also stateless since the same time, unsuccessfully re-applied for Turkish nationality.[11] The eve of the next world cataclysm is thus not the first year that the Canettis were forced to change their national allegiance. In the end, they both died as British citizens.

They were also desperately short of money after the death of Veza's mother in October 1934. Her stepfather, who had died five years earlier, cut Veza out of his will, in revenge, Canetti writes, for her self-assertion against him, which her young admirer found so inspiring.[12] Lack of money was a constant source of worry for the couple until Veza's death. According to one account, they spent a winter in the late 1950s living in desperate poverty in France while their small upstairs flat in Hampstead's Thurlow Road was sublet.[13] Veza earned small sums from translations and freelance editorial work, while Canetti's wealthier friends very often supplied money and hospitality. She claimed to have charge of the "business" side of his writing and correspondence with publishers regarding translations, regretting in 1947 that she did not learn to forge his signature years before (to Georg, 31 December 1947; *BG*:302).

It is possible that Veza gave up writing or stopped trying to publish in 1934 and was then encouraged to try again by the relaxation in the censorship rules. The new Chancellor, Kurt von Schuschnigg, was neither a philistine nor an anti-Semite: Musil respected him because he read Homer in Greek;[14] Alma Mahler is suspected of having had an affair with him. Shortly before he died, Canetti even claimed that Mahler had given Veza the love letters that Schuschnigg had written her for safekeeping. Schuschnigg certainly posed for her and they holidayed together in the summer of 1935.[15] Until the Anschluss he was not unpopular with non-Communist Viennese Jews who knew only too well what was happening in Nazi Germany. These dangerous times led to strange pairings: to Canetti's disgust, Karl Kraus supported Dollfuß as an Austrian bulwark against Hitler.

When the *Arbeiter-Zeitung* closed, Veza was working on *The Ogre*, which she first wrote as a chapter for *Yellow Street*. It was too critical to be performed under the new regime, however. She may have believed there was a possibility that her second play, *The Tiger*, would be accepted by a theatre. The dissimilarity to *The Ogre* suggests she wrote with performance in mind. Similarly, the stories published in 1937 differ from those from 1932 through 1934. Other pieces of short fiction found among Canetti's papers seem to be from the period before the Nazi Anschluss. Two, "The Seer" and "Pastora," are set in Seville, while the more autobiographical "Three Quarters" and "The Flight from the Earth" are Viennese, the latter is an attempt to complete one of Canetti's abandoned projects from his Balzacian *Comédie Humaine of Madmen*. "The Seer" was broadcast on Austrian radio in 1949 as "short story of the week." She must have thought highly of it, but it contains nothing that could have raised a censor's eyebrow.

In his letter of condolence, Fried told Canetti: "I am sorry that none of Veza's plays has been published, but she always deliberately held herself back, which meant it was almost what she wanted."[16] She told him that she did not want her own work to be known until her husband was famous. There are some signs that she was writing as late as 1956; Canetti insisted it was a new novel that was sent back unwanted.[17] There is also an intriguing note found among Motesiczky's papers. The note is in German, but it refers to an English title:

> My novel "The Response" is dedicated to the artist Marie-Louise Motesiczky. For the quiet magic which emanates from her inspired one of my characters and her refinement tamed my wildness and determined the characters and the music of my book.[18]

This novel is almost certainly lost.

In her letters to Georg, Veza discusses her husband's literary projects at far greater length and with far greater frequency than she does her own. While she sends Georg a copy of "The Tiger" chapter from *Yellow Street* (16 December 1933; *BG*:14), she never subsequently elaborates why the book, which she said would be finished by the following month, was never published. In fact she never mentions it again at all. A year later almost to the day she alludes to her two Viennese plays (20 December 1934; *BG*:28) but, again, does not describe any attempts to have either of them (*The Ogre* or *The Tiger*) performed in Vienna. Even more striking is her silence regarding the three stories that were published in 1937 and the novel that she wrote on arrival in England in 1939, *The Tortoises*. Her only other reference to her work in the prewar letters is to Jean Hoepffner's high opinion of it, which, two months after the death of his mother, she fears will irritate Canetti if Hoepffner expresses it in his presence when he visits (23 August 1937; *BG*:81). When the correspondence with Georg resumes in January 1945, she tells him that she wrote a novel in English in which he was the hero, a famous doctor who is very attractive to women, but that she lost faith in it and did not correct her first draft. In the same letter she mentions a play in English but says that she will not be able to finish it because she is ill (6 Janurary 1945; *BG*:118). It is difficult to know how seriously to take either of these projects; telling Georg that she has written about him may be a way of expressing her feelings for him. She tells him on another occasion that he is the leading character in a play (she must mean *The Ogre*), which, in a rare moment of self-confidence, she is convinced will be performed all over the world (August 1946; *BG*:221). By the summer of 1945 she reports that her "second play" written in English, a comedy, is almost ready (22 July 1945; *BG*:131). Two months later she discusses a musical comedy about a certain Mrs. Lancaster, a wartime landlady of Veza's who kept her work as a prostitute secret from her husband, seeing five different soldiers a day. Veza wrote love letters to them on her behalf, as Mrs. Lancaster was illiterate (21 September 1945; *BG*:146). Mrs. Lancaster sounds a fascinating figure, but telling Georg that she became a character in a musical comedy may just be a rhetorical ploy. A year later she confides to him the idea for another play, initially suggested by Canetti, about Friedl Benedikt, whose behavior at this time was driving Veza to despair and distraction, but it is clear that she has no intention of writing it (10 November 1946; *BG*:247). In contrast, she tells Georg repeatedly about the habits of Mr. and Mrs. Milburn, in whose house she and Canetti spent most of the war, without saying that she wrote a story, "Toogoods or the Light," about them (e.g. 27 October 1945; *BG*:158). Feeling for once almost boastful she lets on that Robert Neumann had told Veronica Wedgwood, the translator of *Auto-da-Fé*, that she was extremely gifted, "more gifted than Canetti" (2 June 1946: *BG*:211). Eight days later she claims that her work is in demand in Austria and that she will have to write in France, during her visit to Georg, because she has no material in German (8 June 1946; *BG*:213), which was quite untrue. In October 1946 she writes that her plays have been sent off to "Vienna, Salzburg etc" and that people in Austria are very keen to read both her and her husband's works because there are so few writers of German left (24 October 1946; *BG*:239). This was a rather naïve statement, and her optimism proved quite unfounded. Her hopes of literary success had been dashed in 1934 and again in 1939, and they came to nought once more in 1946. The following summer she mentions that a respected Englishwoman is having one of her plays translated into English because her mother is an actress and wants to perform in it. But she adds that Georg should not tell anyone else about this and that she is only telling him because he is the only person she trusts completely; she has been disappointed before (27 August 1947; *BG*:283). She carries on writing regularly to Georg for another year before she abruptly breaks off, but does not refer again to her own work. When Canetti began to write *Crowds and Power* in 1948, after more than twenty years preparatory research, Veza dedicated herself to it and assisted by dealing with his correspondence (he was a dreadful letter writer), and reading and correcting his text. He recalls her "obsessiveness" (*PiB*:112) in pursuing his literary career. Living through him appears to have given her life meaning. She made him sit at his desk, sometimes putting off his visitors without his knowing or writing letters on his behalf that her correspondent is enjoined to keep secret. Her role in the publication of an anthology of his writings that was intended to re-establish his reputation in Germany in the wake of *Crowds and Power* extended beyond writing the introduction. She selected the texts; similarly, she prepared the first collection of his "jottings."

In the introduction to *The World in the Head*, the very last piece of writing before she died, she expressed frustration that Vienna, the city of her birth, ignored expelled writers. Typically, she did not make the statement on her own account, but on her husband's, just as she also did not write under her own name. She recommends *Comedy of Vanity*, her favorite of her husband's three Viennese works, to contemporary theaters, finding

> it barely credible that this grandiose comedy was not performed long ago in Austria. Perhaps no-one has taken the trouble to read it. The characters mostly speak Viennese dialect. Where else can such a play be put on stage? (*WK*:17)

It ends with an assertion that the manuscript indicates was written by Fried, but it would have been even more poignant had it come directly from Veza:

> I cannot close without mentioning at least in one sentence the ideas and inspiration which Canetti has given and continues to give in conversation to a great number of writers, creative artists, academics, and researchers from all parts of the globe, some of them already world famous. The lives of many of these people cannot be imagined without his instruction, his advice and his direct creative help. I count myself among their number. (*WK*:22)

On 1 May 1963, Veza Canetti died in New End Hospital in the London borough of Hampstead. Her funeral took place at Golders Green crematorium. The cause of death is given as "left pulmonary embolus," her occupation as "wife of Elias Jack Canetti, an author." He wrote to Frank and Suse Underwood that she "fell ill at Easter and was taken to hospital a week before her death." That and the cause of death make it unlikely that she took her own life. Photos taken in London show her to have been overweight and a smoker. She was sixty-five years old and life since emigration had been testing in numerous ways. She wrote to Georg that by the end of the war she had moved twenty-seven times (27 November 1945; *BG*:157), changing houses if not countries more often than she changed shoes, to adapt the line from Brecht's poem. In her letters there are recurrent references to financial problems, a weak heart that had been broken when she was forced to leave what had once been the "happiest" city in Central Europe (*SK*:27), which is the reason why she could not bear to return. There are numerous other health problems, both of a physical and mental nature, which either she or her husband discuss in their letters to his brother. Nassauer thought she had been tired of life and, when it came to her health, did not help herself. Canetti ended his letter to the Underwoods: "You will never know anyone of her generosity and [. . .] goodness. Nor will I. But I had her with me for 38 years and this is more than any human being deserves." He intended to keep her ashes with him forever.[19] The flat they shared in Thurlow Road became a shrine; its occupant showed visitors her photos and returned to it from his travels to be with her memory.

Hanuschek leaves the question of suicide open, since it is possible that Veza had sleeping pills with her. She had threatened her husband with suicide since their arrival in England.[20] He reveals in another unpublished autobiographical fragment that before they left Vienna she wrote to influential individuals, such as Thomas Mann, that she would kill herself if they did not help her husband, which strongly suggests that the pattern of self-sacrifice on his behalf had begun by the time they married.[21] Jeremy Adler sees the completion of *Crowds and Power* as a natural ending and Canetti's survival as by no means the most likely outcome:

> With the publication of *Crowds and Power*, which she had worked so tirelessly to promote, and which he had finished as much thanks to her bullying and badgering as to his own obsession, her life's work was essentially done. In a moral sense the book constituted the sacrifice that they made in return for their deliverance from the terrible fate of their people. With the book's publication, her life fulfilled its purpose; when she died, his own life lost its meaning, and he came close to ending it.[22]

Canetti never hid the fact that Veza was a writer. On the contrary, in a draft of another letter (to Jill?) in his notebooks, he extols her talent:

> I have been in a state of near paralysis since Veza's death and unable to do anything at all.
> You never heard Veza speak in her own language in which she was a highly gifted and often even brilliant writer.[23]

When he was asked about his late wife in 1968 he replied: "She was a writer herself and understood something about the métier" (*X*:217), which is hardly the statement of a man who wants to hide her literary activity. It is curious, though, that H. G. Adler and Fried seem only to be aware of Veza's plays, which suggests that there is another reason that it took the world so long to find out about her work. In their efforts to interest publishers and theaters in her writing, neither she nor Canetti recognized the superior merits of her prose. Both believed *The Ogre* to be "the best thing that she ever wrote," as Canetti wrote in the copy he gave to Nassauer, which is not a view shared by critics since its publication. In 1950 they gave a copy to the young Ingeborg Bachmann when she passed through

London. Among H. G. Adler's papers are notes for an interview on Canetti dated 7 June 1979 that include the following: "Veza Canetti was for her part a highly talented author of dramas which have not yet been published (tragedy 'Ogre')."[24] The only letter we have documenting the Canettis' shared efforts to re-establish Veza's reputation in German-speaking countries concerns *The Tiger*, which the Zurich Schauspielhaus that premiered *The Ogre* in 1992 turned down in 1950. *Yellow Street* has been translated into seven languages and is the superior piece of writing, its highpoint the *prose* version of the ogre story that has attracted more critical comment since 1990 than anything else she wrote.

Toward the end of Bachmann's celebrated novel, *Malina*, the nameless narrator is telling her male alter ego how women suffer in relationships with men. She cites the case of a certain "Erna Zanetti" who tried to kill herself after having been left by a man she had been seeing for a few months: "just think of Erna Zanetti, who swallowed forty sleeping pills all on account of a lecturer in Theater Studies, just think of that, a lecturer in Theater Studies!"[25] In the narrator's view, Erna Zanetti should have been pleased to be rid of him since he had sought to impose his will on her by making her give up smoking and, as far as she knows, eating meat as well. As Canetti wrote *The Numbered* shortly after meeting Bachmann in London during the winter of 1950 and 1951, his views on death and suicide are likely to have featured in their conversations. Since Bachmann also met Veza and was given copies of *The Ogre* and his *Comedy of Vanity*, the "lecturer in Theater Studies" who spurns Erna Zanetti could plausibly refer to the German theater world's indifference to the exiled literary couple.[26] The unlikely sounding name Erna Zanetti is a conflation of theirs.

The twenty-four-year-old Bachmann, who had just completed her doctorate on Heidegger and begun to publish poems, met Canetti through Ilse Aichinger. He in turn introduced her to Fried. She had come from Paris where she had visited Paul Celan, whose poetry, personality, and background were to have a profound and well-attested influence on her writing. Canetti wrote in the two books he gave her: "For Ingeborg Bachmann, who has brought Vienna near to me once more and from whom I expect many beautiful things" (in *Auto-da-Fé*, which was reissued in German in 1948) and "For Ingeborg Bachmann, so that she recognizes Vienna again" (in the freshly published *Comedy of Vanity*).[27] In the first message he suggests that she has done him a service, but in the second the roles are reversed and he imparts a lesson to her.

Canetti is not the only person who could have done more to get Veza's writings published. After 1945, Herzfelde returned to East Germany, where he died in 1988 at the age of ninety-two just a year before its collapse. There is a letter from Veza among his papers but no evidence that he thought to recommend her stories to East German publishers.[28] When an East German press re-issued *Thirty New Writers from the New*

Germany on the fiftieth anniversary of its first publication, Veza Magd was one of the names the editor was unable to identify.[29] Similarly, there is a question mark next to Veronika Knecht in a bibliography of the Malik Press published at the end of the 1980s in West Germany.[30]

Ernst Fischer's reference to Veza Magd enabled Eckart Früh, the archivist at the Viennese Workers' Record Office, to identify the author of the stories he had already found in the *Arbeiter-Zeitung* when Helmut Göbel approached him in 1989. Yet while Fischer uses her nom de plume, he does not indicate that she published stories under this name in the very same paper he helped to edit:

> Veza had adopted the surname Magd [Maid]. This choice of name was in keeping with her nature. For all her pride, she was extremely modest. Her goodness was the distillation of a dark, smouldering passion. [. . .] She loved Elias, worshipped him, suffered at his hands, reproached herself for thus suffering and, while longing to be the only woman in his life, refused to let this feeling get the better of her.[31]

Fischer does quote, however, from Canetti's *Auto-da-Fé* and he recalls discussing with him ideas that would enter *Crowds and Power* a quarter of a century later when the street battles between police and workers raged outside on the night of 12–13 February 1934. Ruth von Mayenburg, who married Fischer in 1932, also recalls discussions of Canetti's work while ignoring Veza's writing that she too must have known. It can only be that neither took "Veza Magd" very seriously as an author. Fischer clearly likes her as a person but respects her husband for his intellect. He makes the soon-to-be-married couple sound like an odd mix of opposites:

> I took Elias Canetti to be an attractive *diable boiteux*, a character such as Goethe describes as "daemonic," with "an evil eye" for all that was evil, finding pleasure in the horrifying, the distorted, the deformed, the mad, in uprooting and in giving pain.[32]

Canetti often provoked extreme reactions, even from friends and lovers, who made him into a figure of mythic proportions even before he mythologized himself at length in his autobiography. Fischer's comment anticipates Bayley's all-controlling "Dr Canetti" or Conradi's account of Murdoch's demon lover, not to mention Murdoch's own Canetti figures.

For all her acuity in dissecting workers' psychology and her solidarity with Austrian Social Democracy, Venetiana Taubner-Calderon was born on 21 November 1897 into a middle-class family in Vienna. She did encounter poverty in her childhood after her father died when she was seven. In her letters to Georg she mentions her childhood only once after reporting that she had cried when listening to the commentary of Princess Elizabeth's marriage to the future Duke of Edinburgh: "Why was

I weeping? Because I too was once a princess. That was at the time of the monarchy and I used to sit every summer in a villa in Ischl and the Emperor used to pass by, and I waved and he waved back and my mother was convinced that he was waving to me. That happened every morning and I was seven years old" (23 November 1947; *BG*:298). Her father must have died shortly after this because her life soon became harder. As a step-daughter she experienced maltreatment and witnessed the effects of an unequal marriage on her mother. Unlike Mathilde Canetti, Rachel Calderon had been obliged to remarry for financial reasons, and for the next twenty years, mother, daughter, and stepfather shared the apartment at 29 Ferdinandstraße. It is striking that two of Canetti's other artistic lovers, Anna Mahler and Marie-Louise Motesiczky, were also brought up fatherless by powerful mothers. The tragic early death of a father was not all Veza had in common with her young suitor. In addition to a passion for books, they shared a Sephardic background, family connections with England, and a childhood spent in the shadow of jealous patriarchs — his two grandfathers in Bulgarian Rustchuk and her mother's third husband, Menachem Alkaley, the original "ogre" who features repeatedly in both their writing. Canetti's family moved to Manchester when he was five so that his father could go into business with his brother-in-law, Salomon Arditti, another ogre, according to his nephew in *The Tongue set Free*, who knew the value of nothing except money. Veza's English relatives included a cousin who married the future wartime cabinet minister, Leslie Hore-Belisha (Veza never met him); another who wrote for the *Manchester Guardian*; and her half-brother from her mother's first marriage, Maurice Calderon, who owned a shop in Surrey and was known as "Bookie" (or "Bucky") because of his proficiency in bookkeeping.[33] As a young adult, Veza visited the country where she would spend the last twenty-five years of her life. Like Canetti, she spoke fluent English. After passing her school-leaving certificate, the *matura*, she gave English lessons — Fischer was one of her pupils — and worked as a translator from English to German. For Canetti, she was the girl next door in two different cities in two different countries. Before the First World War, his mother had taken them to live a stone's throw from the Ferdinandstraße. Ten years later when the family returned to Vienna from Frankfurt, they lodged in an apartment owned by Veza's aunt. His paternal grandfather, who came up from Rustchuk on a Danube boat, was a well-known figure on the Leopoldstadt's bustling streets, accosting residents for money for young Jewish women who could not afford a dowry.

In a discarded chapter from *The Torch in the Ear*, "First Visit," he reveals there was an even eerier coincidence. Veza had an "uncle" who lived in West Didsbury, Manchester, where Canetti had first attended school, and on Burton Road no less, where Canetti's family had lived until his father's shocking death:

> I heard from her lips the same names which I remembered as my father's last words. They were the names which made up our address, and he said them for my little brother Georg to repeat so that he could practice the language on them.[34]

The experience of hearing Veza say these words in 1925 was that of a deliverance from the "war" his mother was waging against him on the subject of his wide-ranging academic interests and lack of professional plans. It was also, astoundingly, the first time he spoke about his father since he had died so cruelly and suddenly twelve years earlier. Jacques Calderon even came to Jacques Canetti's funeral, but his presence stuck in the seven-year-old son's memory for unfortunate reasons: Jacques Calderon laughed as if he did not take the death at all seriously. Veza explained it was a nervous reaction to the unspeakable tragedy and recalled that she wondered what was going to happen to the three little boys now that their father was dead. This "uncle" appears twice in *The Tongue Set Free*, first as "Herr Calderon who had the longest moustache and was always laughing" (*VII*:66) when he attended family parties, and then at the funeral where Canetti angrily tries to hit him because of his apparent lack of solemnity.[35] Neither here nor in the next volume where Veza is introduced does he say that the laughing man with the longest moustache is related to Veza.

Veza's immediate family was not as large as her future husband's, but it embodied the cosmopolitanism of the Habsburg Monarchy in similar ways. While her father was from Hungarian Ashkenazi stock, her mother's ancestors were welcomed into the expanding Ottoman Empire in 1492, to which the province of Bosnia-Herzegovina and its unique mix of Muslims, Jews, Catholics, and Orthodox Christians still belonged until 1878 when the Congress of Berlin passed its administration to the Austrians. These Jews could also be called "Turks," as she terms the stepfather in "Money — Money — Money" who moves from Sarajevo to Vienna when he gets married. Veza's maternal relatives lived in both Belgrade, capital of independent Serbia, and in Sarajevo, capital of neighboring Bosnia-Herzegovina where the shots that unleashed the First World War were fired when Veza was sixteen. Between them the Canettis straddled numerous fault lines in Europe's political geography. They both had family on both sides of the First World War. It seems superfluous to point out that their multilingual internationalism, which was reflected in their selection of favorite authors, contradicts the chauvinistic nationalism that caused that war.

Veza and Canetti married in the same month as another couple in Vienna with British connections who made an impact on world affairs: the scion of British Imperialism, Kim Philby, and the working-class Viennese Communist, Lizzy Kohlmann. The future Foreign Office official turned spy needed to get his Austrian girlfriend a British passport so that she could leave the country with him. Their marriage did not last long and both had numerous affairs.[36] The Canettis' marriage lasted twenty-nine years and only he was unfaithful, but their reason for marrying was not entirely dissimilar. It was a time for sticking together. Canetti explained to his brother that by marrying she became officially "stateless" like him and that paradoxically removed the immediate threat of deportation.[37]

His explanation in one of the unused chapters for *The Play of the Eyes* is rather different. Veza was against the idea of marriage because she wanted them both to retain their freedom and independence. She formally left the Jewish religion in May 1931 and rejoined it hastily in order to marry in a synagogue. She gave her consent only for her mother's sake and with the condition that it should not change the way they lived together:

> For really it had been the case that we lived in complete freedom with one another. Veza wanted to keep us away from any of the usual pressure to be tied down. A poet, she believed, had to be free under all circumstances. He could only feel tied insofar as his inner necessity allowed him, and when that was no longer so, he should feel himself free to love another woman without conflict and to preserve his feelings of trust and friendship for the first woman, who would always mean very much. It should be possible for him to turn to her in emotional distress without shyness; he should continue to speak to her about everything which uplifted or troubled him. Nothing should change between them apart from the one thing, for which there are no rules and no laws, at the very most tides.[38]

Such a radical experiment in lifestyle that flouted bourgeois conventions in the name of poetic freedom was not unique in the 1930s. Again, one is reminded of Sartre and de Beauvoir's famed "open relationship," except that in contrast to Veza, de Beauvoir also took lovers, or Brecht's polygamous liaisons with his female literary collaborators. Brecht, however, often went to great lengths to keep the arrangements secret, since he and his co-worker girlfriends were fearful of public opprobrium. The scandalized reactions of posterity that anticipated the criticism of Canetti seems to vindicate their caution.[39]

The freedom that both Canettis cherished determined their *modus vivendi* from this point onwards. The cryptic reference to "the one thing, for which there are no rules and no laws, at the very most tides" apparently signifies their sex life that ended by this time on Veza's own insistence. By recommending that they make this agreement, Veza protected herself, her pride and dignity, as he recognized; perhaps she knew that she could not have him under any other terms. Given the criticism of his behavior, his explanation sounds like special pleading, except that he wrote it before his critics had heard of his wife. Veza also stepped back in horror from the monstrous heroine of *Auto-da-Fé*, whose marriage to the novel's hero ends his intellectual career. If her younger lover feared that she would similarly destroy him, then she was determined to prove him wrong.

In a paragraph from "Marriage (late marriage)," Canetti explains the apparent contradiction in Veza's behavior between the clear feminist sympathies she expresses in her fiction and her seemingly undignified role as a subordinated wife in her married life. He argues that she believed equally in poets and in women. Poets create the world anew and, were it not for them, the world would dry up and wither away. Her love of literature was, after all, what attracted him to her: her own character, he felt, was made from her favorite characters of the books she loved. But she associated women with understanding and a unique kind of intelligence different from the male variety that was dominant in the world. In the author of *Auto-da-Fé*, however horrifying she may have found some of the novel's contents, a genuine poet stood before her and she decided to take him on.

According to Hanuschek, Veza suggested the unconventional form of their relationship eighteen months before they married, in a "letter" she scribbled at the back of a notebook he used for his jottings in the autumn of 1932. The existence of this text indicates that she had access to Canetti's notebooks. It seems that she had a miscarriage in the spring and she gave up the hope of ever having her own child. "I would have been the cleverest mother," she affirms, before adding more mysteriously, "and I will prove it to you." It is not obvious what she means since she goes on to propose that they no longer be lovers even though he will continue to be the most important and the "kindest" person in her life, his "breath as necessary" to her as hers is to him. He should have the freedom, however, to see other women:

> If we determine that now once and for all, then my hysterical reactions will no longer have any grounds. What often worries me is the linking of your youth with my maturity and what I often wish for you is that you have the opportunity to rejuvenate yourself.[40]

Veza, however, wants to know who these women are and get to know them as well. Her relationship with him will fulfill another function: she has no need to give birth herself to prove herself as a mother because she has her younger boyfriend. "For you I will be the best mother and nothing can take you away from us."[41] He often refers to Veza as a "mother," as he does in a letter to Georg explaining his decision to marry (2 March 1934; *BG*:18). She had replaced Mathilde Canetti as partner in his literary conversations long before.

Anna Mahler was the first of his girlfriends Veza befriended after Mahler ended the eight-week affair, which had hurt him deeply. Veza orchestrated his affair with Friedl Benedikt in order to take her husband's mind off Mahler, whom she claims to love as much as Canetti does (to Georg, 20 December 1934; *BG*:28). She advised him what to do with respect to both women. After Mathilde's death in June 1937, she encouraged him to see both Mahler, whose statue of a standing woman was on display in front of the Austrian pavilion at the World Exhibition, and Benedikt, who traveled to Paris to see him.

> I was certain that Veza had encouraged Friedl to undertake this journey, she wanted to have her there as a counterbalance to Anna, she did not care what it took to distract me from what had happened and the intensity of my feeling for Georg, even if it was only for a few hours.[42]

Veza knew and, on the whole, liked Motesiczky, who painted her with a sour expression and a crown on her head, as well as Murdoch, for whom Veza cooked after her trysts with Canetti in Thurlow Road, a detail that shocked many readers of Murdoch's biography.[43] She fell out with her husband's lovers only if they threatened her own position, as Motesiczky did in the late 1940s, or were distracting Canetti from his work, as Benedikt was doing at the same time.[44] In return, Canetti gave her emotional support. She reported to Georg that she wept uncontrollably in his presence after another change of address (27 November 1945; *BG*:157). Her emotional demands often kept him from his desk, to which again, like Kafka, he would retreat in the late evenings to work until the small hours. He was repaying a debt because Veza saved him in Vienna, not only by showing herself ready to take her own life if it would help him, but through the example of her behavior after the Nazi occupation:

> Veza showed her real stature when Austria was occupied and we had to leave Vienna. The half year between March and November 1938 was her heroic period. The word is justified here. Her courage saved my life, as I was not courageous at all, I was filled with the blackest thoughts, and as was shown soon afterwards they were not black enough.[45]

This belongs to the debt of gratitude that filled his thoughts and notebooks after her death.

Unlike her husband, Veza loved the Vienna, where she was born, brought up, and lived most of her life. She felt its loss more than he did. In Britain, she took to signing her name "Veza J Canetti" to embrace the identity that was forced on her. The "J" was short for *Jüdin* (Jewess). After the hardships endured since February 1934 and the humiliations that culminated in the Kristallnacht, when she witnessed Nazi thugs ransack Jewish property and beat up the owners, the prospect of involuntary exile was horrifying, especially for someone who writes. There are several passages in *The Tortoises* that read as if they come straight from the heart. The most personal concerns the fate of the poet who has to flee his native land:

> Leave the country.
> This sentence and this commandment are on everyone's lips in the city in Middle Europe which used to be known as the happiest. The man in the street hears it. He leaves behind his modest bliss and prepares to emigrate with cheeks pale with fear. This sentence upsets the doctor and

the doctor lowers his head in shame. For there are not as many cobble-stones in the streets as wounds that he has healed. And the doctor decides to go. The barrister hears this sentence and sees his life in ruins. The man on the street may begin his life again on foreign soil, the doctor may build a new clinic, the barrister arrives in a foreign country where there are laws which are not laws here. None of his knowledge is knowledge there, nobody will listen to him. He is made worthless.

The sentence is heard by the artist, who has chosen the landscape here. His eye has joined the gentle colors of this stretch of earth together, his pictures tell of this city's history. The artist folds up his easel and decides to emigrate. And the decision weighs heavily on him.

It falls heaviest of all on the poet. His soul is made of language; the characters that he creates are his body. He can only breathe where his language is alive and his life is extinguished when he can no longer understand and be understood. Perhaps this is why this sentence affects the poet so much, although he has been ready to make the decision for a very long time. Although he forces everything in himself toward a separation, although he regards it as a stroke of fate if he succeeds in emigrating to a foreign country, if a new world opens its doors to him, if he is granted entry and not turned away on the threshold. If his good name smoothes his path to a new homeland. For he is sure of one thing: he will not begin his journey lightly. He will fall back in weariness, there will be struggles, fear unto death. Fear now holds sway at the heart of Europe, whose inhabitants used to be known for their kindness. Whose houses were history. Whose women sang songs by Schubert. Fear wears a brown uniform and the swastika. The higher form wears a black uniform with death's-heads. It reaches its apogee in a leader who has nothing human about him apart from his inhumanity. (*SK*:27–28)

Veza's own fears are projected on to her male, central character, another one of her portraits of her husband. What carried him through these long years of exile and obscurity was his seemingly indestructible sense of his own talent and his belief in his mission as a *Dichter*. Veza did not possess similar self-confidence and supported him instead. In both their semi-fictionalized accounts of settling in England (his *Party in the Blitz*, her "Toogoods or the Light"), he is serene and in control, while her identity is fragile.

The Tortoises is all about fear of knocks at the door, of thugs in the street, about the pain of forced departure, and the torture of waiting in uncertainty before permission is granted to leave the country that the narrator loves. That wait in the autumn of 1938 ended happily for Andreas and Eva Kain, even though they crossed the border clutching the ashes of Andreas' older brother, who had been killed by the Nazis, who mistook the older brother for him. A year later in England, Veza wrote to Franz Baermann Steiner: "Yes, my novel is ready and now the waiting begins."[46] That particular wait would go on for a long time: the novel would not be published for another six decades when both she and Steiner had been dead for many years.

Notes

[1] H. G. Adler, "Brief an Veza Canetti v. 5.6.1950," in *Veza Canetti*, edited by Ingrid Spörk and Alexandra Strohmaier (Graz/Vienna: Droschl, 2005, 211–15).

[2] Conradi, *Iris Murdoch*, 643 n. 82. Rubens avoids the word "abortion" in her own memoir, however, recalling only how Veza had told her that Canetti "took steps" to avoid having babies. Bernice Rubens, *When I Grow Up: A Memoir* (London: Little Brown, 2005), 68.

[3] Hanuschek, *Elias Canetti*, 266.

[4] The correct date is 19 February 1934. Angelika Schedel, who has written biographical sketches of Veza's life for three different publications, originally wrote 29 instead of 19, which Hanuschek seems to have copied (Hanuschek, *Elias Canetti*, 265). E-mail from Schedel to the author, 15 September 2005.

[5] Sibylle Mulot, "Leben mit dem Monster," *Facts* 5 (1999): 122–25.

[6] Hanuschek, *Elias Canetti*, 391.

[7] Armin Ayren, "Vom Toten und vom Tod. Erinnerung an Elias Canetti," *Allmende* 46/47 (1995), 146–57; here: 150 and 151.

[8] "Veza und Georg," 11/12 December 1983, ZB 60.

[9] Ruth Beckermann, *Die Mazzeinsel: Juden in der Wiener Leopoldstadt 1918–1938* (Vienna: Löcker, 1984), 11.

[10] "Heirat (späte Heirat)," 14 September 1983, ZB 60.

[11] Angelika Schedel, *Sozialismus und Psychoanalyse: Quellen von Veza Canettis literarischen Utopien* (Würzburg: Königshausen & Neumann: 2002), 155.

[12] "Heirat (späte Heirat)," ZB 60.

[13] Jeremy Adler, "J. as in Jew," *Times Literary Supplement*, 28 February 2003.

[14] Karl Corino, *Robert Musil: Eine Biographie* (Reinbek bei Hamburg: Rowohlt, 2003), 1153.

[15] Peter Stephan Jungk, *A Life Torn by History: Franz Werfel 1890–1945*, trans. Anselm Hollo (London: Weidenfeld & Nicolson, 1990), 153.

[16] Fried to Canetti, 31 May 1963, quoted by Schedel, *Sozialismus und Psychoanalyse*, 202.

[17] Ibid., 172.

[18] Undated note in the papers of Marie-Louise von Motesiczky, quoted by Ines Schlenker, "Painting Authors: The Portraits of Elias Canetti, Iris Murdoch, and Franz Baermann Steiner by Marie-Louise von Motescizky," in *Franz Baermann Steiner Celebrated*, edited by Jeremy Adler, Richard Fardon, and Carol Tully (London: Institute of Germanic Studies, 2003), 105–21; here: 108.

[19] Elias Canetti to Frank and Suse Underwood, 17 June 1963.

[20] Hanuschek, *Elias Canetti*, 457–58.

[21] "Allgemeines: Bedenken. Veza. Das System," ZB 60.

[22] Jeremy Adler, "Introduction," *Party in the Blitz: The English Years*, by Elias Canetti, trans. Michael Hofmann (London: Harvill, 2005), 1–41; here: 33.

[23] 11 June 1963, ZB 22.

[24] DLA Marbach.

[25] Ingeborg Bachmann, *Malina* (Frankfurt am Main: Suhrkamp, 1971), 287.

[26] For H. G. Adler's brief account of meeting Bachmann at the Canettis' flat, see Marcel Atze, ed. *"Ortlose Botschaft": Der Freundeskreis H. G. Adler, Elias Canetti und Franz Baermann Steiner im englischen Exil* (Stuttgart: Marbach, 1998), 126.

[27] Peter Beicken, *Ingeborg Bachmann* (Munich: Beck, 1988), 69.

[28] Schedel quotes from a letter from Veza to Herzfelde dated 13 January 1947. Schedel, *Sozialismus und Psychoanalyse*, 157 and 165.

[29] *Dreißig neue Erzähler des neuen Deutschland: Junge deutsche Prosa*, introd. Bärbel Schrader (Leipzig: Reclam, 1983).

[30] Frank Hermann, *Der Malik-Verlag, 1916–1947: Eine Bibliographie* (Kiel: Neuer Malik, 1989).

[31] Ernst Fischer, *An Opposing Man*, trans. Peter and Betty Ross (London: Allen Lane, 1974), 204.

[32] Ibid.

[33] In *Party in the Blitz*, Canetti calls him "Bucky," which to a German ear is a transcription of "Bookie." I am grateful to Frank Underwood for this information.

[34] "Erster Besuch," ZB 226.

[35] Frank Underwood believes Jacques to be Maurice (or "Bucky"/"Bookie") Calderon, who also had a long moustache. This is certainly possible given the difference in age between him and his half-sister, Veza. As Canetti changed the names of most of the characters in his autobiography, he could easily have turned "Maurice" into "Jacques."

[36] Barbara Honigmann, *Ein Kapitel aus meinem Leben* (Munich: Hanser, 2004), 60–61.

[37] Letter from Elias to Georg Canetti, 2 March 1934.

[38] "Heirat (späte Heirat)," 14 September 1983, ZB 60.

[39] For the fairest treatment, see Sabine Kebir, *Ein akzeptabler Mann? Brecht und die Frauen* (Berlin: Aufbau, 1998).

[40] Hanuschek, *Elias Canetti*, 266.

[41] Ibid.

[42] "Veza und Georg," ZB 60.

[43] Ines Schlenker, " 'So grüss ich vom Herzen meinen Hofmaler Mulo und küss ihn auf die Palette': Die Freundschaft zwischen Elias Canetti und Marie-Louise Motesiczky," *Text und Kritik* 28 (Elias Canetti issue) (2005), 126–39.

[44] Jeremy Adler, "Nachwort," *Aufzeichnungen für Marie-Louise* by Elias Canetti (Munich: Hanser, 2005), 67–113; here: 86.

[45] "Allgemeines: Bedenken. Veza. Das System," 6 September 1982, ZB 60.

[46] Letter from Veza to Steiner, 8 November 1939. DLA Marbach.

2: The Case of Veza Magd

> *They* know *what there is to find before they've seen it.*
>
> —A. S. Byatt, *Possession* (1990)

AFTER SO MANY YEARS OF obscurity Veza Canetti could not have anticipated that more than a quarter of a century after her death her story
would become a feminist cause célèbre. Yet there is no other way to
describe her impact in Germany when her writings began to appear in the
1990s. On the publication of *The Tortoises* in 1999, Anna Mitgutsch, a distinguished Austrian writer and critic, author of a contemporary feminist
classic on abusive family relationships, wrote a scathing attack on her husband. She accused him of direct responsibility for Veza's neglect both
before and after her death, of writing condescendingly about her in the
foreword to *Yellow Street*, and of comparing her realistic stories unfavor-
ably with his own celebrated modernist novel of cultural and mental disintegration, *Auto-da-Fé*. While the great man created, his wife merely
"reported," she alleged Canetti had written.[1] Even if we put aside the
other grounds for her polemic, it remains a peculiar way to greet a novel
which contains one of the most powerful literary accounts of the
Kristallnacht since Günter Grass's *The Tin Drum*.

Mitgutsch was not the first reviewer to think that Veza's "case" was more
interesting than anything she had actually written. The opinion was first
expressed in the pages of the *Frankfurter Allgemeine Zeitung* in response to
Yellow Street.[2] Nor was she the first Austrian woman writer to empathize with
a literary colleague from the 1930s who apparently suffered at the hands of
her husband. Speaking in a lecture series organized in Vienna by Elisabeth
Reichart, entitled "Women Poets on Women Poets," Elfriede Czurda had
made similar allegations against Canetti in 1992.[3] They were also made in *Die
Zeit* in a review of *Patience Brings Roses*, which reportedly upset Canetti.[4]
Reviewing *Yellow Street* for the same newspaper, Sibylle Mulot had noticed
Veza's antagonistic attitude to Knut Tell, whom she identified as a Canetti
portrait.[5] The fact that Veza's work remained unknown for so long seemed
to be evidence enough for these critics that her more famous and longer lived
husband stifled her literary ambitions. His explanation of why she chose the
pseudonym Veza Magd was all one needs to know about his attitude to her.
While he claimed it indicated how she wanted to "serve" the people she
wrote about, these critics knew better: it was her husband "Veza, the maid"
was to serve first and foremost.

Mulot entitled her response to *The Tortoises,* which was printed in the popular Austrian news magazine *Facts,* "Life with the Monster," after Bayley's epithet for the *Dichter* who, to her dying day had enchanted his wife. Bayley had echoed the title of Benedikt's second novel written under Canetti's guidance, ignoring that *The Monster* was not about Canetti himself but about power, his all-consuming preoccupation. This does not concern Mulot, who argues that Veza's attitude to Andreas Kain in *The Tortoises* is even more ambiguous than to Tell in the earlier stories. She contends that Eva Kain, in a tiny part of her soul, identifies her husband with the Nazi Baldur Pilz who evicts the couple from their house. This happens on two separate occasions, according to Mulot: "At the beginning when the external oppressor on the balcony elides for the reader for a brief moment with Eva's husband. Another time later in the garden." Mulot believes that Veza — through Eva — sees "male sex as the oppressive principle, irrespective of political differences."[6]

Two years later, this time in *Der Spiegel* in response to *Der Fund,* Mulot repeats the gossip that Conradi relegated to his footnotes — that Canetti had forced Veza to have abortions. She associates him with Herr Iger from Veza's *The Ogre* — just as Iger metamorphoses into Oger when he signs his name, so the first letter of Elias is said to have change from "E" to "O" when he signed his. She encourages the view that all Veza's fiction is coded autobiography and her marriage the only part of her life she wrote about. Because she believes she can see inside Veza's mind and consequently knows the truth about her feelings for her husband, she rails with her for not having written about Canetti in the way she "should have done," accusing her of largely "bracketing out" the Kains' marital tension: "Why? Self-harming discretion? Or because she had fallen in love with Canetti's brother Georg in Paris? Whatever the reason it is a significant weakness in the novel which augured badly for her future writing."[7] Andreas and Eva Kain are indeed based largely on Canetti and Veza. *The Tortoises* is indeed autobiographical fiction in a number of other ways as well. But the Kains are, above all, characters in a novel and products of the novelist's imagination; it is impossible for a critic to know that there is tension in their fictional marriage that can be "bracketed out." How does Mulot know there was such tension in the Canettis' marriage? She offers no evidence, instead she merely makes assertions.

The attacks fed on a mixture of half-digested fact (that Canetti destroyed not only Veza's correspondence but his own memoirs of their time in London), rumor (that Veza took her own life), speculation (that she destroyed her own writings in 1956 because of Murdoch's success that year with her second novel, *The Flight from the Enchanter* and Canetti's with the premiere of *The Numbered* in Oxford), and incompetent literary criticism (Andreas Kain is in fact portrayed with deep, even cloying affection, meanwhile his elder brother Werner who is murdered by the Nazis is by no means his nobler other self). For Canetti's critics, his worst omission was failing to mention in his autobiography that his wife was a writer.[8] He might have replied that he had done so in draft chapters that he subsequently discarded (as we now know from his papers to be the case), or that he broadcast the fact to Swiss radio listeners more than twenty years ago. A sentence in the foreword to *Yellow Street* is quoted frequently to illustrate his "monstrous blindness" and "uninhibited egocentrism."[9] Yet his recollection of how Veza began to write the stories that fed into *Yellow Street* in response to his preoccupation with his own novel is open to a kinder reading: "In order not to sacrifice her own identity, she began to write herself, and in order not to jeopardize the concept of the grand project, which I needed, she treated her own work as if it were nothing" (*GS*:5). Could he have reached this realization without a degree of self-awareness and self-criticism. This is evident in his qualifying phrase: "which I needed." He was recalling a time sixty years ago; when he wrote that he was no longer the man or the author he had been then. Furthermore, his recollection of the sequence of events and Veza's behavior might well be accurate.

The argument is not only about Veza, however. There are other allegations: that Canetti had excised the negative references to himself in Hermann Broch's published letters and, as part of a program of rewriting his own left-wing past, he "denounced" Ernst Fischer by claiming that he happily sent his comrades in the Communist resistance to their deaths.[10] A surviving friend of Fischer's calls this a "defamation," but does not deny its substance. He argues that Canetti was angered by Fischer's published critique of *Crowds and Power*, which, as it is a piece of Marxist dogma typical of Fischer's writing after 1945, he had every reason to be.[11] The two friends had fallen out long ago after taking very different paths after February 1934, when Fischer joined the Communist resistance to Dollfuß and Schuschnigg's "corporate state."

The Canetti scholar and former intimate, Gerald Stieg, identifies a "campaign" against Canetti that he dates to the publication of *The Play of the Eyes* in 1985 and an essay by the influential critic, Gerhard Melzer, on "the potentate Elias Canetti," which Mitgutsch cites numerous times.[12] Melzer locates misogynistic leanings in a memorable chapter from the beginning of *The Tongue Set Free*, where the five-year-old narrator tries to kill his cousin Laurica because she would not reveal to him the secrets of reading and writing. As an adult Canetti became a writer who "kills when he writes," needing to assert his intellectual superiority over others in elaborate verbal and psychological power games. Unless he submits willingly to another person, such as Karl Kraus, he must emerge as the "victor" and "survivor," with all the implications the term "survival" has in *Crowds and Power* of triumphing over the deaths of others.[13] This claim overstates the link between Canetti's life and his writing in a way that later becomes routine. Veza was the first to use the tactic, however, during her bitter quarrel with him in the early 1930s. In "The Victor," Siegfried Salzman gloats over the death of the powerless Anna Seidler, who clandestinely learned to write in order to serve him better and improve her own prospects. Canetti responds by self-mockingly calling himself "victor" in *Comedy of Vanity*, which was his literary gesture of reconciliation.

Canetti's last volume of his autobiography, which covered the period in which *Comedy of Vanity* was written, concentrates on overcoming such power-based attitudes toward other human beings. Exemplary figures who have achieved this in their life, conversation, or writing are the artist Georg Merkel, who painted a portrait of Veza (13 April [?] 1938; *BG*:111), Dr. Abraham Sonne, Canetti's last and greatest mentor, whom Veza disliked, and Robert Musil, whose mammoth unfinished novel, *A Man without Qualities*, Canetti greatly admired and Veza mildly parodied in *Yellow Street*. One might argue that the recollection of his attempt on his cousin's life reflected his fascination with the printed word that dates to his infancy. When he meets Laurica as an adult, her inability to remember what for him was a formative experience that now has immense symbolic power in his autobiographical narrative, does not betray her feminine frivolity, as Melzer asserts. Instead, it shows how two individuals can appreciate the past very differently. Whatever the precise rights and wrongs of these cases, Canetti, who was no stranger to controversy in his lifetime, posthumously generated debates in the usually staid confines of the academic journals. When the debates concerned Veza, they spilled over into the more sensationally minded sections of the press.

A number of academic feminists were quick to claim that Veza's story vindicated their understanding of the literary past. Writing about her became the preserve of women critics: the first two monographs are by Eva Meidl and Angelika Schedel; a special issue of *Text und Kritik* had a clear majority of women contributors in 2002; an edited student guide from 2005 contained no contributions by men whatsoever.[14] On the other hand, when men did express an opinion, they sometimes reacted on cue by downplaying Veza's achievement in just the way Canetti had feared. Ulrich Weinzierl not only found her "case" more interesting than her first novel, he recommended Canetti's foreword to *Yellow Street* over the text of the novel itself. Meanwhile the playwright Rolf Hochhuth found the Zurich premiere of *The Ogre* dull and felt that it was only performed (and *Yellow Street* published) due to her widower's intervention.[15]

The topic of the literary marriage was in vogue at the end of the 1980s. In 1988 Klaus Theweleit published his multi-volume account of how male writers from Dante to Freud had used and abused their real-life female "muses" to create art. Eva Meidl characterized the Canettis' relationship by quoting from Inge Stephan's classic study of "literary marriages" that was published the year before *Yellow Street*.[16] For Theweleit, the leading exponents of German high Modernism, such as Kafka, Rilke, and Gottfried Benn — all at least a generation older than Canetti — are guilty of bad faith in their dealings with women, but they all wrote better poems or novels as a result of their involvement with them. This practice reaches back to the mythic beginnings of Western literature. The first poet in the Western tradition valued his song more than his mistress and sang all the more powerfully after he looked back to glimpse her stumbling up from Hades. In Stephan's case studies, the younger gifted woman abandons her creative projects when she links her fortunes to those of the already famous man. Two reviewers of *The Tortoises* cited Theweleit: one to say that he now had material at his disposal for another installment of his book; another contended that, on the contrary, he had written the script for the scandal in advance.[17] Or, to put it another way, and feminists fitted what they deduced from Veza's case into a ready-made paradigm of husband-and-wife literary collaboration.

They also found a set of reasons to account for Veza's long disappearance that led them to welcome her first three posthumously published books for a number of negative reasons. For Czurda it was significant that Veza failed to publish after her marriage. However, we now know that she published three stories in 1937 and carried on writing for at least fifteen years after that — whereas he published nothing of significance for twenty-five years after becoming her husband. Czurda identifies the couple as the characters Leda Frisch and Heinrich Föhn in *Comedy of Vanity* and quotes Heinrich's words to Leda:

> You shall have your own song, Leda. I had to deny it to you up to now, it would have disturbed me too much. By now I am so firmly established that nothing can throw me off my course — unless it is a sun which is more powerful than me and I haven't yet found one which is. (*II*:136)

She adds: "Venetiana's sin against Canetti is that she began to write herself, and is not, like Leda, merely the voice for his song."[18] She misreads *Comedy of Vanity* on a number of counts: Heinrich Föhn is a satirical self-portrait and by the end of the play it is Dr. Leda Frisch who "cures" her patient of his guilt and — by extension — can return the sense of identity and self-respect to the rest of the population that was subjected to a ban on all images of themselves and all means of producing them. Through Föhn and Frisch, Canetti explores, in part, his relationship with the woman who was soon to become his wife. He is offering her a literary olive branch after their exhausting falling out over *Auto-da-Fé* rather than endorsing the subjugation of women in literature.

By claiming that marriage prevented Veza from continuing to write, Czurda also ignored the greater obstacle to the literary career of any Jewish or socialist author after February 1934, namely, the "corporate state," which among other oppressive measures closed down the *Arbeiter-Zeitung* that published Veza's stories. All that they, but especially Veza, had hoped and worked for politically was crushed. This defeat affected her writing more than her marriage to a young, unpublished novelist. It blocked her avenues for publication.

There is indeed a connection to Theweleit that runs through the writer who fascinated Canetti more than the triumvirate of modern Viennese greats (Kraus, Broch, Musil) in the pantheon he cited in his Nobel acceptance speech: Kafka.[19] Theweleit quotes Canetti several times concerning Kafka's *Letters to Felice*.[20] He senses that one can read *Kafka's Other Trial,* Canetti's first major piece of writing after Veza's death, as displaced autobiography. This is why in *The Torch in the Ear* and *The Play of the Eyes* Canetti wove in references to Kafka's epistolary obsession with the Berlin businesswoman he met at Max Brod's house on the evening he corrected the proofs of his first collection of stories.[21] Theweleit quotes the following passage in order to imply that Canetti could only have known the truth of what he wrote from his own experience, and that he wrote about himself more than Kafka:

> It is thus, and not only judging from our later point of view, a magnificent period; there are few times in his life which can be compared with it. If one may judge from the results, and how else is one supposed to judge a poet's life, then Kafka's behavior in the first three months of the correspondence with Felice was exactly the right thing for him. His feeling told him what he needed: a point of security in the distance, a source of strength, which did not disrupt his sensitivity, a woman who was there for him, expecting nothing more from him than his words, a kind of transformer, whose miscellaneous technical shortcomings he knew and controlled well enough to negate them immediately with letters. The woman who served him for this purpose could not be exposed to the influences of his family, from whose proximity he suffered; he had to keep her away from them. (*VI:*173)[22]

Kafka wrote *The Judgement, Metamorphosis,* and *The Man who Disappeared* during this time; he began *The Trial* shortly after he broke off their six-week-old engagement nearly two years later. For Canetti, Kafka's "other trial" is what he submitted himself to as a consequence of his treatment of Felice and what consumed him with guilt and fed directly into his most famous novel.

The circumstances under which Canetti wrote *Auto-da-Fé* in his lodgings on the Hagenberggasse are not dissimilar to Kafka in Prague writing to Felice in Berlin: he had his own key to Veza's family apartment to reassure himself that he could call on her at any time should a personal or creative crisis drive him to do so. In this light, *Auto-da-Fé* corresponds with *The Trial* and Therese Krumbholz becomes Peter Kien's Fräulein Bürstner, the elusive object of Josef K.'s predatory attentions, who shares Felice

Bauer's initials. Canetti claims to have come across Kafka's *Metamorphosis* after beginning to write and to have found immediate affinities with it, but *Auto-da-Fé* has just as many with Kafka's own bachelor novel, which he claims he read later. Josef K. is arrested on his thirtieth birthday; Peter Kien is forty when crisis strikes him. Both novels begin with the disruption of a daily routine that proves permanent, both central characters die on the last page after completing an odyssey through the city in search of salvation.

There are other striking points of comparison in their lives and writing that Canetti was only too well aware of. They shared an interest in China, Chinese literature, and Sinology; they blurred the boundaries between species by writing about animals as if they were human (in part a reaction to their status as Jews in an anti-Semitic environment); and they were both interested in power.[23] They both came from Jewish families who pushed their eldest sons towards a career in business and both studied vocational subjects (Law, Chemistry) while listening to lectures in other fields which interested them more. While Kafka subsequently exhausted himself by combining work by day at the Workers' Insurance Institute of the Kingdom of Bohemia with a nocturnal existence as a writer, Canetti shunned regular employment in favor of a life of the mind. Kafka chose writing over marriage because marriage would have entailed the beginning of an ordered bourgeois existence and spelt the death of his writing. Canetti found a better solution because Veza agreed to grant him the same freedoms in marriage that he had enjoyed outside it. These were the freedoms due to a poet, to a *Dichter*, and, as we have seen, she only consented to get married if he promised to retain them. If Europe's political horizon had not darkened, he would have had the best of both worlds, something that Kafka never believed to be possible.

Kafka's Other Trial was Canetti's first new work to be dedicated "For Veza Canetti." He writes on the first page that he has been more captivated by the letters than by any work of literature for many years and that:

> these letters have entered me as if they were a real life, and I now find them so puzzling and so familiar as if they had belonged to me since the time when I started to try to absorb people completely into myself in order to begin anew, time and time again, to understand them. (*VI*:165)

Reading *Letters to Felice* shortly after Veza's death was a cathartic experience. Presenting Veza through Felice shows the same self-awareness and self-criticism, which he had already shown more than thirty years earlier in *Comedy of Vanity*.

Veza forced Canetti to reflect on his use of her as muse for *Auto-da-Fé*. She angrily objected to his depiction of women and was disturbed by his personal behavior toward her while he was writing. She believed, with some reason, that he used her memory of her mistreatment at the hands of her stepfather to depict his profoundly self-deluded and congenitally stupid anti-heroine. Veza, the novel's first reader, recognized her young boyfriend in Kien and feared Canetti was exploring an aspect of his feelings for her through Kien's relationship with his housekeeper turned wife. By calling herself Veza Magd, she ironically embraced this identity: Therese Krumbholz from Canetti's novel began her career as a maid. There are also traces of Veza's stepfather, who had died a year before Canetti started *Auto-da-Fé*, in the violent, money-grabbing caretaker, Benedikt Pfaff, the "kind father" who murders his wife before "marrying" his daughter and beating her to death. Veza could have seen herself portrayed twice: first as illiterate wife, then as abused and murdered daughter. She knew that all his characters had their real-life models and that their "acoustic masks" were taken from everyday speech. Canetti never made a secret of her negative reaction to the novel, but the reasons for that rejection, the nature of her response, and his reaction to it can only be reconstructed through a close reading of the texts they produced together in the first half of the 1930s.

Only one episode in their long relationship, that is while writing his novel, fits the feminist paradigm elaborated in the late 1980s by Theweleit and Stephan. Theweleit's judgments on Kafka have not gone unchallenged (Felice, for example, was an independent-minded individual and successful businesswoman who did not let herself be used for long).[24] There are a number of ways in which the Canettis' case differed from the others that Theweleit analyzes. Canetti and Veza *both* wrote and at the beginning of their writing careers they carried on a dialogue with one another in their writings. It was only in exile in England, when she was losing hope of finding publishers that *she* dealt with *his* correspondence, as he helped her by trying to interest publishers in her work. When she destroyed her own writing, she was already working on *Crowds and Power* with him. There is no sign that she worked for him on his projects while they lived and wrote in Vienna, where she was successful in her own right. "The Flight from the Earth" is her mildly satirical version of one of his abandoned projects, not a story she wrote to help him. She was, after all, his senior by eight years and was initially the senior intellectual partner. He read her his poems, which she often inspired, then chapters from his novel, and she responded with advice and encouragement. She even commented on his work in his notebooks. Felice only saw Kafka's published fiction and then she disappointed him with her reactions, as she did with her insensitive praise of other authors. By the end, Veza and Canetti had been close for thirty-eight years, in contrast, Kafka knew Felice for only five.

There is evidence that the conflict ended by the time they married and that Canetti lost the battle. Veza's response was swift. Knut Tell, her ironic portrait of Canetti made his first appearance in the *Arbeiter-Zeitung* in April 1933. She reacted to themes, motifs, and the general narrative tone of *Auto-da-Fé*, critically or correctively, and gave her own account of the behavior of predatory patriarchs in "The Victor" and subsequently in two chapters of *Yellow Street*, "The Tiger" and "The Ogre," both of which she made into plays. As I will show, "The Ogre"/*The Ogre* is both her response to his chapter "The Kind Father" and a fictionalized version of her mother and stepfather's marriage, not an account of her own. In *Comedy of Vanity*, Canetti indicated he wanted a reconciliation with a positive and more explicit portrait of Veza in the character Leda Frisch and a revised treatment of gender, especially as related to housemaids, that shows appreciation of the impact their working conditions had on their psyche. He completed it in early 1934 while she wrote *The Ogre* and while the political circumstances in Austria worsened. Thereafter they appear to have worked together as seen in her writings of the mid- to late 1930s and later in his *Crowds and Power*. *The Ogre* and *Comedy of Vanity* are both optimistic diagnoses of the political crisis of 1934; both feature doctors (in his play, this is Leda Frisch) who carry out acts of healing which can be read allegorically. The political circumstances in Austria at this time hardly warranted their shared optimism, as expressed in these plays, which was possibly more an expression of their private contentment, however short-lived that would prove to be given the outside pressures that would force them out of the country within five years.

Veza's role in the writing of *Crowds and Power* has never been a secret. In 1962 H. G. Adler dedicated his autobiographical novel *A Journey*, "For Elias and Venezia Canetti" and congratulated *both* on the publication of the English version of *Crowds and Power*.[25] His son, Jeremy, who knew both of them, calls their relationship a "literary partnership" and *Crowds and Power* the magnum opus to which they both "sacrificed their lives as novelists."[26] In the draft of a letter to Kathleen (Raine?) after Veza's death, Canetti wrote (in English):

> I want her to exist in the memory of the world when all my own works are dead and forgotten. Whatever compassion and love for other human beings I had came from her. She died, of course, in the worst possible moment, when my own work, which was half her work, was beginning to bear fruit.[27]

He repeated the assertion many times, including in a Swiss radio interview in 1968. When he told the German critic Hermann Kesten, he specified that her role was as intellectual partner in discussion:

> I am now finally sending you a copy of *Crowds and Power* which has cost me more than twenty years of my life. Perhaps, if you read it, you will find that my wife's miserable life was not completely for nothing. Her intellectual part in it is as great as mine. There is not a syllable in it which we did not consider and discuss together.[28]

Kafka's Other Trial was as close as he came to giving an account of his and Veza's own work together. The second two volumes of autobiography are largely missed opportunities for a posthumous dialogue with her because he decides to omit the key chapters. The literary life he in the end decided to write (as opposed to that we know from the unpublished chapters that he considered writing) is too stylized and too symbolically unifying for it to contain the disturbing, contradictory chunk of reality that Veza represented. He does, however, deal at length with characters and motifs which, as is evident from her writing, the pair discussed half a century earlier.

Canetti's other female literary partners, like Brecht's, were not there "to transform manuscripts into typescripts," as Felice told Kafka she liked to do.[29] Instead they wrote, or painted, or sculpted — and at least one, Iris Murdoch, became more successful. Benedikt and Mahler were excited that Canetti had written a novel; his being a writer made him more attractive to both of them, as if writing and sex were contiguous domains. Veza's knowledge of literature had also attracted him to her when they first met at the Karl Kraus performance. Neither Mahler nor Benedikt can be called muses whose role was limited to catering to their artist lover's practical or emotional needs. His experience with them does not appear to have helped him write. On the contrary, Mahler's rejection contributed to his lack of productivity in his remaining Viennese years; Benedikt's demands kept him from his own project in London. He had a literary partnership with Benedikt, albeit an unequal one. At his behest, she kept a journal from May 1942 to December 1944 that she entitled with ironic pathos, *The Wretched Work of a Besotted and Lazy Pupil*, parts of which show resemblances to passages in *Party in the Blitz*. 1942 was also the year that he began to devote himself on a daily basis to his "jottings." *The Monster* can be read as a variation on a theme for *Crowds and Power* and shows an engagement with his ideas rather than with his personality, in particular the central concept of the "sting" left behind by the command in the person of the commanded. In his desire to compete with God, Jonathan Crisp resembles the real-life paranoiac, Daniel Paul Schreber, whose case Canetti discusses at the end of his "big book." Veza claims to Georg repeatedly that Canetti wrote all three of Benedikt's novels for her, but the quality of her writing in her journal shows that she possessed talent of her own.

When Canetti's women speak about him, a different picture sometimes emerges from the one painted by his feminist critics or the male champions of his female "victims." Kathleen Raine considered herself "one of Canetti's failures" because he had been so generous with his advice and teaching and she was unable to live up to his expectations. She recalls that their mutual friends admiringly called him "the Master" or "the Professor":

> It was at one of William Empson's parties at Hampstead I first met Elias Canetti, sometime during the war. I had never seen anyone quite like him;

as if tremendous energy had been compacted into his small but dynamic person. "He is like a little lion," that same Frederica [Rose] said; but with all the energy of a large lion, or a whole pride of lions concentrated in his immense mental vitality. It was this vitality, coupled with an equally immense interest in people, which first impressed me in him, and no doubt I, like many others, found irresistible his evident interest in what I thought, did, was; an interest at once concerned and disinterested; for Canetti's concern (again like Socrates) is with the discovery and evocation of the essence of each person, with what Ibsen calls the vital illusion, seeing each as one more manifestation of the variousness of life. For those who want simple answers Canetti has none to give; he was essentially "the Master" for those who wanted complex answers. Those who conversed with Socrates must all have left him not only with a clearer, but with an essentially more interesting notion of who and what they themselves were; and so it was with Canetti. Are we not most indebted to those masters who chip our statues out of our marble? So, as with Socrates, those who loved him did so principally for own sakes, because he had the magical power of evoking for us, ourselves. Yet the converse is, perhaps, also true; as Gavin [Maxwell] once said, "none of us needs Canetti as much as Canetti needs us." We were, indeed, his raw material, which every artist needs supremely.[30]

Canetti's relationships with his "disciples" were a matter of give and take: he gave "his intelligence, his compassion, his time" and in return he observed them as objects of study.[31] From Raine he learnt about William Blake, whom he places high in his personal pantheon in *Party in the Blitz* and on whom she would publish numerous books.

He also had male confidants and students. Nassauer's *The Hooligan* bears Canetti's stamp as much as Fried's *A Soldier and a Girl*, both published the same year as *Crowds and Power* (Fried's novel with the same Hamburg publisher). Another young male poet, fresh in cosmopolitan London from his native South Wales, was as captivated by the Hampstead "master" as Canetti had once been himself by his Viennese mentors, Kraus and Sonne. The experience of listening to him in the Hampstead cafés, where the atmosphere of smoke, coffee, talk, and newspapers recreated a lost Central Europe, left no scars on Dannie Abse, as he recalled after revisiting Canetti's favorite haunt:

After I left The Coffee Cup, I kept remembering how kind Canetti had been to me when I was young: had shown me texts I would not otherwise have encountered; listened to my youthful, opinionated vapourings as if they were important; told me of writers I had not yet heard of, such as Cesare Pavese and a not yet published young novelist called Iris Murdoch; introduced me to Kathleen Raine, thinking she might be a useful person for me to know; even arranged for a desperately flawed verse-play of mine to be presented at the Institute of Contemporary Arts. I was in debt to him for many long-ago things — remembered and unremembered, not least a 1905 book of Bushmen legends.[32]

Abse was well aware too that in studying human nature, in particular people's responses to displays of power, Canetti was collecting material for his
book, and that he *toyed* with others to test their reactions.

Abse and Raine are positively disposed in their recollections of Canetti,
though Raine's memory of their friendship soon soured. Nassauer became a
lifelong friend but he and his then wife, Bernice Rubens were bruised by their
Canetti experience, as Benedikt, Murdoch, and Motesiczky all were at various
times. Nassauer's *The Cuckoo*, a lesser novel than *The Hooligan* that followed
quickly on its heels and partly describes its genesis, centers on a series of
unequal artistic partnerships: between Klein and E. (Canetti and Benedikt),
which is over by the time the action of this roman-à-clef begins; between the
authorial narrator and Klein (Nassauer and Canetti); and between Aaron
Fawkes, the artist-cuckoo based on Allan Forbes, Benedikt's lover at the time
of her death, and the narrator's wife Ria (Rubens also published her first novel
in 1960, which is something of an *annus mirabilis* for this North London
coterie).[33] Both Nassauer's authorial narrator and his wife Ria are teachers to
Aaron Fawkes who comes to live in their house at Klein's instigation and
begins an affair with Ria that her husband affects not to mind. But why does
Nassauer call his Canetti figure Klein (meaning small), as Murdoch had done
the previous year in *A Severed Head* (a novel in which she also splits her
Canetti character into two)? Why does he give the gentile Allan Forbes the
Jewish name Aaron? He is surely exploring complicated aspects of his feelings
towards Canetti, and in particular Canetti's use of literary pupils and partners.

Nassauer projects Canetti's personality differently on to several characters, positively on to the benevolent Klein who is the obvious Canetti portrait, a little less appealingly on to the choleric narrator who tolerates Aaron
in his house because he feels superior to him, and more insidiously on to the
parasitic Aaron. This strategy of narrative splitting gives Nassauer the leeway
he needs to criticize his friend's behavior while ostensibly praising him. He
discretely draws his readers' attention to the connection between Aaron and
Klein, and specifically to Aaron's contribution to our understanding of
Klein's character: "Klein was an enormous mosaic we were constructing, for
which Aaron brought us a hundred new pieces every day."[34] Aaron's artistic
method seems very familiar to anyone who knew Canetti, as he has "the gift
of acute and fast observation."[35] Capturing photographic images of anonymous individuals on the city's streets recalls Canetti's ability to record
"acoustic masks":

> He was the passive recorder, a hunter, the gasman who collects the pen-
> nies in the slot, the laundry-man, the collector in whatever field you like,
> the clerk of art, uncreative, the cuckoo who needed Ria to hatch his
> artistic, speckled eggs.[36]

Only through a female can the male artist be productive. In a bizarre and
not entirely clear comparison, the narrator says that Aaron reminds him of

a friend he once had who made sausage skins because he absorbs and reprocesses his material like a sausage maker.

The Cuckoo is an homage to Canetti which contains numerous references to his preferred reading (Stendhal and Dostoyevsky) as well as themes from *Crowds and Power* (transformation and survival). The narrator wants to be Klein's friend, is delighted when he calls to collect a manuscript he has written, and even more pleased when he praises it. He enjoys too their journey to Germany and Austria. Rubens herself behaved not altogether differently from her former husband in her posthumously published memoir. She claimed to have hated Canetti because of the way he interfered in other people's lives, especially her own after she had married Nassauer. But, in a bizarre recollection, she confides that she refrained from running him down in her car when he was wandering across Haverstock Hill "deep in filthy thought" because "I needed him around so that I could go on hating him."[37] It seems that he was useful to her for her art as a kind of anti-muse, a figure she had created for her own purposes in her imagination.

While Nassauer's Klein is apparently not married, Veza's attitudes to the women who threatened to crowd her out of her husband's life were friendly: this was part of their agreement of autumn 1932. She portrayed both Benedikt and Mahler as strong, resourceful women in "The Tiger"/*The Tiger* and *The Tortoises* respectively. Canetti depicts them in *The Play of the Eyes*, where he makes plain his disappointment at Mahler suddenly dumping him. In his account, the Hungarian poetess, Ibby Gordon, was the first artist-girlfriend to compete with Veza for his attention, though he insists a little implausibly that their relationship remained platonic ("we never kissed," *VIII*:291).

His affair with Motesiczky generated art too. In 1939 in the Surrey town of Amersham he again found a partner who encouraged him with his own writing, while adapting his ideas in her own work, as Veza had done a decade before. While Canetti presented Motesiczky with a notebook of jottings on her birthday in October 1942, Veza, dedicated a novel to her. Jeremy Adler writes:

> They lived for art — if we may for the sake of argument count *Crowds and Power* as a work of art — and the friendship they had with one another consisted for the most part in mutual encouragement, whether of a practical or intellectual nature. Canetti coaxed his girlfriend, who was tortured by self-doubt, to paint and more than once helped her win an important commission; she served the poet, on the other hand, as a patron.[38]

Like Mahler, Motesiczky ultimately had little time for *Crowds and Power*, which she appears not to have read when it was finally published. She also had a low opinion of his views on painting, just as he did not value her views on literature, but she painted him numerous times, once in conversation with Steiner, who was Murdoch's fiancé when he died suddenly in 1952. In other paintings she makes no attempt to disguise her disappointment that he refused to formalize their relationship or pay her more attention. It was shortly after Steiner's death that Canetti began his own affair with Murdoch. When her old Oxford college wanted a portrait of their famous philosophy fellow, Motesiczky won the commission.

These artistic and biographical interconnections give some impression of the unusual nature of the Canettis' marriage and creative partnership. Art and his status and demands as a *Dichter* sometimes took precedence over more conventional considerations. In a letter to Steiner a year and a half after they had arrived in Britain, his friend Kae Hursthouse reveals that Benedikt, his present mistress, is sharing one of the two rooms in their new flat and helps Veza cook, while former girlfriend Mahler "is around alot."[39] Their agreement was evidently working nearly ten years after they had made it.

The literary links run not only from Canetti to each of the three women writers, Veza, Benedikt, and Murdoch, who each knew his early published work and his opus in progress, *Crowds and Power*: they also knew each other and read each other's work. They put each other in their fiction. Conradi identifies Veza as the refugee dressmaker Nina in *The Flight from the Enchanter*, one of the female "creatures" whom Mischa Fox (the enchanter in the novel's title) keeps at his beck and call, and we might recognize her too in the Polish brothers' deaf and blind grandmother, who sits at one end of an L-shaped room while her sinister sons take turns to make love to the heroine, Rosa Keepe. Nina kills herself in despair, fearing that she may be deported. In life she sacrificed her independence to Fox, who pays her rent and expects her to comply to his every whim in return. This construction reverses the Canettis' own straitened financial arrangements since Veza was more likely to pay for their modest upkeep. A poverty-stricken enchanter could have found no place in Murdoch's imagination.

While Murdoch was not aware that Veza was a published author, she revered her as a person. Benedikt knew Veza's stories and her first two novels focus on housemaids, whose lives Veza Magd chronicled in her Viennese fiction. She mentions Veza once in her journal and once again in a letter, where it is obvious that the pupil-mistress has fallen out with the partner-wife. To Canetti she distances herself from Veza's moral and political commitment: "By the way, I think that is one of the things about Veza which half attract and but then again repel me — her partisanship, her exaggerated partisanship."[40] In a letter to Steiner, she is less guarded and gives a glimpse of the tensions which existed in their triangular ménage. Steiner wonders why Canetti, ever the poor correspondent, has not replied to his letter. Benedikt gives her view:

> The reason that he has not answered your letter is that he is ashamed to tell you that Veza does not want you to come. You know what she is like.

She does not approve of anybody Canetti likes to spend time with and talk to. As he still hoped to persuade her, he didn't want to write you off completely either. The devil take her![41]

For her part, Veza spills out her venom for Benedikt on page after page of her letters to Georg, but her concern is for the effect Benedikt's behavior is having on Canetti. In friendlier times Benedikt was the model for the "young girl" Hilde in *The Tortoises* who competes with Eva for Andreas Kain's attentions. Benedikt returned the compliment by portraying Veza, rather less flatteringly, as Veronica Cressfield in *The Dreams*, the middle-aged widow who sits alone in the White Ship every evening.

The case with Murdoch is different from that with Benedikt: she was thirty-one rather than nineteen when she met her late fiancé's best friend and, if she added Canetti to her list of powerful and knowledgeable older mentors whose mistress she became, she knew exactly what she wanted from him and took no instruction. He comments to this effect on her use of her lovers in *Party in the Blitz*. She needed ideas and characters and she gets this "booty" from them, exchanging sex for one-sided conversation. She was a passionate listener, which irked Canetti because he felt she took without giving and that is why her books in his opinion are such a "stew" of others' thoughts. After they had first made love she confided to him that she had imagined him to be an Oriental pirate who held her captive in a cave before ravishing her. This amuses him at first, he says, as it certainly was due to his account of his childhood in the Ottoman Balkans that inspired her fantasy. But his amusement was short-lived: he recognizes that she is using him in the role of muse and finds that "Every way to love was blocked for me by her dream" (*PiB*:181). Soon he sees her as a pirate who robs each of her lovers not of his heart, but of his mind.

This gives us another insight into those figures Canetti is said to have inspired. The point about Mischa Fox in *The Flight from the Enchanter* is that he is what those enthralled by him want to make him, whereas Honor Klein in *A Severed Head* is ultimately a pathetic figure. The repeated descriptions of her Jewish features and "tawny breasts" are unwittingly borrowed from caricature, which is surely a reason that Canetti recalls with distaste how Murdoch exoticized him. For the evil genius Julius King in *A Fairly Honourable Defeat*, she uses Canetti's Sephardic origins and his foreignness in English surroundings in ways that he had good reason to find distasteful: King's malign obsession with power is revealed at the end of the novel to be a consequence of his spending the war in Bergen-Belsen.

Canetti was not always the dominant partner and he often benefited from his female contacts. Benedikt introduced him to her editor at Cape, C. V. Wedgwood, who introduced him to English readers by translating *Die Blendung* into *Auto-da-Fé*. Cape published *Let thy Moon Arise* and *The Monster* in 1944 before *Auto-da-Fé* in 1946. At a literary party towards the end of the war, he was introduced as her "friend and teacher, to whom she had dedicated both her novels" (*PiB*:70), but nobody among the twenty or thirty writers and poets assembled had heard of *him*. His debt to Murdoch was similar. She reviewed the translation of *Crowds and Power* for *The Spectator*, one of only two positive reactions to it in the English literary press, as Conradi pointedly notes.[42] Her endorsement of *Auto-da-Fé* has adorned its cover ever since its first re-issue in 1965 and it is not the only one of his books which her blurbs helped to sell (she also helped Nassauer similarly with *The Hooligan*).

When Veza's writings began to appear in 1990, critics were right to sense a massive disjunction between the couple's respective oeuvres. Canetti's literary work stretched over nearly six decades and he was known for his disdain of commercialism in the literary media. Even now that all her surviving writings are published, Veza's output is slim by comparison. She preferred shorter forms, wrote for a daily newspaper rather than posterity, and has little to set against the sheer scope of his major books.

Canetti answered the charge of delaying an earlier publication of Veza's work by replying that he wanted her work to be appreciated for her own sake, not because she shared his name. He did not want to present her as a failed author, given her complete lack of success after leaving Vienna. Allusion to her writing might have interested a publisher just because she was called Canetti — not, of course, that she had published under her married name while she was alive. The attention that was paid to him each time one of her books appeared has borne this out; reviewers were never entirely sure they would be reading her work at all had she not married a "famous man." His reticence does not bespeak a low opinion of her fiction and drama, though one might imagine that his confidence in its merits was dented after her years of frustration, first in Austria, and then in England. After *Yellow Street*, *The Ogre*, and *Patience Brings Roses* were published in the early 1990s, he was unwilling to release either *The Tiger* or *The Tortoises* because he felt they were less successful and he wanted her reputation to establish itself before letting others read them.[43] His intentions can be interpreted differently: either he still exercised the same insufferable control over her estate as he always had, or, he acted honorably and in Veza's best interests. No admirer of her work could dispute that some of the material that was eventually included in *Der Fund* does not match the quality of *Yellow Street*. Yet he was wrong about *The Tortoises*, which is a uniquely poetic and sober account of the plight of Vienna's Jews between the Nazi invasion in March and the pogrom of the Kristallnacht in November 1938.

Veza's case was always likely to return to haunt Canetti. Göbel reveals that he was wounded by Mulot's comments in *Die Zeit*. Ayren reports how Angela Praesent's comments in *Die Zeit* in April 1992 also upset him because she got so much *wrong*.[44] He blamed Göbel for telling Mulot about Veza's missing arm, even though Göbel's source was Fischer. Canetti's autobiography ultimately played a role in getting Veza's work published: Göbel was prompted to write to him after finding a scribbled note "Veza Magd (Veza Canetti?)" in a bookseller's catalogue. He had already been contacted regarding the identity of Veza Magd after the re-issue of the East German anthology edited by Herzfelde for the Malik Press, *Thirty New Writers from the New Germany*, which included Veza's novella, "Patience Brings Roses." Canetti suggested a meeting and he proposed the publication of *Yellow Street*, which he could now honorably present as Göbel's find, as was clearly very important to him. Once the novel was published and Göbel had served his purpose, Canetti refused to speak to him.

Canetti claims that he saved at least some of Veza's works that were not published in her lifetime when she wanted to destroy them. He kept them carefully among his papers just as he kept Benedikt's notebooks and the reviews of her novels. He stressed too that they both tried to get her stories into print and her plays performed. "In spite of everything which we both, she and I, undertook, she had no luck" (*DO*:100). A letter from the Zurich Schauspielhaus dated 9 June 1949 regarding the possibility of a production of *The Tiger* confirms his role. It is addressed to *both* "Herr und Frau Canetti." The signatory does not discount the possibility that *The Tiger* will be performed:

> Hirschfeld loves it very much and would like to convince the other gentlemen at our institution of its merits.
>
> He asks for that reason to be able to hold on to the Tiger for a while longer; so that views for and against it can be settled one way or the other.[45]

Kurt Hirschfeld was present at Canetti's reading of his first play, *Wedding*, in Zurich and is mentioned in *The Play of the Eyes*. He was Canetti's, rather than Veza's, contact. Canetti told Georg in March 1935 that he had done his best to sell Veza's *The Ogre* to Wladimir Rosenbaum, in whose Zurich house he had given a reading in the presence of James Joyce (4 March 1935; *BG*:37). He alludes to her writing proportionately more often than she does (given that she wrote to Georg far more frequently than he did) in their published letters. He tells Georg that she is "a born dramatist of the highest rank" (31? August 1946; *BG*:227) and holds out to her the prospect of both of them having time to work on their own projects if they moved to France (3 May 1948; *BG*:334).

Canetti was not her only contemporary who could have alerted the world to Veza's work after her death. Neither Herzfelde nor Fischer, both influential men in the German-speaking Left, made any attempt to draw attention to her writing after 1945. In 1984 Erich Fried told an interviewer that it saddened him that Canetti had not done more to publish somehow the manuscripts of his wife Veza, Venezia Canetti, who died — and whom he loved. She said that she did not want anything of hers published until Canetti himself had received due recognition. In my view, now, that he is so famous, he should something with Veza's manuscripts.[46]

Fried died in 1988 and these comments were not published for another seven years. But this was not an exclusively male conspiracy of silence. Hilde Spiel claims to have known Veza's work but she did not think to mention it before and she confusingly refers to "two novels" by Veza that she says were published by Zsolnay, the publishing house owned by Anna Mahler's third husband. Zsolnay had nothing to do with Veza, however, until they published her translation of Graham Greene's *The Power and the Glory* shortly after the war.[47] Ruth von Mayenburg also worked for the *Arbeiter-Zeitung* and like Fischer, whom she married in 1932, knew both Canettis well. She passes over Veza in a single sentence of her autobiography, noting only that she bore most of the financial burden for supporting Canetti.[48] Like Ingeborg Bachmann, she was more interested in Canetti.

The next generation was less forgiving and quicker to draw what appeared to be obvious conclusions. Like Anna Mitgutsch (b.1948) and Elisabeth Reichart (b.1953), Elfriede Czurda (b.1946) made her name with a novel about an emotionally and sexually abusive relationship.[49] Mulot (b.1950) wrote a Ph.D. on the "Young Robert Musil" and introduced two books by a forgotten female Viennese author of Canetti's generation, Gina Kaus, who died in California in the early 1990s. All felt Veza's case resonated with their own fictional or critical writing. The views on contemporary feminists that Canetti expressed at age eighty-five in his foreword to *Yellow Street* sounded conservative and were as predictable in their way as were their subsequent reactions to him. He took pains to distance Veza from the same women who soon took issue with him:

> Her convictions were not far from those one finds often, and in a militant form, among women today, but she held them in those days. Nor did she display them in that rebellious manner that gives rise to divisiveness and aggressive splinter-groups, for she sacrificed nothing of her admiration of beauty, seductiveness, or devotion. (*GS*:6)

If he recognizes in the first sentence that it was a greater achievement to speak out for women's rights in the 1930s than in the 1980s, the second sentence sounds provocative, though that may have been unintentional. He wrote most of these words in encoded form in the notes for *The Play of the Eyes*, which indicates how private the recollection was; he may have expressed a contradiction in Veza's personality as he watched it develop. Nonetheless "beauty," "seductiveness," and "devotion" were not attributes independent women were likely to value at the end of the twentieth century.

In a note from 1992 in the last volume of "jottings," he shows that he certainly noticed the brickbats thrown at him: "V. — *Each* mention of her name makes me happy, even if it is linked with insults aimed at me" (*A*:37). His joy at her posthumous success and recognition of her suffering while alive are moving, but one can detect a sense of mischief too:

> When lack of consolation has no reason it disguises itself as disappointment, disappointment about a life which is said not to merit the name.
>
> But it was more than one life, it was a life for many different people, fear for many, expectation for many, and, if only very rarely: success. Even celebrity was not completely lacking in this life, you were with her, the woman whose breath you held, in Stockholm, and she was the most beautiful of the laureates' wives. [. . .] And then, two years ago the most beautiful thing: Veza's name on books, even in other languages — Veza who now bears your name and remains united with you forever —, what could be more wonderful, this resurrection twenty-seven years after her death? (*A*:10–11)

His comment on the laureates' wives sounds like a jab at his critics since it assumes that the Nobel Prize is male territory. But in 1981 the winners were all men. His remarks may still show unease at being confronted with what his wife had written up to sixty years earlier. He may have been reminded of a battle they had waged with one another precisely on the subject of gender because of the way he treated it in *Auto-da-Fé*, their financial struggle and shared battles with despair after emigration to Britain, not to mention her years of literary failure. He also believed that she saved his life and knew that she offered to sacrifice her own for his sake, which explains why the overwhelming impression is one of recollected sadness.

After 1999 the controversy over Canetti's role in Veza's career abated. Mulot's *Der Spiegel* review notwithstanding, *Der Fund* did not provoke comparable outbursts in 2001, not least because the material disproved one or two of the criticisms that were made about him. Angelika Schedel is conciliatory towards him. Another critic, in a chapter on their partnership for an academic volume on "literary couples," had already turned the tables on his detractors:

> When some representatives of contemporary women's studies claim that the lives of so-called career companions were "unlived lives," an "oppressive example," a "depressing result," a "second-hand life," their blanket moral condemnations say more about themselves than about the women they are judging, notwithstanding that they are expressing their disappointment at finding so few positive role models in the past to guide them in today's society.[50]

The phrases in quotation marks are all from Inge Stephan's book. Canetti's own biographer continues the counterattack, questioning whether Veza's despairing auto-da-fé really took place, since we have only her husband's account and it turns out that a remarkable amount of material did elude her destructive grasp. He is sceptical too about her determination after the war to find German-language outlets for her work, pointing out that there is no sign that she tried to follow up her success with "The Seer," which was broadcast on Austrian radio in 1949. She and Canetti knew the commissioning editor, Ernst Schönwiese, from the 1930s. He reviewed or published their writings in *Das Silberboot* (*Die Blendung* in 1936; *The Power and the Glory* in 1949) and was aware of Veza's other work. Hanuschek even found indications that it was Canetti who felt his work suffered since his marriage — after all, he did not complete *Crowds and Power* until twenty-five years after marrying.[51]

The dust would have remained on *The Tortoises* had it not been for Murdoch's biographers. Conradi's animus against her lover of three years is as powerful as that of the Austrian feminists, even though he wrote his authorized biography unaware of them. That Elias Canetti was an unpleasant individual goes unquestioned by writers on Murdoch. After A. N. Wilson joined the fray with an anti-Bayley memoir that contains three errors of fact (and as many put-downs) in its paragraph on the Canettis, the British journalist David Aaronovitch declared he would cross *Auto-da-Fé* and *Crowds and Power* off his list of books to read because he had learned that Veza would sometimes be in the flat when her husband made love to Murdoch and even prepare the couple a meal afterwards.[52] Yet it is a fact of Western literature that great books, like *Crowds and Power* or *The Tortoises*, even Murdoch's own novels come to that, have often been written by authors with unconventional home lives.

Notes

[1] Anna Mitgutsch, "Veza Canetti (1897–1963)," *Literatur und Kritik* 335/336 (1999), 99–109; here: 109. *Die Züchtigung* (*The Punishment*) was published in 1985.

[2] Ulrich Weinzierl, "Ins Gesicht gebrannt: Späte Gerechtigkeit für Veza Canetti," *Frankfurter Allgemeine Zeitung*, 1 June 1990. Reprinted in Spörk and Strohmaier, *Veza Canetti*, 159–60.

[3] Elfriede Czurda, "Veza Canetti: Ein ferner Stern, unleserlich," in *Buchstäblich: Unmenschen* (Graz: Droschl, 1995), 112–35, esp. 122. First published as "Veza Canetti — Dichtung und Wahrheit," *manuskripte* 117 (1992), 114–20.

[4] Ayren, "Vom Toten und vom Tod," 152.

[5] Sibylle Mulot, "Das Leben vor der Haustür. Nach mehr als einem halben Jahrhundert erschienen: der unbekannte Roman einer unbekannten Dichterin — *Die gelbe Straße* der Veza Canetti," *Die Zeit*, 6 April 1990.

6 Mulot, "Leben mit dem Monster," 124.

7 Sibylle Mulot, "Befreundet mit den Geliebten," *Der Spiegel*, 22 December 2001, 190–92.

8 See also Suzanne Schaber, "Wer ist Veza Magd?" *Die Presse*, 10 April 1999, reprinted in Spörk and Strohmaier, *Veza Canetti*, 171–75.

9 Czurda, "Veza Canetti," 122.

10 Willi Winkler, "Die Kraft und ihre Herrlichkeit," *Süddeutsche Zeitung* 17/18 April 1999, quoting from a posthumously published interview with Peter Stephan Jungk, "Fragmente, Momente, Minuten. Ein Besuch bei Elias Canetti," *Neue Rundschau* 106:1 (1995), 95–104. See Deborah Holmes, "Elias Canetti in Red Vienna," in *The Worlds of Elias Canetti: Centenary Essays* (Newcastle: Cambridge Scholars Publishing, forthcoming), edited by William Collins Donahue and Julian Preece. She concludes: "Unable to contain and ultimately deride Red Vienna in retrospect, as was the case with his contemporary experiences of the left-wing scene in Berlin, Canetti tried, not entirely successfully, to ignore it instead."

11 Thomas Rothschild, "Offener Brief an Peter Stephan Jungk," *Neue Rundschau* 106:2 (1995), 177–79 and Peter Stephan Jungk, "Elias Canetti und Ernst Fischer," *Neue Rundschau* 106:3 (1995), 154–55; Ernst Fischer, "Bemerkungen zu Elias Canettis *Masse und Macht*," *Literatur und Kritik* 7 (1966), 12–20.

12 Gerald Stieg, "Kain und Eva: Eine Replik auf Anna Mitgutsch," *Literatur und Kritik* 339/340 (1999), 36–40; Gerhard Melzer, "Der einzige Satz und sein Eigentümer. Versuch über den symbolischen Machthaber Elias Canetti," in *Die verschwiegenen Engel: Aufsätze zur österreichischen Literatur* (Graz: Droschl, 1998), 83–100. First published 1985.

13 Melzer, "Der einzige Satz," 85 and 98.

14 Spörk and Strohmaier, *Veza Canetti*.

15 Weinzierl, "Ins Gesicht gebrannt"; Rolf Hochhuth, "Nur ein bißchen tot," *Die Welt*, 5 June 1992. Reprinted in Spörk and Strohmaier, *Veza Canetti*, 164–66.

16 Eva Meidl, *Veza Canettis Sozialkritik in der revolutionären Nachkriegszeit: Sozialkritische, feministische und postkoloniale Aspekte in ihrem Werk* (Frankfurt am Main: Lang, 1998), 16; Inge Stephan, *Das Schicksal der begabten Frau im Schatten berühmter Männer* (Stuttgart: Kreuz, 1989).

17 Winkler, "Die Kraft und ihre Herrlichkeit"; Andreas Breitenstein, "Nationalismus für Anfänger," *Neue Zürcher Zeitung* 8/9 May 1999. On Veza as Eurydice, see Czurda, "Veza Canetti," 125.

18 Czurda, "Veza Canetti," 127.

19 Elias Canetti, "Dank in Stockholm. Rede bei der Verleihung des Nobelpreises für Literatur am 10. Dezember 1981" (X:115–16).

20 Klaus Theweleit, *Buch der Könige: Orpheus und Eurydike* (Basel/Frankfurt am Main: Stroemfeld/Roter Stern, 1988), 978, 979, 980, 983, 993, 994–95, 996.

21 Schedel, *Sozialismus und Psychoanalyse*, 127–36.

22 Also quoted by Theweleit, *Buch der Könige*, 996.

23 Rolf J. Goebel, *Constructing China: Kafka's Orientalist Discourse* (Rochester, NY: Camden House, 1997).

24 Rainer Stach reveals that there were multiple crises in the Bauer family that directly beset her and that she kept secret from her correspondent. Working from new documentary sources, he shows that Felice was nobody's fool and possessed great inner strength. Rainer Stach, *Kafka: Die Jahre der Entscheidungen* (Frankfurt am Main: Fischer, 2002), esp. 182–90.

25 H. G. Adler, *Eine Reise: Erzählung* (Bonn: bibliotheca christina, 1962).

26 Elias Canetti, *Party in the Blitz: The English Years*, trans. Michael Hofmann, introd. Jeremy Adler (London: Harvill, 2005) 32 and 12.

27 Draft letter, 27 June 1963, ZB 22.

28 4 December 1963, quoted by Schedel, *Sozialismus und Psychoanalyse*, 187.

29 Quoted by Theweleit, *Buch der Könige*, 92.

30 Kathleen Raine, *The Lion's Mouth: Concluding Chapters of Autobiography* (London: Hamish Hamilton, 1977), 53–54.

31 Ibid., 51.

32 Dannie Abse, *Goodbye, Twentieth Century: An Autobiography* (London: Pimlico, 2001), 228.

33 Bernice Rubens, *Set on Edge* (London: Eyre & Spottiswoode, 1960).

34 Nassauer, *The Cuckoo*, 38.

35 Ibid., 65.

36 Ibid., 67.

37 Bernice Rubens, *When I Grow Up: A Memoir* (London: Little Brown, 2005), 112.

38 Jeremy Adler, "Nachwort," *Aufzeichnungen für Marie-Louise*, 83.

39 Kae Hursthouse to Franz Baermann Steiner, 30 May 1940, quoted by Schedel, *Sozialismus und Psychoanalyse*, 175.

40 Friedl Benedikt, "Das armselige Werk einer vernarrten und faulen Schülerin," ZB 217, 54.

41 Quoted by Atze, *"Ortlose Botschaft,"* 34.

42 Conradi, *Iris Murdoch*, 455.

43 Letter from Elias Canetti to the author, 18 July 1993.

44 Ayren, "Vom Toten und vom Tod," 152.

45 Letter to Herr and Frau Canetti from Peter Löffler, Schauspielhaus Zurich, 9 June 1949, ZB.

46 Erich Fried interviewed by Mechthild Curtius. Quoted by Gerda Marko, *Schreibende Paare: Liebe, Freundschaft, Konkurrenz* (Zurich: Artemis and Winkler, 1995), 226.

47 Hilde Spiel interviewed by Robert Scheding (1988), *Gegenwart* 23 (1994), 15–16.

48 Ruth von Mayenburg, *Blaues Blut und rote Fahnen: Revolutionäres Frauenleben zwischen Wien, Berlin und Moskau* (Vienna: Promedia, 1993), 111.

[49] Elfriede Czurda, *Kerner: Ein Abenteuerroman* (Reinbek bei Hamburg: Rowohlt, 1987); Elisabeth Reichart, *Februarschatten* (Salzburg: Müller, 1985).

[50] Marianne Kröger, "Themenaffinitäten zwischen Veza und Elias Canetti in den 30er Jahren und im Exil. Eine Spurensuche in den Romanen *Die Schildkröten* von Veza Canetti und *Die Blendung* von Elias Canetti," in *Das literarische Paar: Intertextualität der Geschlechterdiskurse,* ed. Gislinde Seybert (Bielefeld: Aisthesis, 2003), 279–308; here: 282.

[51] Hanuschek, *Elias Canetti,* 264, 389–90, and 321.

[52] A. N. Wilson, *Iris Murdoch as I Knew Her* (London: Hutchinson, 2003) 87–88; David Aaronovitch, "The Iris Troubles," *The Observer,* 7 September 2003.

3: Shared Beginnings

Elias and Veza Canetti began to write at the same time; he started with his only novel, while she wrote short stories for the workers' newspaper in Vienna. After graduating in chemistry in the summer of 1929, he initially began to work on an even more ambitious eight-volume project he had called (after Balzac) the *Comédie Humaine of Madmen*. In the end he wrote only one volume, initially called *Kant catches Fire*, which he completed between 1930 and 1931. It is about an eccentric academic whose mind is so warped by reading and his sequestered intellectual life that he marries his ignorant housekeeper and consequently brings about his personal, professional, and financial downfall. Veza enthused, the year before she died, that

> It is unheard of for a twenty-six year old to have written a novel of such maturity and weightiness, which inhabits its own complete world so perfectly. One may almost call it unique in world literature. (*WK*:9)

For a novel of such overweening proportions to be its author's first piece of literary writing is all but unprecedented. That Canetti wrote no more fiction makes its status more unusual still.

Veza was not always so sanguine on the subject, not least because she bore the brunt of the mental collapse Canetti almost endured as he narrated Peter Kien's disintegration. She responded by publishing prose fiction, short stories, and novellas, in the *Arbeiter-Zeitung* from June 1932, which she continued to do until November 1933, three months before the paper was closed. According to Hanuschek's interpretation of her letter in Canetti's notebook, the beginning of her writing career also coincided with the loss of her unborn child: her last miscarriage was in the early part of 1932. Her first story was published at the end of June and she wrote to curtail her sexual relationship with Canetti in November. Her writing could have been the reason she needed to change the nature of their relationship, and it did not necessarily please her boyfriend.[1]

The self-assured tone of her stories belies her personal modesty that in turn contrasted with his all-conquering confidence. When she gave Canetti her first play to read, "it was the first time that she showed me something without saying that she did not think it was any good" (*DO*:99). He insists that his role in helping her to believe in her own abilities had been positive:

> I had encouraged her to write in every way: I praised what she showed
> me with conviction and had to defend it against her. For a long time she
> was determined to think her stuff was no good. (*DO*:99)

He claims credit for her first publication successes because he recommended her stories to Fischer at the *Arbeiter-Zeitung* and Herzfelde at
the Malik Press.[2] After all, for years before he set to work on *Auto-da-Fé*,
she had similarly encouraged him by taking "the bad poems seriously
which I brought to her" (*GS*:5), so convinced was she that this juvenilia
would one day bear fruit. It was only after finishing *The Ogre* that she over-
came — temporarily at least — her own low self-esteem as a writer. The
unkindest comment on her writing that he ever made was to Georg when
he claimed that Veza was finally outgrowing his influence (25 April 1946;
BG:193). In the same letter, however, he is also concerned that she should
receive the recognition that was her due.

Canetti writes in *The Torch in the Ear* that he met Veza Taubner-
Calderon five years before he started his novel, shortly after starting his
degree at Vienna University. He notes that on the same date, 17 April
1924, he saw Karl Kraus, whose journal, *Die Fackel* (*The Torch*), gave him
the title for the middle book of the autobiography, perform his three-hun-
dredth public reading. From May 1925, when he paid his first visit to
Veza's flat in the Ferdinandstraße, he extended his knowledge of life and
literature in endless conversations with her, alongside learning chemistry in
the university's laboratories. Veza also showed him something he valued
much more than anything his professors could teach him: how it was possible to liberate oneself from a domineering family member, in her case her
mother's tyrannical third husband. Later, they both transmuted Veza's
experience into literature: Menachem Alkaley is the subject of the last story
she published and a chapter in his autobiography, which he wrote more
than forty years later. Meanwhile, Kraus held his new disciple entranced,
but Veza, always seated in the front row, listened intently without ever
relinquishing her own views and opinions.

Veza's stepfather is a foundational figure in their literary imagination.
Both were inspired to write *against* all that he represented: his petty misuse of power, his self-obsession, his fixation on the dead and inert, crystal-
lized in his worship of money — all that defined him as an ogre and
demonstrated his social hypocrisy. For Veza, it entailed an allegiance with
oppositional left-wing politics; for Canetti, whose politics were universally
oppositional, it meant — at least in his work written after leaving Vienna
— empathizing with the victims of abusive power. In one of his first jottings from 1942, included in the selection Veza introduced in the early
1960s, he wants to see the tables turned in these unequal power relationships: "My greatest wish is to see a mouse devour a cat alive. But not
before she has played with it long enough" (*WK*:110).

Canetti's graduation in 1929 provided the opportunity to devote himself to a task he believed in. First, however, he had a commission from Herzfelde to translate two books by the American socialist writer, Upton Sinclair, one an extended political essay on the commercialization of literature in contemporary America, the other a novel. Both *Money Writes!* and *Love's Pilgrimage* appeared promptly, in 1930, with Malik. *Love's Pilgrimage* was reprinted and sold a total of 30,000 copies; it was the sort of success all Sinclair's titles enjoyed in Germany, where his sales outstripped those in the United States. Canetti got paid well enough to meet his modest needs for the next two or three years, "but the content of these books touched me only on the surface, sometimes I caught myself during the work on them thinking of quite other things" (*VIII*:295). He acknowledges that Sinclair was a "muckraker," but adds that his best known novel, *The Jungle*, led to improvements in the working conditions in the Chicago slaughterhouses where it was set (as was Brecht's *St. Joan of the Stockyards* in imitation). Nevertheless, he does not rate Sinclair as a literary talent and credits him only with preparing the ground for other novelists, such as "Dos Passos, Hemingway, Faulkner, writers of incomparably higher rank" (*VIII*:252). It is bizarre that he ignores Sinclair's politics, but Canetti's autobiography teems with other such omissions. As a campaigning author of the Left, Sinclair was in fact far more to Veza's taste. The Canettis' divergent approach to politics in their literary writings was one cause of dissension prior to Hitler's takeover in Germany, which concentrated Canetti's mind. Gender was another bone of contention between them.

Thanks to Ibby Gordon's invitation to join her in Berlin, Canetti moved in leftist circles in the summer of 1928. Herzfelde, whom he was hired to help research a biography of Sinclair to mark the author's fiftieth birthday, was a member of the German Communist Party; Malik was a workers' press that published well-produced but cheap mass editions of committed texts intended to serve the coming proletarian revolution. Sinclair was a model for the writers of these books and his influence in Germany was immense. He was by far Malik's most published author with a total of seventy-two titles or reprints, more than his two closest rivals combined, the Russians Maxim Gorki (forty) and Ilja Ehrenburg (twenty-four).[3] Canetti worked at the heart of the Malik project, albeit as a lowly translator on commissions he termed *Brotarbeit* (bread-and-butter work). It is also striking that his literary progress developed through his relationships with women, in particular, women who wrote. While on his first visit to Berlin, he was in the tow of the enchanting Ibby Gordon, on his second, much shorter stay the following summer, he fell into the clutches of another older writer, Grete Bernheim, and this time they certainly did kiss. Bernheim belonged to the Malik stable, as did her husband, F. C. Weiskopf, who contributed a story to Herzfelde's anthology, in which Veza's

"Patience Brings Roses" was published; they both settled in East Germany after 1945.[4] Canetti's first exposure to the literary world was the result of a partnership. Gordon pleaded with him to come to Berlin because of the success she was having with his German versions of her poems. His role was clearly subordinate, like his position at that time with respect to the older Veza. Hanuschek writes that "in effect she made him the offer of coming to Berlin as her ghostwriter in case she could not think of any more poems in Hungarian."[5] Canetti lists eight titles of Gordon's poems in *The Torch in the Ear*, but only "Pamela!" was published at the time and place he recalls. Most of the rest are not recorded, which perhaps indicates that he exaggerated her impact. "Pamela!," however, did appear in *Die literarische Welt* on 28 September 1928, the same week that he made his own debut with a mini-article on Sinclair's fiftieth birthday in another fashionable literary journal, *Der Querschnitt*. The fact that he gets the details of only this poem right, however, indicates its importance to him and perhaps his role in its composition.

Veza was jealous of Gordon. Canetti writes that she broke into his room to reclaim the letters she wrote him in exchange for his poems because of the time he was spending with her rival. By taking back her textual gifts to him, Veza temporarily ended their literary romance. It was a highly appropriate gesture in response to Canetti's literary infidelity in translating Gordon's poems. But it was because of Gordon that Malik became not just his but also Veza's first publisher. According to a contemporary, it was Ernst Fischer and not Gordon who provided Canetti with the Malik contact, but even if this is true, Canetti would often benefit from his girlfriends' greater stock of cultural capital.[6] If he snubbed Fischer by ignoring the role he played, he acknowledged a debt elsewhere or one of a different nature.

"Pamela!" is a short narrative poem addressed to a young country girl who wants to move to the big city to work as a maid. The poet invokes her to remember the people she has left behind and assures her that she will be welcomed home if she wants to return:

> When you in white apron
> Serve up the middle-class meal,
> Or when you run to the door
> At the ring of the electric bell,
> When you scrub the stone flags,
> When someone caresses you,
> Think of us and do not cry.
> We have not let the shepherd's fire go out
> So that you will not lose your way
> When you come home.

> Come back and do not be afraid,
> For your child, the meadow will provide.[7]

Thousands of country girls left the meadows of Central Europe every year in search of work and a husband. The tragic fates of maids made pregnant by their employers were a common subject in fiction. Nonetheless the parallels with what Veza Magd — and, a little later, Friedl Benedikt — wrote are remarkable. Even more remarkable, perhaps, is that Canetti made his own modest literary debut at the same time as a girlfriend who had helped him by getting him literary work in recognition of his assistance with her writing. Given his role in the production of the German versions of Gordon's poems, might he have had a hand in suggesting the maid motif to his two other collaborators, Veza and Friedl?

At the end of his three months in Berlin in the summer of 1928, Canetti attended the premiere of Brecht and Weill's *The Threepenny Opera*. Rather than reading it as an attack on gangster capitalism, police complicity in crime, and a satire on bourgeois happy ends, he finds that it "glorifies everything that is normally hidden shamefully away" (*VIII*:287) and was the apotheosis of the corrupt values (fame, egomania, self-centeredness, money, and cynicism) that he had encountered while working for Herzfelde. Yet he does admit to a negative influence; only after reading Brecht's poems in *The Household Breviary* did he stop writing the juvenile verse he passed on to Veza. The cheating low-life characters in the middle book of *Auto-da-Fé*, who include a "blind" beggar who murders the Jewish Fischerle for having double-crossed him, are not very far removed from the frauds in *The Threepenny Opera*, although the narrative approach is rather different from Brecht and Weill's. Veza's "The Seer" centers on a blind beggar of an altogether different stamp.

Canetti wrote *Wedding* in the winter of 1931–32 immediately after finishing *Auto-da-Fé*. It beat the novel into print by three years, appearing with Samuel Fischer in late 1932, too late in the life of the Weimar Republic for it to be performed on stage. Although he nowhere admits to it, he adapts his basic idea (and title) from a Brecht one-act play, originally called *The Wedding* and later *The Petty-Bourgeois Wedding* that was written in 1919 and premiered in Frankfurt in 1926. In Brecht's play, the newlyweds' furniture collapses about them piece by piece as their reception party descends into acrimony and the social order fractures. In Canetti's *Wedding* the building itself disintegrates and the wedding guests are swallowed up by the rubble. It is not the characters' acquisitiveness, though they plot to inherit the property from their landlady, but their inability to control their lust for one another that causes the house to crumble and invalidates the institution of marriage, which they have come to celebrate. While Brecht's critique is Marxist, Canetti's is apocalyptic, as it is in *Auto-da-Fé*, which ends with Kien setting fire to himself and his precious library.

Unlike Brecht, Canetti does not diagnose social ills, he exaggerates them and leaves any diagnosis to an audience whose judgement he refuses to guide.

Auto-da-Fé had to wait four years before a small press was prepared to take it. Meanwhile, *Money Writes!* and *Love's Pilgrimage* were followed by another Sinclair doorstopper, *Wet Parade*, in October 1932. Veza also worked on these translations, most intensively on *Wet Parade*, "large parts" of which were translated by her, Canetti told Göbel, even though it is only his name that appears in any of the books.[8] Malik did eventually publish her name or rather her favorite nom de plume, when "Patience Brings Roses" was included in the anthology of socialist fiction published the month after *Wet Parade*. *Thirty New Writers from the New Germany* was edited and introduced by the prodigiously busy Herzfelde, for whom "new" was synonymous with socialist. When making his selection from the one thousand he claims were submitted, he "asked himself not only, is this well written? Is the topic of interest? He asked at the same time: can the story awaken or strengthen the urge to change the world?"[9] Like all Malik books it had a cover design by Herzfelde's brother, John Heartfield, whose montages have shaped our perception of the Weimar Republic that Hitler soon swept aside.[10]

Veza also mentions working as a translator without specifying her involvement in her husband's Sinclair translations. Translation was the only field in which she could re-establish herself in Britain after 1945. It is coincidental that Graham Greene's *The Power and the Gory* also concerned Prohibition, the same subject as *Wet Parade*, and had the word "power" in the title (but as *Kraft* rather than *Macht* in German) like the great work her husband was writing. One assumes she would not have declined the commission for Greene's Viennese story, *The Third Man*, whose most famous episode is set on the big Ferris wheel in her beloved Prater. But that was not to be. On the title page of *The Power and the Glory*, she is named next to another translator in three editions: the first with Bernhard Zebrowski, the re-issue with Walter Puchwein, and subsequently with Käthe Springer in the version that is still available today. *Wet Parade* remains in print in the original. On this evidence, as a translator Veza worked better with her husband than without him.

In the critical writing on Canetti, little attention has been paid to his translations that are often wrongly referred to as "three novels" if they are mentioned at all. Perhaps it is because he did not take the work seriously. Yet there are passages in *Auto-da-Fé* like the beginning of the key chapter set in the Theresianum (modeled on Vienna's auction house cum pawn shop, the Dorotheum) that would not have looked out of place in a text by Sinclair, or any other author published by Malik. Notwithstanding this trenchant stance on the profit made on the few belongings of the destitute by pawnbrokers, his account in *The Torch in the Ear* of his time in Berlin is taken up with a critique of the self-congratulatory Marxist clique around Herzfelde. Veza continued to work with Herzfelde as a freelance copy editor and reader, however, after he moved to Prague in 1933.

As Göbel remarks, Veza must have written extremely quickly if the two novels she mentions in the biographical notice that teased critics since the republication of her work had also been completed between 1930 and 1932. Yet had she indeed finished them in this short time, she would have written no more quickly than her future husband. She says she sent her *Kaspar-Hauser* novel to "a famous critic," as Canetti sent the manuscript of *Auto-da-Fé* to Thomas Mann, but the critic did not reply and that led her to make her own conclusions as to the quality of her writing.[11] She claims her second novel, *The Enjoyers*, had already appeared (by November 1932) "in the German and Austrian workers' press." Canetti told Göbel that the *Arbeiter-Zeitung* was going to publish it in installments in 1933. It could be that Herzfelde, who edited the biographical notes on his contributors, considered it published even though it had not yet appeared. No trace of either has been found despite extensive searches since 1990. She did produce *Yellow Street* in this period, two chapters of which appeared in the *Arbeiter-Zeitung* in 1933, and a number of other short stories now published in *Patience Brings Roses* and *Der Fund*. Like her husband, Veza began with prose before moving on to drama. The subject of her first play is also marriage.

The autumn of 1932 was an inauspicious moment for two Jewish German-language writers to begin their literary careers. Born out of military defeat and named after the tiny Saxon city that cradled the German cultural renaissance at the time of Goethe, the German Republic had entered its last desperate phase. The German-speaking rump of the former Habsburg Empire ("l'Autriche est ce qui reste," the French Prime Minister Clemenceau had famously said at the peace negotiations) was barely better off. Austrians did not inwardly accept the consequences of defeat in the First World War and the resentment against the postwar settlement ran high. Like the rest of Europe, the new country was hit by economic crisis: productivity decreased by more than a third between 1929 and 1932 and unemployment all but doubled. The crisis of the country's largest bank, the Creditanstalt, which needed to be baled out by the government and the Bank of England, rumbled on through 1931 and 1932.[12] For those who had work, wages and salaries were cut and strikes often banned.[13] Like the rightwing parties, the Social Democrats had their own fully armed paramilitary force, the Republican Defense League, but they were unable to offer national leadership despite their strength in the capital. Their power base did not extend far beyond "Red Vienna" and they were in opposition virtually since the state's founding and declined an invitation to join a coalition with Ignaz Seipel's Christian Socials. Austria was threatened by homegrown Nazis (as Veza hints in "New Boy"), but the possibility of joining Greater Germany, which was officially banned by international treaties, was less attractive to the non-Nazi right after the rise of Hitler. Dollfuß was no friend of the Nazis but he looked to Mussolini for protection. Dollfuß had little sympathy for democratic forms or the aims of the organized working class. In March 1933 he suspended parliamentary democracy and eleven months later outlawed the Social Democratic Party; then in May 1934, he proclaimed a Catholic-dominated corporate state: two months later he was assassinated.[14] When Veza published her first story, he had been Chancellor for a month.

Within six months of publication, *Thirty New Writers from the New Germany* was added to the Nazis' bonfire of the books in Berlin. Herzfelde had fled into exile, where he struggled to re-establish his publishing house in Prague. The anthology's title indicates both the recognition Veza had achieved and the false hopes of a literary and political revival on the German Left. Herzfelde dates his rousing introductory comments 9 November, a date now associated with the Kristallnacht of 1938 and Hitler's failed Beer Hall putsch of 1923. In 1932, Herzfelde's readers would have recognized it as the day the German Republic was founded after the Kaiser's Abdication in 1918. It was like Bastille Day for German republicans — the last they celebrated in freedom.

At Malik, Veza would have struggled with socialist sexism that subordinated women's emancipation to the revolution that would liberate everyone. *Thirty New Writers from the New Germany* contained just three stories by women — one of these was by Elisabeth Hauptmann, one of Brecht's mistresses-cum-collaborators. Herzfelde hints that he is aware of this lack and he comments on his rejection of no fewer than seventeen submissions that concern the anti-abortion Paragraph 218, most, if not all — one assumes — must have been written by women. The slogan, "Your body belongs to you," he argues, should apply in all circumstances of life. Instead of an abortion story, he picked Wolfgang Tureck's tearjerking first-person account of how a little boy's baby brother dies of starvation at the age of three weeks because his parents cannot afford to feed him. Veza's critique in "Patience Brings Roses" is carefully balanced between class and gender. Its main thrust is class politics, as exemplified in the disparate fortunes of the Mäusle and Prokop families and their respective low self-esteem or arrogance generated by their social positions. The Prokops' collective mistreatment of the Mäusles denies both their daughter Tamara and niece Ljubka our full sympathy.

Gender, as explored by Veza Magd in "The Ogre" and "The Tiger," does not have a place in his campaigning volume, though his bad conscience on this point does not leave him in peace. A few lines further down, while arguing the necessary connection between politics and aesthetics, his simile betrays him: "Uncommitted art can, like sterile women, be delightful, but it can never bear any fruit."[15] Women appear to be defined by their bodies, which have two purposes: to delight men and to produce babies.

The story Veza published in *Neue Deutsche Blätter* as Veronika Knecht could have been called "Three Heroes and a Woman" to make this point to the journal's own heroic editor. The "heroes" in her story are male Viennese police officers. It is a socialist *and* a feminist story that details the devastation wrought on ordinary working-class families as a consequence of the failed workers' revolt in February 1934.

The Canettis shared contacts through their remaining years in Vienna. In April 1937, *Sonntag*, which published Veza's "Clairvoyants" in March, interviewed Canetti, which suggests that she passed the contact on to him, although the same paper had interviewed him on the subject of his novel on 2 February 1936 (reproduced in *BG*:383). Their careers only began to diverge in exile. Unlike Veza, Canetti soon succeeded to attract interest from literary journals in his work after 1945. Both *Die Fähre* and *Das Silberboot*, which reviewed Veza's translation of *The Power and the Glory*, reprinted extracts from *Auto-da-Fé* and *Wedding* in the late 1940s. It is a sign that once again they were approaching publishers as a couple, but for whatever reason nothing followed from that for Veza. The poorly supported Weismann Verlag re-issued *Auto-da-Fé* in German in 1948 and published *Comedy of Vanity* two years later. In Britain and America, *Auto-da-Fé* found more readers than *Die Blendung* in Germany or Austria. The French translation won the Grand Prix International du Club Français du Livre in 1949. Jack Isaacs, whose BBC lectures Veza wanted to translate into German, championed Canetti's works in Britain.[16] On his fiftieth birthday, the *Deutsche Rundschau* published a "tribute." In 1956 the first extract from his jottings appeared in *Wort in der Zeit*, which also published the first brief memoir of his visit to Morocco with Aymer Maxwell in 1953, which became a chapter in *Voices from Marrakesh*. *The Numbered* premiered in Oxford that year. Spread over a decade, this hardly seems greatly significant, but it meant that the name Elias Canetti was not unknown in German or English-speaking literary circles. In contrast, Veza did not have success in translation, and she had no chance to get translated because she never published a book in her native tongue. Her Viennese works were perhaps too closely attached to the country she had left behind — a problem encountered by other exiled writers. *The Tortoises* was on a subject postwar Europe was trying to forget.

According to Canetti, Veza's writing initially reacted to his, perhaps both to what he was writing about as well as to his very activity of writing, which took him away from her physically (in that it took up all his time) as well as emotionally and intellectually. In order to keep her peace of mind, to regain her mental equilibrium, Veza put pen to paper and wrote on what ultimately are similar themes, the state of Austria during the Depression on the eve of Nazism, viewed, however, from the perspective of the economically dispossessed. His last year of frenzied work from 1930–31 produced what is by any measure a substantial novel. It is indeed, as he says, a "grand project," entirely in keeping with his own epic personality, which is responsible for two more grand oeuvres over a long and ultimately productive life. Veza's own "project" was more modest in scope. While he wrote for posterity in competition with the classics of the previous century, she published stories based on observations of everyday life in a daily newspaper. "He wants to become immortal," Marlies Acker, his London secretary in the late 1950s, remembers Veza saying frequently to her as she prepared the manuscript of *Crowds and Power*.[17] In 1965 he explained during an interview with Horst Bienek that it was his "greatest wish to be still read in a hundred years time" (*X*:166).

What is of greater significance than the possibility that Canetti underrated Veza's work is the revelation that his literary activity prompted hers. While he omits to say that she initially enjoyed greater success than he did, he recalls that he started first, and in the absence of any evidence to the contrary, we will have to take him at his word.

Notes

[1] Sven Hanuschek, "'Alle grossen Beziehungen sind mir ein Rätsel.' Paarverweigerungsstrategien bei Elias Canetti," *Text und Kritik* 28 (Elias Canetti issue) (2005), 110–17.

[2] Ayren, "Vom Toten und vom Tod," 150.

[3] Hermann, *Der Malik-Verlag*.

[4] Hanuschek, *Elias Canetti*, 171.

[5] Ibid., 154.

[6] Eduard März, *Wiener Zeitung*, 23 January 1987.

[7] Ibby Gordon, "Pamela!" *Die literarische Welt*, 28 September 1928.

[8] Göbel, "Zur Wiederentdeckung Veza Canettis," 5.

[9] Wieland Herzfelde, ed., *Dreissig neue Erzähler des neuen Deutschlands: Junge deutsche Prosa* (Berlin: Malik, 1932), 10.

[10] Upton Sinclair: *Das Geld schreibt: Eine Studie über die amerikanische Literatur* (Berlin: Malik, 1930); *Leidweg der Liebe* (Berlin: Malik, 1932); *Alkohol* (Berlin: Malik, 1932). All translated by Elias Canetti.

[11] Schedel's research does not confirm Canetti's recollection that the critic was Hermann Kesten at Kiepenheuer & Witsch. Schedel, *Sozialismus und Psychoanalyse*, 146–47 n. 470.

[12] F. L. Carsten, *The First Austrian Republic 1918–1938: A Study Based on British and Austrian Documents* (Aldershot: Gower, 1986), 152–56.

[13] Alfred Pfoser, *Literatur und Austromarxismus* (Vienna: Löcker, 1980), 26–27.

[14] Barbara Jelavich, *Modern Austria: Empire and Republic 1815–1986* (Cambridge: Cambridge UP, 1987), 192–208 ("Dollfuss and Austrofascism").

[15] Herzfelde, *Dreissig Neue Erzähler*, 11.

[16] Jack Isaacs, *An Assessment of Twentieth-Century Literature: Six Lectures Delivered in the BBC Third Programme* (London: Secker & Warburg, 1951).

[17] Quoted by Meidl, *Veza Canettis Sozialkritik*, 30.

4: Workers' Writer: Veza at the *Arbeiter-Zeitung*, 1932–33

IN THE VIENNESE *Arbeiter-Zeitung* of 29 June 1932, seven months and a day before Adolf Hitler was appointed Reichskanzler of Germany, the thirty-five-year-old occasional English teacher and freelance translator, Venetiana Taubner-Calderon, published her first short story. It was on the tragic fate of a young working-class woman, but she entitled it "The Victor" after her protagonist's more powerful male employer. This was the same title as a recently released blockbuster from the UFA film studios starring German cinema's leading matinée idol, who soon became Nazi Germany's greatest box office draw and male poster-boy, Hans Albers. Judging from a line in *Comedy of Vanity*, the title also alludes to her fiancé's interest in the subject and exercise of power. As Canetti elaborates in *Crowds and Power*, anyone who survives the death of another individual, as Siegfried Salzman survives that of Anna Seidler, experiences a sense of victory over him (*III*:267–329). When Anna's body is carried back to the factory by a young worker who found her in the snow, Salzman takes satisfaction from her death because it confirms his own more powerful position. There may be a further dimension. In Canetti's *Comedy of Vanity*, it is Heinrich Föhn (his self-portrait) who joshes to Leda Frisch that she considers him a "victor." What's more, according to Heinrich, Leda likes him in this role. Yet Veza's Anna kills herself as a consequence of Salzman's refusal to confirm her secretarial skills, which she acquires independently, through private study, and which denies her the chance of finding work with another firm. Could it be that Veza feared Canetti did not recognize her ability as a writer, or did she project her own lack of self-confidence on to Anna's experience of rejection?

"The Victor" was signed "Veza Magd," as were six more stories that appeared in Viennese newspapers over the next five years. In structure, style, and subject matter, it is typical of the ten stories that appeared in the *Arbeiter-Zeitung* up to November 1933 under this name or her other noms de plume, Martina (sometimes Martha, once even Martin) Murner. In some of them, she recounts a moment of triumph in the life of a child or worker. "The Victor," in contrast, chronicles the defeat of its resilient heroine by the economic forces embodied by Salzman. The title is ironic and the story subverts the premise of Albers' escapist film.

Canetti described the *Arbeiter-Zeitung* as Vienna's best written newspaper in the interwar period (*GS*:8). It was read by blue-collar workers and intellectuals, who comprised the Left of "Red Vienna" under the Social Democratic Mayor, Karl Seitz. *Arbeiter-Zeitung* contributors included Joseph Roth, Erich Kästner, Ernst Toller, and Jura Soyfer, who published both journalism and, like Veza Magd, original literary texts. As the Social Democrats attracted the support of up to three-quarters of Vienna's Jewish population, the party newspaper had a disproportionate number of Jewish readers.[1] Yet, just as Veza was advised to write under a false name to hide her Jewish heritage, Jewish themes were all but taboo by the early 1930s. Consequently, it is only in her later work, especially *The Tortoises*, where she refers openly to Jewish identity.

Writing for the workers' daily newspaper entailed restrictions on the form as well as subject matter. The tight word limit fostered a disciplined style. Every word had to count and the stories are held together by a single narrative thread. Her success at the paper, which awarded her a prize in March 1933 for "A Child Rolls Gold," must have made her more ambitious in terms of length and textual complexity. Left to her own devices, as she shows in her two surviving novels, she wrote on subjects other than class politics, and she favored more complex narrative forms. Her use of perspective in some chapters of *The Tortoises* follows from the contemporary high modernists, Joyce, Woolf, and Faulkner. She already termed two of her stories "novellas": "Patience Brings Roses," which was published in installments in August 1932, and "The Canal," which first appeared over November 1933 and became chapter three of *Yellow Street*. In its interweaving of interconnected lives and focusing on a complete urban community, *Yellow Street* is a modernist text. It stands in the contemporary tradition of novels about the alienating modern metropolis started by Dos Passos (*Manhatten Transfer*) and Alfred Döblin (*Berlin Alexanderplatz*). We may read "New Boy" as a mini homage to Döblin's modernist epic of Berlin street life. Like Franz Biberkopf, her protagonist gets into trouble with the law, goes from job to job as he struggles to make an honest living, and ends up selling newspapers in the center of the city (outside Vienna's Stephansdom in his case; on Alexanderplatz in Biberkopf's). The three chapters of *Yellow Street* that did not find their way into the *Arbeiter-Zeitung* either focus on bourgeois marriage ("The Ogre" and "The Tiger") or more multifaceted moral dilemmas involving the misuse of power ("The Monster"). These are subjects Veza largely avoids when the hero or heroine battles in the class war.

"The Victor" is about the economic precariousness of working-class life and the exploitation of vulnerable young women. Anna Seidler's hopes of preferment on account of her dedication and skill come to nought; her hard toil to help feed her six younger siblings brings her only short-lived success. When her next prospective employer refuses to accept that she has the secretarial skills she claims without a piece of paper confirming that it is the case, she has nowhere to turn. The chief clerk at this firm does not have the authority to accept her word nor the imagination to test her. His pusillanimity is typical of a certain type of Viennese bourgeois who features in Veza's prose.

If Seidler is a Dickensian victim, Salzman has the air of a modern-day pasha. He brings to mind the absolutist Prince in Lessing's Enlightenment domestic tragedy, *Emilia Galotti*, who is ready to sign an execution warrant he has not read because he is distracted by thoughts of a young woman. Salzman lavishes his attention on a champion greyhound whose fussy eating requires the employment of a personal canine chef. But, as he is no less fond of young women, Anna could have caught his eye had her posture not been so hunched and her dress so drab. It does not help that she is his most talented and versatile worker and, like the Mäusle family in "Patience Brings Roses," resolutely moral. She in fact lives according to an ethic of self-help and hard work, precisely those capitalist values that Albers's film ostensibly promulgates.

When Salzman's export markets shrink after the Great Crash of 1929, he surveys his production line workers looking for a someone to fire. He casts a proprietorial eye over the ranks of young women who have taken turns satisfying him:

> There was Fräulein Schmerler, a redhead, who had great influence over her workmates; she had to be kept on, she would kick up a fuss otherwise. There was Fräulein Pilz, who despite her hunchback, was very useful as she reported to the boss all sorts of things the employees had said. Then there was Käthe Schmidt, he recognized her from behind, as he had had her already. And Salzman wetted his lips and his fat face grew larger when he saw Mitzi Sperl, seventeen years old and built very daintily. He thought how sweet she had been that time he had given her strong wine to drink. He went further and one after another came girls who had surrendered to him the blossom of their youth (which the daughters of the well-off sell for a high price) for an evening meal, and — even more important — for the great advantage that came from the boss's goodwill. None of these girls, Siegfried Salzman decided, shall lose her job. And then he saw a figure which he did not know from behind. His eyes rested on the girl's full legs. Although clothed in cheap ribbed stockings, something roundly youthful attracted him to her calves and he stepped forward briskly. He saw a spotty complexion, reddened eyes, a broad nose, and a hunched figure. (*GbR*:51)

Had it not been for her diligence and sense of duty, Anna could have exploited the only asset in her possession that Salzman values, her youthful physique.

In the first chapter of *Yellow Street*, Anna has a beautiful namesake who loses her job for the opposite reason, as her employer, one of the chapter's two eponymous monsters, is jealous of the attention she gets from men. Frieda Runkel's tiny legs dangle from the edge of her chair, as she observes Lina Seidler's beautifully curved lips, warm brown eyes and soft oval cheeks. She had the body of a young mother, her blouses were made from coarse material but their whiteness dazzled. She was what every healthy young man wished for himself. (*GS*:22)

When Lina slaps a man in the face after he tries to steal a kiss, Runkel dismisses her. Herr Vlk, the chapter's other eponymous "monster," has already complained about her opening the shop too late in the morning. It is not just Salzman who ignores Anna:

> no man in the tram ever looked twice at her. For she had that impure complexion, those permanently reddened eyes, which had become chronic, she had a broad nose, and still wore that dark-colored dress. (*GbR*:50)

Whether a woman is a feast for men's eyes, like Lina, or invisible to them, like Anna, is ultimately immaterial.

Anna's body reveals itself to the male gaze only after her death, confirming the injustice of her original situation. The worker who finds her "looked at the girl's young figure and her heavy hair and thought regretfully how she could have caught his fancy" (*GbR*:56). This gesture belongs to that nineteenth-century tradition of admiring the beauty of women's bodies after their death that is exemplified in English literature by the parish surgeon who delivers Oliver Twist in the workhouse. "She was a good-looking girl, too," he comments to his assistant moments after she dies, before asking: "Where did she come from?" The genteel background of Oliver's mother may have been very different from Anna Seidler's, but her outward circumstances appear to have been similar:

> "She was brought here last night," replied the old woman, "by the overseer's order. She was found lying in the street. She had walked some distance, for her shoes were worn to pieces; but where she came from, or where she was going to, nobody knows."[2]

The fate of Hans Christian Andersen's little matchgirl, who dies in the snow after the matches she burns to keep warm have run out, anticipates Anna's as well. Unlike Andersen, Veza spells out the social and economic forces that cause her character's death.

Whether or not they noticed the depiction of the predatory power of the male gaze, "The Victor" would have given the readers of the *Arbeiter-Zeitung* much to fire their sense of aggrieved injustice at the end of June 1932. Regardless of the Austrian Left's reluctance to talk about anti-Semitism, it does touch on the subject of race in addition to class and gender as the story's villain and his erstwhile sidekick are both Jewish. Like New York and London, the rag trade in Vienna was predominantly run by Jews.[3] Siegfried Salzman is also a name that the paper's readers would have understood as Jewish. Salzman is the type of name Jews adopted on emancipation or were forced to adopt by Habsburg officials. Naming a child after a Wagnerian hero indicates that the parents want their son to inte-grate into gentile society.[4] Salzman's foreman, who first promotes Anna and tries to intercede on her behalf, is named Etzel (the German for Atila). The real name of the would-be assimilationist, hunchbacked Jewish dwarf "Fischerle" in *Auto-da-Fé* is Siegfried Fischer, who is the embodiment of every poisonous anti-Semitic prejudice. The revelation of Salzman's Jewish origins are presented simply as a given and ostensibly suggest nothing more. Nothing in his behavior denotes his origins: he is simply a capitalist who follows the laws of capitalism. But a Jewish capitalist all the same.

Salzman is involved in clandestine currency deals with the help of a less sophisticated partner, a certain Herr Topf from the firm "Gold & Topf," who does not think to disguise his Yiddish inflections when pleading with his former partner on Anna's behalf. The problem with Topf is that he does not have sufficient self-awareness to speak standard German to Salzman:

> "Miss Seidler did not work as a secretary with me," he then said in a loud voice.
>
> "Make a leetle exception," Topf intoned, making no effort to tone down his Yiddish expression, he had no tact whatsoever and did not know how to raise himself up to the manufacturer's level. (*GbR*:54)

The German word Veza uses for his German speech is the pejorative *judeln* that equates his Jewishness with his inferior speech. While Topf may be only partially assimilated, his easy good nature and willingness to help are related to his Jewishness. For his part Salzman dissociates himself from his onetime partner immediately after hearing his Yiddish-German. This in turn partially humanizes Salzman: it appears he cannot bear being reminded of the background he is determined to leave behind him. Successful and assimilated Viennese Jews disparaged the *Ostjuden* and "Orientals" from Eastern Europe with the reflex reaction of the insecure erstwhile immigrant to the new arrival, an expression of the present self's revulsion at his former condition. Topf may be more Jewish but he is less good at business, which is why he loses the argument. Veza's critique of the unscrupulous assimilated Jewish businessman is tempered through the kindly but incompetent Topf: by appearing to pander to the anti-Semitism of some of her readers, she gently undermines it.

Salzman and Topf are her most overtly Jewish figures prior to "The Oriental" in *The Tiger* who is a comic stereotype and the quintet of char-acters in *The Tortoises* who are forced during the Nazi period to accept a separate Jewish identity. The low profile of Jewish figures in her pre-1934 writing can only be a reflection of the difficulty discussing Jewish issues. Since the real-life model for her "yellow street" was her Ferdinandstraße in the Leopoldstadt, most of the characters in the novel must be Jewish too. The color yellow has been identified as a code word that draws attention to the plight of the Jews.[5] Runkel's disability may also be a displaced expression of her Jewishness given that the word "cripple" had a prominent place in Nazi terminology. When Pilz sees reproductions of paintings by Breughel in the Kains' flat, he exclaims "These cripples here! Painting cripples!" (*SK*:116) because the painting contradicts his dogmatic aesthetic sense. "Cripples" such as Runkel were murdered by the Nazis like the Jews. Ritchie Robertson comments on *Auto-da-Fé* that "The word 'Krüppel' ('cripple') recurs obsessively [. . .] What Canetti has done is to bring home the reality of anti-semitism by a kind of alienation-effect in which anti-Semitic mass feeling is displaced on to cripples."[6] Veza adopted a similar strategy in her novel. The only direct reference to Jews in *Yellow Street* is in the last chapter, where the grocer blames the disappearance of Helli Wunderer on the Jews, who, he says "have murdered her." He uses the word *abgeschlachtet* (*GS*:163) which means "butchered" or "slaughtered" and is used in connection with animals killed for their meat. This allusion to the "blood libel" (that Jews sacrificed a child to use its blood to make unleavened bread) gives a hint of the intercommunal tension that informs the novel. While Canetti makes Fischerle into a physically and morally repulsive embodiment of every anti-Semitic caricature and thus engages directly with distorted projections of Jewish identity,[7] Veza is more circumspect and more subtle. The kindly, devout, and rather simpleminded Felberbaum in *The Tortoises* can be read, as I argue, as a corrective to the monstrous Fischerle.

In spite of its terse, matter-of-fact tone that is schooled in the new style of *Neue Sachlichkeit*, "The Victor" is distinctly literary in the richness of its allusions. The firm "Gold & Topf" makes Anna's would-be rescuer into a grotesque from the world of E. T. A. Hoffmann. "The Victor" begins with an evocation of a well-known episode from Goethe's *The Sufferings of Young Werther*, where the lovelorn hero first gazes on the unobtainable object of his desire while she cuts bread for her adoring younger siblings. Veza subverts Werther's account of the incident:

> One is not always reminded of Werther's Lotte when hungry children stand around their sister waiting for bread. When Anna distributed bread it looked different. Her brothers and sisters may have stood around her, but they were more absorbed by the bread itself than by the favor of receiving it from her. Nor did she joke as she cut the bread, as she was full of worries. Seven souls had to satisfy their hunger and bread was their staple nourishment. (*GbR*:47)

Goethe was writing for readers with full bellies, who, like Frau Prokop from "Patience Brings Roses," "always knew where [their] next meal would be coming from" (*GbR*:7). If you are hungry, you cannot suffer the delicious torments of Goethe's tragic hero if your mind is consumed by the bread and the prospect of eating it.

Veza often wrote against a well-known model text. Göbel identifies Theodor Storm's "Late Roses" as a source text for "Patience brings Roses." Veza, however, inverts Storm's sense of love belatedly fulfilled with Tamara throwing secondhand roses on to the coffin in order to save money.[8] On the first page of *Yellow Street* she rewrites the famous opening from Musil's great Viennese novel, *The Man without Qualities*, which was published just two years earlier in 1931. In the accident Musil invents the victim is unnamed and the two passersby whose conversation the narrator reproduces do not even know if he survived it, still, the man assures his female companion that he looked alive as he was carried into the ambulance. There are two aspects of Musil's witty account that would perturb Veza: the impersonal depiction of the accident and the woman's need for male reassurance and explanation (she does not understand, and does not even want to understand, what "braking distances" are). Musil has a place in Canetti's modern pantheon next to Kraus, Kafka, and Broch, though he appears not to have made an impression on the great novelist when they met in person. In *Yellow Street* Runkel's maid is run over by a motorbike after Runkel makes her cross the street at the wrong moment and "the faithful soul pushed the pram containing the cripple in what was literally the last moment of her life, shielded it with her own body and so brought about her own death" (*GS*:15). Unlike Musil, Veza does not make a philosophical point but concentrates instead on the victim. This too constitutes part of a dialogue with her husband.

There are echoes of another famous male contemporary, Thomas Mann, in "Hush Money" (*Tristan* and *The Magic Mountain*) and in "Clairvoyants" (*Mario and the Magician*). Canetti confirms Mann's importance for Veza: "Even though she did not like Kafka she enjoyed reading Thomas Mann" (*PiB*:111). She was attached to one novel in particular, which prompts him to recall how her passion for a book could provoke an antagonistic reaction in him:

> Veza loved *Buddenbrooks* almost as much as *Anna Karenina* and when her enthusiasm took on such dimensions it often put me off from reading the book. Instead I read *Magic Mountain*; its atmosphere was familiar to me from mother's tales as she had spent two years in the forest sanatorium in Arosa. (*IX*:249–50)

The Magic Mountain does leave its marks on *Auto-da-Fé*, but "Hush Money" is soaked in the "atmosphere" of the sanatorium. In "Patience Brings Roses," Ljubka's status as an indigent, orphaned niece recalls more strongly the dependent niece Klothilde in *Buddenbrooks* whose silent disappointment with life is expressed at every family gathering in her appetite, which never makes her fat and never makes her satisfied, no matter how much she eats. Ljubka and Tamara's skivvying prompts Veza's first comments on those family female servants who inspired her nom de plume:

> Tamara did not tolerate a maid. A maid was a great danger for the valuable jewelry, the furs and the currency in the flat, she explained to astonished guests. Ljubka did the hard work, and Tamara was not lazy herself, she cooked and scrubbed and was not too proud to clean the floor, and looked after her mother [. . .] (*GbR*:10)

Within her own class of the Russian haute bourgeoisie displaced by the Bolshevik Revolution, Tamara's role is determined by her sex. While she scrubs floors by day and dons her finery in the evening to attend social functions and search for a husband, her brother Bobby degenerates at the gaming tables. When Tamara weds a wealthy lawyer twenty years her senior, the arrangement recalls the financially motivated dynastic marriages in Mann's novel. Toni Buddenbrook's resilience also contrasts with the decline of her brothers, Christian and Thomas.

Veza incorporates elements from fairy tales too. The dog in "A Child Rolls Gold" who guards little Hedi after she has found the stash of money is called Grimm, which is a sign that only in a fairy tale could a child stumble upon such a sum and hang on to it. The children in the orphanage where Hedi lives perform scenes from fairy tales in order to earn money for their upkeep. Once their performance is over, they put their orphans' clothes back on and return once more to reality. After "Cinderella," they perform "Three Wishes," in which a peasant couple waste all the wishes granted them by a fairy through foolishness. It is the only fairy tale from the Grimms' *Children's and Household Tales* that the popular Enlightenment author, Johann Peter Hebel, adapts in *The Treasure Chest*, a book that plays an important role in Canetti's autobiography. In a letter to H. G. Adler, Veza reveals a fondness for another author of fairy tales when she describes Adler's wife: "Bettina always reminds me of Andersen's little mermaid, she has the same eyes that were painted on her in my book of fairy tales."[9] Whereas Andersen's little match girl dreams of joining her grandmother in Heaven, Anna Seidler is mocked through the worker's gaze by those same mercilessly material forces that condemn her. Veza thus writes against the grain of the male bourgeois tradition epitomized by Goethe, Andersen, or Dickens.

"Patience brings Roses" is an anti-fairy tale that counters the proverbial wisdom of the title expressed in the line from Milton that "they also serve who only stand and wait" by literalizing the metaphor. The poor Mäusle family waits with inexhaustible patience only to reap the rewards of a society that believes the poor deserve their poverty. In Tamara's words: "when a person has it in himself, he can step naked on to the street and come home in a fur with a car, and if he hasn't got it in him, then he will go to the dogs anyway" (*GbR*:34). The singing diva Pudicka Pasta in *The Tiger* tells Andrea Sandoval that "patience brings roses" (*DF*:81) after engaging her to play piano for no pay. It is an empty phrase that means the opposite of what it is supposed to mean. Pasta echoes Tamara when she rejects the notion that artists live in poverty: "Whoever has an idea, gets ahead, the others are not capable of life" (*DF*:99). Veza was clearly angered by the glib inhumanity of this ethic. The Nazi Baldur Pilz adapts it only slightly when he explains that the Jews should be grateful to Hitler for initiating a natural process:

> The *Führer* is only scraping off the rust; if someone has it within himself, then he will find a way out, you can rely on that Herr Doktor, the Jews know lots of tricks. The ones who kill themselves, you have not lost much with those who will immediately go and kill themselves. The *Führer* is just cleansing their ranks, he is a benefactor of all Jewry. (*SK*:97)

In 1932 Veza's critique was still economic and class based. Herr Mäusle tries everything to get a new job after he has been dismissed when Bobby "borrows" money from the cash box he faithfully delivered for the last quarter of a century. Like Anna Seidler, Herr Mäusle plays by the rules and pays the price.

"The Victor's" final and most influential intertext is the UFA musical *The Victor*, which stars Hans Albers. Veza turns the film's plot inside out, subverting each of its narrative and ideological premises. Her highly critical absorption of motifs from this film is part of a wider critique of the German and American film industries that she develops over the decade, which was fully in keeping with the ethic of the paper where she published. While the *Arbeiter-Zeitung* believed in the collective victory of the working masses, UFA's *The Victor* showed a humble postal clerk triumphing against the odds entirely on his own, trusting only to luck or supernatural intervention. Directed by Hans Hinrich and Paul Martin with a screenplay co-authored by the novelist Leonhard Frank, *The Victor* passed the censors on 15 March 1932 and premiered the following week. It was first screened in Vienna at the Scala-Kino on 27 March where it stayed for three weeks before beginning its peregrination through the picture houses of the Viennese districts. From 17 through 19 May it was shown at the Leopoldstädter Volks-Kino, Rotensterngasse 7A, a three minute walk from the Ferdinandstraße, which had shown other Albers vehicles earlier in the year.

Lady Fortune smiles on the postal clerk as he first wins and then loses a fortune before getting that second chance that is denied Anna by marrying the daughter of a billionaire American banker. In Central Europe during the Depression, this was pure escapist fantasy, of the sort that made Albers, "the incarnation of the fairy-tale prince," a crowd pleaser on both Berlin's Kurfürstendamm and in working-class districts across German-speaking Europe.[10] By the summer of 1932 he was at the height of his fame. He played Marlene Dietrich's lover in *The Blue Angel* (1930) and starred in such films as *Der Greifer* ("The Grabber," 1930) and *Der Draufgänger* ("The Dare-Devil," 1931), and *Der Liebes-Reporter* ("The Sex Reporter," 1932) which became vehicles for his signature roles. He embodied a type and became his own legend: he was the "grabber," "the dare-devil," "the victor." A song from *The Victor* became indelibly linked to his own success:

> Hoppla, I'm on my way —
> open all doors, open all windows,
> and the road ahead is free.[11]

While the German film industry once threatened to surpass Hollywood (and still produce critical masterpieces such as *The Blue Angel*), as the Weimar Republic tottered, UFA specialized in ostensibly apolitical fantasies. Since 1927 the film studio was owned by Hitler's intimate, the media magnate Alfred Hugenberg, whose politics increasingly left their mark on its films. A Jewish socialist like Veza Taubner-Calderon had every reason to react critically to UFA blockbusters in the dying days of the Weimar Republic. Her version of "The Victor" is in line with the *Arbeiter-Zeitung*'s view of UFA: the paper called Albers the "hero of a Hugenberg wish-dream film" and the studio itself a "wish-dream factory" or "the people's stupefaction institute."

A reader of the *Arbeiter-Zeitung* did not need Upton Sinclair to explain the reactionary politics behind these fantasies of individualism. Nevertheless, at the beginning of *Money Writes!*, which Canetti (with some help from his girlfriend) had translated two years earlier, Veza would have read:

There have been great empires prior to capitalist America; the number of them is buried under the sands of ages. But we may safely make the assertion, that never in all history, or pre-history, has there been an empire in which the victims of exploitation were kept so continuously face to face with their loss. Now, as ever, the poor are huddled in slums, far from the palaces of the rich; but now, for the first time, the rich have been vain enough — future times will say insane enough — to devise "Sunday supplements," "tabloids," and home editions, to enable the poor to share imaginatively in the lives of the rich. The factory slave, having hung for an hour to a strap in a crowded street car, and eaten his tasteless supper of processed food, props his stockinged feet upon a chair, lights his rancid pipe, and spreads before his eyes a magic document — the twenty-four hour record of all the murders, adulteries, briberies, betrayals, drinking, gambling and general licentiousness of the exploits of the world. It is all made as real life to him — the palaces and shiny motor-cars, the soft-skinned "darlings of luxury" in their ermines, and also in their lingerie; their elegantly groomed escorts in opera costume, and also in underdrawers — no intimate details are spared.

And then once a week the wage slave takes his wife and children to a moving picture palace, where they see people spend upon a supper party more than a working class family earns in a year. Old time fairy tales dealt with far-off things, but the modern movies deal with the instant hour, and why they do not lead to instant revolution is a problem that would puzzle a man from Mars. The explanation is the conviction, deeply rooted in the heart of ninety-nine out of every hundred persons in the movie audience, that he or she is destined to climb out upon the faces of the other ninety-nine, and have a chance to spend money like those darlings of luxury upon the screen.[12]

Sinclair's writing could easily be applied to UFA on the eve of the Nazi takeover.

The *Arbeiter-Zeitung* gave Fritz Rosenfeld's review of *The Victor* some prominence on 30 March 1932. Its "World of Film" feature did not often appear on week days and individual films rarely merited more than a paragraph. *The Victor* receives a whole column. Rosenfeld titled his angry comments "Jung-Siegfried 1932," a reference Veza appropriates with the name she chooses for her triumphant villain. Rosenfeld finds Leonhard Frank's involvement "puzzling" and laments that Erich Pommer should have lent his name to this poor quality production with a deeply reactionary message. He sees their involvement as evidence of the sad decline (a *Götterdämmerung*, no less) of Germany's once proud film studio. Albers is a new Siegfried because of the way he masters his own fate, just as the Nibelungen hero, immortalized for UFA by Fritz Lang, overcomes the dragon and subdues Brünnhilde on behalf of his king. His parting comments to the post office colleagues he leaves behind especially annoys the *Arbeiter-Zeitung* reviewer:

> On making his farewell, he gives his colleagues less favored by Lady Fortune some good advice: "Work hard and don't despair." After all not everybody can be a darling of the gods, a "victor," a Hans Albers.

The film invites mythological comparisons through its use of offscreen voices for expressing the hero's conscience and — another device that Veza adapted — Fate itself. She sometimes mythologizes the inevitability of their destiny, even though she shows the primacy of economic factors in determining what happens to her characters and how petty decisions directed against the weak can assume cosmic proportions. The lord of the cosmos mocks Anna when she is offered a new job: "The Great Tormentor is concerned that his material should not go to rack and ruin, and so fate bequeathed Anna a new position" (*GbR*:52).

Fate can sometimes smile on the weak. In "New Boy" it seems that a hidden hand is directing the destiny of a third member of the Seidler clan when he is rescued twice by a nameless *deus ex machina* figure who appears to offer advice and guidance. This "friend was still grateful to him from his time at the factory" (*GbR*:68), when Seidler had let him through the gates with stolen yarn. He first appears after Seidler loses his second job at the jeweler's shop to tell him about an opportunity selling newspapers. When Seidler is arrested on suspicion of stealing from the jeweler's shop, the man appears again, but Seidler does not realize who he is:

> It was not until he opened his mouth that he recognized his friend from the factory. "What are you doing in jail," said the friend, "when I can remember very well that you once arranged the shopwindow without putting on your gloves. Instead of speaking out you let yourself be locked up! I have made a statement, this is not the place for you." Seidler was released less than an hour later, as they could not find a scrap of evidence against him. (*GbR*:70)

"New Boy" was Veza's last story to be published in the *Arbeiter-Zeitung*. By November 1933 there were reasons to cheer up the readership with an encouraging ending.

On 29 June 1932 readers of the *Arbeiter-Zeitung* would recognize the title of the story published under the name "Veza Magd" and appreciate how she exposes the film's political subtext by inverting its structure. Anna takes the role of Albers's clerk. What he gains through a lucky bet on the horses, she achieves through self-help and hard work. As he loses his fortune, she is dismissed from her job. But while he gets a second chance and acquires another fortune by marrying an heiress, she is denied her reference for a second modest position and dies in the snow. While he wins by dint of his strong personality and sex appeal, her inability to exploit her modest youthful charms and misplaced faith in the capitalist ethic of self-help seal her fate. Veza has thus taken the film story, shaken it inside out, and inserted sexual and class politics into a new counternarrative. She repeatedly writes in this manner for her early stories, whether or not there is a specific literary model or antimodel.

Veza returns explicitly to the theme of film in *The Tortoises*, in which the kindhearted Felberbaum is said to have owned his own cinema until the Nazis dispossessed him of it. After his release, Felberbaum takes a room in Werner Kain's flat on the Leopoldstadt. It sounds like Yellow Street, as we read: "The street in which he now lived was also affected by the urge to destroy which the new Reich sanctioned." A soap shop, "which he had particularly liked" (*SK*:162–63), has been ransacked by the Nazi mob. Could this be where Runkel used to spy on Lina across the road in the newsstand and where she was killed when her boxes collapsed on top of her? There is another connection between Runkel and Felberbaum. Going to the movies cost money and the two "monsters" from the first chapter of *Yellow Street* are the novel's only regular cinemagoers. Runkel is said to go every day, Vlk once a week.

As employers or property owners Runkel and Vlk can afford cinema tickets, unlike little Georgie Burger in "The Criminal," who sneaks into a showing of *Emil and the Detectives* without paying. It is Veza's only text to mention a film by name. Based on Erich Kästner's popular children's adventure story and with a screenplay by Billy Wilder, Gerhard Lamprecht's *Emil and the Detectives* (1931) would seem to be a rather different sort of film than any Albers vehicle. Kästner was a fellow contributor to the Malik anthology and also wrote regularly for the *Arbeiter-Zeitung*. Siegfried Kracauer sees evidence of a "democratic spirit" in the adaptation of his novel.[13] Yet *The Victor* also had a screenplay co-authored by the novelist, Leonard Frank, who also published with Malik and who earns a portrait in *The Torch in the Ear*. Frank was no less distinguished than Kästner. There would thus have been no reason for Veza to show critical loyalty to Kästner because of the shared connections with Malik and the *Arbeiter-Zeitung*. Frank has been identified as the model for the nurse, Leopoldine, in *Yellow Street*, who is so taken with Knut Tell's good looks.[14] When Canetti met him in Berlin, he stood out from the crowd because of his handsome appearance. His novel *Der Bürger* (1922) may help explain why Veza chose the surname for the two teachers in "The Difference."

Like *The Victor*, *Emil and the Detectives* makes use of the traditional fairy tale. Twelve-year-old Emil is sent to Berlin by train with money for his grandmother. The money is stolen. When he successfully pursues the thief, the film shows how light triumphs over darkness. By calling her story "The Criminal," Veza inverts the narrative focus by highlighting the role of the thief, a stereotypical villain in Lamprecht's film. Here we come upon another motif that recurs in her fiction: theft, accusations of theft, the character of the thief, and by extension, the ethics of ownership and the distribution of wealth. Ownership and theft are major themes in *Auto-da-Fé*.

There are several evildoers in "The Criminal." One is the resourceful young Georgie whose impecunious father runs an exotic animal show at the Prater fairground. The Burgers' poverty and the facility shared by father and son for telling tall stories are their defining characteristics. When Georgie asks to go on the various rides, his father conceals his lack of money by telling him how dangerous they all are and what dreadful accidents have recently taken place. Georgie then runs from one to another scaring off prospective customers with the same hair-raising tales. After attaching himself to a group of better-off youngsters he creeps into the picture house with them even though he does not have a ticket. *Emil and the Detectives* happens to be showing, which, with its focus on a resourceful young hero and a gang of street children, apparently mirrors the action of Veza's story. Georgie, however, relying on class based instinct and another lesson his father taught him, takes on the role of political detective and turns out to be a different sort of character than Kästner's Emil. When a man who "was not wearing a collar" and who, given his emaciated appearance, "had gone without a meal to buy his ticket" (*GbR*:62), is accused by a well-dressed lady of spending too long in the cinema, Georgie takes his side. He wants to help the collarless man by giving him his ticket but quickly remembers that he does not have one — luckily for him it turns out tickets are not transferable anyway. When the manager arrives, Georgie expresses social solidarity and demonstrates forensic skill in identifying the real criminal elements in the situation:

"But he did come in with us," said Georgie to the boys, looking threat-eningly at the manager, "I'm not staying a moment longer, lads. George always says you don't have to start looking among the common folk if you're looking for criminals."

The audience laughed, but Georgie didn't care about all the people, he shook Peterheinz and the other boys by the hand and strode out of the cinema as if he were wearing seven-league boots. (*GbR*:63)

As he himself is ticketless, Georgie the detective is also Georgie the crimi-nal. At the end of *Emil and the Detectives* the young hero is greeted by cheering crowds and is integrated into a collective that has expelled the evil thief, whereas at the end of "The Criminal" Georgie stands alone after questioning the administration of justice in a poverty-ridden society.[15]

In her stories on criminality Veza inverts the motif of the thief from commercial, popular culture and challenges bourgeois attitudes about theft. In "New Boy," Seidler is wrongfully arrested for burglary. In his first job as foreman, however, he let his fellow workers leave the textile factory each evening with stolen spools of yarn concealed in their clothes, which Veza presents as demonstrating his humanity and sympathy with his fellow workers. When the detectives later accuse him of breaking into the jew-eler's, the narrator explains how easy it is for such a man to appear guilty to his accusers in such circumstances:

> When a human being has to struggle all his life against the temptation of ending his misery by putting his hand in the till, which would not signif-icantly have harmed anybody, by removing a piece of jewelry, whose removal would hardly have been noticed, when a human being defies all these temptations, he can feel himself brought so low by a false accusa-tion, that he blushes, stutters, tears come to his eyes, he does not know what to say and behaves just as if he were guilty. And that is what Seidler did. (*GbR*:70)

This is possibly an allusion to one of Albers's earlier roles in *The Grabber*, where his character apprehends a jewelry thief. The parallels in the series of titles for his films and Veza's stories are striking: he stars in *Der Greifer*, *Der Draufgänger*, *Der Sieger*; she writes "Der Sieger," "Der Verbrecher," "Der Neue."

Her last surviving text *The Palanquin* is a comedy of morals which turns on definitions of crime and the criminal. It is set among a group of upper-middle-class London households, all of which conceal a criminal secret or two and are preyed on by a professional thief who yearns to be found out, arrested, and sent to jail. The victims of his burglaries are too complicit in his crimes to denounce him to the law. In *Yellow Street* her analysis was firmly socialist. She satirizes the Dostoyevskyan attitude to crime through Knut Tell: when an opportunistic thief bangs on his door with a stolen bunch of bananas Tell takes him for an existential Romantic who has "experienced something." When the police arrest the banker Schleier, who disposes of his money where little Hedi Adenberger accidentally finds it, the assumption is that bankers deal with money in the same way as thieves. In "Patience Brings Roses" the real thief is Bobby Prokop who, against Herr Mäusle's repeated entreaties, first unseals the envelope containing the money and then removes the notes he needs to pay his gambling debt. Bobby is not aware of his wrongdoing and believes his own promises: he is only borrowing the money and will return it before anyone has noticed it has gone missing. When he fails to do so because he loses it all at the gambling table again, he has no bad conscience. Since he has never been held accountable for such losses in the past, he cannot imagine that Herr Mäusle will be either. Economic strength or weakness affects the ways individuals interact with others and moulds their psychology. The Mäusle family does not break the law, Herr Mäusle will not even give Bobby's name to his employers because that could have unpleasant consequences for the gentleman. When Herr Garaus calls on Herr Mäusle to find out what has happened to the cash box, he only needs to glance at their hovel to be certain that Herr Mäusle is guilty of taking the money. He could not be more wrong since Frau Mäusle even returns the food packages left outside her door by the Prokops, who *are* guilty, because she believes that they *are* someone else's property.

Veza's exploration of the dialectics of thievery continues in *The Tortoises*. When Pilz is reprimanded by his superiors for stealing "currency, gold chains as thick as your finger, precious stones the size of cherries, silver cutlery" (*SK*:177) while on a "requisition" his defense is that he believes that the owner is Jewish. It turns out that despite his Jewish appearance ("dark, small, with wide nostrils and a belly"), he is a catholic Italian, as he claimed all along, and Pilz must answer for his actions at the Italian Consulate. His wife's conscience is not quite deadened: she wants to salve what remains of it by buying the Kains' furniture cheaply, thus convincing herself that she is not stealing. Felberbaum, on the other hand, momentarily subverts the Nazi sacking of Jewish property by buying back the furniture of a dispossessed family and carrying it back to their flat before he is stopped by a zealous neighbor who is intent on buying it up for a fraction of its value.

In June 1932 the *Arbeiter-Zeitung* was preoccupied with the political and economic developments in Germany. The paper reports there were 5.6 million unemployed, an increase of 1.4 million since June 1931 (Great Britain had 2.8 million, an increase of 300,000 since the previous year). Von Papen replaced Brüning as Reichskanzler early in the month and the Nazis were poised to make gains in the new elections. On 29 June when "The Victor" was published, the paper speaks of a "civil war" between Nazis and forces of the Left on the streets of Germany's cities. Shots had been fired in Leipzig, Berlin-Steglitz, and Wuppertal, while in Mannheim there were stabbings. In the past week, eight Social Democrats and Communists had been killed by Nazis and three workers shot by police after they joined the funeral procession for one of the victims. The police claimed they had been attacked by the mourners and their procession contravened the ban on demonstrations.

Poverty was endemic. In that same month, the *Arbeiter-Zeitung* reported that a three-year-old child had died of starvation. The Social Democrats tabled a parliamentary question on the police's use of tear gas in the town of Donauwitz against a family unable to pay their rent. According to the Christian Social Justice Minister, one Kurt von Schuschnigg, a Donauwitz landlord acted legally by enforcing the eviction, even though the father had been unemployed for two years. The paper compared the government's adherence to the letter of the law in this case with the announcement that state employees will no longer be paid in one but in two monthly installments. In Austria Dollfuß had been Chancellor for a month. The country he ruled was under threat from homegrown Nazis who exploited resentment over the consequences of defeat in the First World War.

As Veza published her first story of working-class defeat, the German and Austrian working class was staring ultimate defeat in the face. She, for one, was not going to give up easily. Not until her last story sixteen months later does she mention Hitler directly. The central character in "New Boy" may be a cousin of the defeated Anna and Lina Seidler, as he shares both their surname and their faith in the good nature and sense of fair play in their fellow human beings. At the beginning of the story he is also working in a textile factory like Anna. When his instinctive class solidarity results in his dismissal, his honest face ensures that he quickly gets another job. The reason that the owners of the jewelery shop dismiss him is that he lets potential customers leave without making a purchase: he cannot understand why anyone should want to buy the jewels in the first place. In his third job selling a workers' newspaper, his sense of class solidarity wins through a third and final time. Yet high politics does not concern either him or any of the other sellers, whose papers support an array of parties:

> There was no political wrangling between them, there was just the hunt for customers, the hunt for bread, and their hatred was reserved for the rain, which was bad for business, for a beggar who distracted the customers, and most of all they hated a newcomer, who could mean competition. (*GbR*:68)

Even though the others have been anything but friendly to him and the aggressive "brown" colleague selling the "German" papers is especially hostile, Seidler covers up for him after police find explosives in his flat. The intervention on behalf of the fellow worker shows that Seidler is seemingly ignorant of the political ramifications of his actions. The point for the

Arbeiter-Zeitung is that his class solidarity transcends differences in allegiance as indicated by their different newspapers. By the end of the story, Seidler has been absorbed and accepted into the group, that is finally prepared to share their change with him.

There is an element of wishful thinking in Veza's story to appear in the *Arbeiter-Zeitung* before its closure. After the defeat of February 1934, many Austrian workers were inclined to put their faith in the Nazis. While the ending of "New Boy" is upbeat insofar as Seidler finds acceptance, the parting comment of one of the detectives that the "German" did not behave so well toward him when he was in trouble is ominous.

Notes

[1] Bruce F. Pauley, "Political Antisemitism in Interwar Vienna," in *Jews, Antisemitism and Culture in Vienna*, edited by Ivar Oxaal, Michael Pollak, and Gerhard Botz (London/New York: Routledge and Kegan Paul, 1987), 152–73; here: 155.

[2] Charles Dickens, *Oliver Twist*, ed. Kathleen Tillotson (Oxford: Oxford UP, 1999), 3.

[3] In 1936 seventy per cent of those involved in textiles in Vienna were Jewish. Pauley, "Political Antisemitism in Interwar Vienna," 155.

[4] Ritchie Robertson, *The "Jewish Question" in German Literature 1749–1939: Emancipation and Its Discontents* (Oxford: Oxford UP, 1999), 347–48.

[5] Helmut Göbel, "Bemerkungen zum verdeckten Judentum in Veza Canettis *Die gelbe Straße*," in Gerald Stieg, ed., *"Ein Dichter braucht Ahnen": Elias Canetti und die europäische Tradition*. Akten des Pariser Symposiums, 16–18.11.1995 (Bern: Lang, 1997), 283–97.

[6] Robertson, *The "Jewish Question" in German Literature*, 343–44.

[7] William Collins Donahue, *The End of Modernism: Elias Canetti's Auto-da-Fé* (Chapel Hill: U North Carolina P, 2001), 106–36 ("The Hunchback of 'Heaven': Anti-Semitism and the Failure of Humanism").

[8] Helmut Göbel, "Nachwort" in *Die gelbe Straße*, by Elias Canetti, 169–81 (Munich: Hanser, 1990); here: 169–70. Veza appears to have adapted the family story of a young writer who joined the *Arbeiter-Zeitung* the same year that she did, Jura Soyfer (1911–38). Soyfer's father owned two factories in the Ukrainian city of Charkow and the family fled by train from the Reds during the Civil War. His elder sister was also called Tamara and, once in Vienna, the family depended on money their mother earned from the sale of her jewelry. Horst Jarka, *Jura Soyfer, Leben, Werke, Zeit,* Mit einem Vorwort von Hans Weigel (Vienna: Löcker, 1987), 19–23.

[9] Letter From Veza Canetti to H. G. Adler, 7 May 1950. Quoted by Atze, *Ortlose Botschaft*, 127.

[10] Siegfried Kracauer, *Von Caligari zu Hitler: Eine psychologische Geschichte des deutschen Films* (1947; Frankfurt am Main: Suhrkamp, 1984), 223–24.

[11] Michaela Krützen, *Hans Albers: Eine deutsche Karriere* (Berlin: Quadriga, 1995), 178–79.

[12] Upton Sinclair, *Money Writes!* (New York: Albert and Charles Boni, 1927), 11–12.

[13] Kracauer, *Von Caligari zu Hitler*, 236–37.

[14] Göbel, "Bemerkungen zum verdeckten Judentum," 286.

[15] Schedel argues that Georgie's success at inventing stories ends in the cinema, which shows how Veza contrasts oral narrative with film, to the detriment of the latter. *Sozialismus und Pyschoanalyse*, 119–20.

5: What's in a Name? On Maids

The name is good. The choice of all the names is good.

— H. G. Adler, "Letter on The Ogre"

IT WAS FAR FROM UNUSUAL in the interwar period for satirical or leftwing German authors to adopt a nom de plume. Indeed there is a long tradition of German literary Jewish writers changing their name to hide their family origins from prejudiced readers.[1] Neither of the other two Jewish women writers from "the 1890s generation," Claire Goll and Gertrud Kolmar, whom Dagmar Lorenz groups with Veza, published under their real names.[2] The greatest satirist of the Weimar period, Kurt Tucholsky, invented a number of writing personae, alternately calling himself Peter Panther, Theobald Tiger, Ignaz Wrobel, and Kaspar Hauser, after the nineteenth-century foundling (that is also the theme of one of Veza's lost texts).

In a letter to Rudolf Hartung after the war, Veza recalls that Dr. König from the *Arbeiter-Zeitung* explained to her that "with the latent anti-Semitism one cannot publish so many stories and novels written by a Jewess, and yours are unfortunately among the best."[3] In such a climate, a change of name was a practical necessity. Pseudonyms could be even more useful to Jewish or oppositional authors after 1933. In order for his book to stand a chance of dissemination in Nazi Germany, Walter Benjamin rechristened himself Detlef Holz (which means wood) to publish an anthology of ostensibly nationalistic letters (*German People*) written by prominent Germans between 1783–1883, which he published in Switzerland.[4] He had already used the name to continue writing for the *Frankfurter Zeitung*. Erich Kästner succeeded in having his plays performed after 1933 by borrowing the real and made-up names that belonged to various friends.[5] Reading between the lines is a skill one quickly develops in such circumstances: Benjamin's critique of nationalist ideology in *German People* is carefully concealed.

An author obliged to forsake her name in order to publish is aware that a name can constitute an identity. Magd and Knecht are not surnames you will find in a telephone directory. It is self-evident that they are made up. They draw attention to themselves while making a statement about the author who hides behind them. It is likely to have been in solidarity with Tucholsky's editor at the *Weltbühne*, Carl von Ossietzky who wrote inter alia as Thomas Murner (after the greatest of German Reformation satirists), that Veza Magd became Martin Murner in January 1933, the month Hitler was made Reichskanzler in Berlin.[6] In December 1932 Ossietzky was released after having spent more than a year in jail on charges of treason for an article he wrote in the paper he edited. He was arrested again on the night of the Reichstag fire, 28 February 1933, and died in a concentration camp five years later. In 1935 after an international campaign he was awarded the Nobel Peace Prize. Veza used variations of the name (Martin, Martina, or Martha Murner) throughout 1933 for her *Arbeiter-Zeitung* stories. It denotes a gesture of defiant, desperate solidarity.

As with Siegfried Salzman, Veza chose fictional names for her stories and plays to comment on the character and his or her background. Names can also designate a type, such as the working-class Seidlers and Adenbergers or the rich Schleiers. Both she and her husband experimented with satirical "speaking names" in their first mature pieces of writing: in "Patience Brings Roses" there are characters called Mäusle (Littlemouse), Unrein (Unclean), and Garaus (Clearout) that her husband uses in *Comedy in Vanity*. Thereafter, Tiger and Pilz (fungus) are rather the exceptions to the rule. In *Auto-da-Fé*, Grob (coarse) is an apt description of Therese's "special person" because of his attitudes to money and women. Therese's own surname Krumbholz (crooked timber) is a Kantian joke: Kant argued that the "crooked timber of humanity" could be straightened through education and the application of reason, whereas within the mental world of *Auto-da-Fé* women are beyond enlightenment. Kien's name could refer to burning since "Kienspan" means kindling wood. Calling the woman-beating caretaker Benedikt Pfaff (priest or cleric) is a less than subtle anti-Catholic jibe that underscores the link between authoritarian politics and Catholicism in interwar Austria.

The names of Veza's characters denote identity in a variety of ways. The Kains have been marked by the Nazis as God marked Cain after he murdered his brother. Kain is also close both to Kien, which links the brothers Andreas and Werner Kain to the brothers in Canetti's novel, but also, as Marianne Kröger points out, to "kein" (meaning no one or none). Werner and Andreas' parents' attempt to assimilate by choosing gentile German names for their children has failed. Their identity as human beings is negated by their persecutors.[7] The identity of the most egregious monster in her first novel merges with his name when his signature ("Iger") mutates into his persona, "Oger." In "The Difference" little Käthi, a name similar in connotation to Pepi or Mizzi and common among maids and prostitutes, is unaware of her poverty, which contrasts with her natural prettiness and intelligence. She is taught through public humiliation by a schoolteacher how she will be treated differently than the better-off "model pupils" in their bright new pinafores. While Käthi has no surname, a lack that makes her stand out in Veza's fiction, two mistresses at her school share the surname Bürger, which can mean both citizen and bourgeois. Historically, the rights of a *Bürger* were conferred only on a privileged minority. While the shorter of the two teachers in "The Difference," "die kleine Bürger" as the pupils call her, shows kindness and understanding to Käthi, her taller namesake, "die grosse Bürger" (the story is called "Die Grosse" in German) is determined to break her spirit. Käthi's treatment at the hands of "die grosse Bürger" is exemplary: her humiliation is an initiation into the workings of bourgeois (*bürger*lich) society, from which as a working-class girl she will be excluded. "You're the last person to put on airs," she is told. "Just you wait until you go into service like your mother, then you will learn how to be humble!" (*DF:*10). Emma Adenberger in "Lost Property" repeats Käthi's experiences when, as a grown-up woman, she relearns that there is a difference between her and her suitor, Dr. Spanek.

Veza chooses a similar surname for the father and son duo in "The Criminal," which also centers on class politics, differences in economic power, and social exclusion. The name is similar but not quite the same, as Georg and little Georgie are called *Burger*, not *Bürger*. The difference between Georgie and the well-dressed lady who gets the collarless man thrown out of the Prater cinema is in a single letter, or the umlaut over a letter: a *Burger* is not quite a *Bürger* — and a *Bürger* is a long way from being a *Magd*.

Maids rarely become writers, but that does not mean their lives are not worth writing about or that they do not have stories to tell. In *The Tortoises* the anti-Nazi Czech cleaning lady Frau Wlk is partial to telling stories, like the other characters who retain their humanity in this novel of inhuman behavior. Her second story is a version of "Three Heroes and a Woman," involving a lawyer, two policemen, and incriminating evidence in the bottom drawer of the lawyer's desk. In the end the lawyer succeeds in diverting the policemen's attention from the all-important bottom drawer in the same way as Frau Schäfer stops the "three heroes" from finding the frightened workers in the flat at the top of the house she is cleaning.

When Veza explores her own self-understanding as a writer, however, she does so through male characters. "The Poet" is a programmatic story on the poet's vocation and concerns a male rather than a female poet. The enlightened writer (a *Schriftsteller* this time rather than a *Dichter*) in "Clairvoyants" is male too. But in both stories the writer or poet *serves* his reading public by playing a role that is socially useful. Her nom de plume, Magd, aligns herself to this role, as Canetti and Fischer partly recognized, except that the choice is also highly gendered, which they overlook or perhaps take for granted. Veronika Knecht denotes a phonetic and existential hardening of Magd and is gender neutral.

Both Canetti and Fischer saw the choice of Magd to indicate no more than a willingness to serve others, as a maid serves those who pay her wages. This is a conservative, not to say highly masculine understanding of feminine service that is more like servitude. It corresponds to the contemporary "idealization of female service as sacrifice," the converse of which can be seen as the demonization of women as prostitutes.[8] It appears to be shared by Werner Kain in *The Tortoises* who regrets there is no maid in his new household:

> They hadn't got a maid either, no, there was no maid. That creature who makes no demands and goes about her work kindly and quietly, the only female being with some entitlement to walk on tiles. Although there was a woman here, a pale and selfish person, she went back and forth aimlessly, started and stopped things aimlessly, picked up this or that aimlessly, poured boiling water and spilt it and when she finally brought the steaming bowl of tea she dropped it. She was no good at anything, this wife of his brother. (*SK*:195)

This "pale and selfish person" is, however, none other than Eva Kain, Veza's authorial alter ego.

In his foreword to *Yellow Street*, Canetti explains (in words he first used in a draft chapter of *The Torch in the Ear*):

> She thought so highly of women whose service stemmed from a love for those she served that she chose the pseudonym Veza Magd for her writings. It stood for dedication in all its forms: to the man she loved, to those entrusted to her protection, but also to those who were disadvantaged by their birth or the dishonest behavior of others. (*GS*:6–7)

Fischer's explanation is remarkably similar, though while revealing that "she called herself Veza Magd," he bizarrely forgets to mention she disguised her true identity in order to become a published author:

> To be a maid is no humiliation if you have dubbed yourself such and take yourself at your own word; pride chooses the garb of modesty, service as a badge of honor, voluntary resignation. Her capacity for love was inexhaustible, never possessive, always ready to help anyone at any time.[9]

I have already put forward an alternative thesis: her choice of name was a reaction to Kien's housekeeper-wife, the former maid, Therese. In her anger Veza threw the label back in her boyfriend's face. Since Therese is female, she reportedly has no mind; after marriage, she keeps her husband from his intellectual pursuits. In real life Veza declined this role; in her fiction she subverted it.

Canetti does seem to have got the message because in another discarded chapter for *The Torch in the Ear* he showed more insight than in the *Yellow Street* foreword. In these unpublished comments, he explained her gift for empathy, her ability to feel the pain and humiliation of others (part of what he called "transformation," a central category in his thought):

> It did not stop with empathy as she lavished praise and presents on anyone who had been humiliated. That was her balsam and her supplies never ran dry. She knew how to lift up someone who had been kicked to

the floor so that he felt on top of the world. She would take a girl who had been cast out into her home to work for her and inspire her with the feeling that she would inherit her own kingdom here on earth. Many found that what she had predicted for them came true, others, who were impatient or had no faith, withdrew and regretted what they had missed out on. She had a hundred ways of getting hold of what she needed for her generosity. She used up what she possessed for her protégés and when she had nothing left, then she was not too proud to beg on their behalf.[10]

The passage, from a chapter he intended to call "Mourning and Enticement," ends with a judgment:

A young girl from the country who ended up in the city, who was in service with cruel employers, who in her innocence had no way of defending herself against the brutes who courted her, who was cheated out of her afternoon off, slept in a stinking room, who was given little to eat and was robbed of her wages, — if she had the good fortune to live in her street, then she heard of her who had become a legend, and went in search of her and found she would help. The protection that she gave to those who could not help themselves was so indispensable to Veza herself that she gave herself the name Veza Magd when she began to write stories about them which she soon also published.[11]

Had Canetti gone ahead and published these words much of the controversy over his failure to alert the world to his first wife's stories might have been averted.

However, there is much more to the matter than her husband suspected even here. The maids in Veza's fiction are not happy with their lot. In "Money — Money — Money," Draga Kozil sets out to avenge her husband who killed himself after the stepfather evicted him for non-payment of rent. Her ruthlessness is signaled by her "small jet-black eyes" that are either covered by the "mask" of her face or hidden behind "thick rolls of fat" (*TK*:22). She has not permanently lost her ability to see, like true villains such as Iger and Pilz. She is playing the role of avenging angel and her disguise is only temporary. Her predecessor, a young Styrian peasant woman of classical beauty, left when she was needed to work in the fields back home after the men had been killed in battle. The stepfather's enjoyment of inventing errands for her was only partly explained by the thrill of imposing his will on an attractive young woman. Also, he could not bear that she sit idle while he was paying her: she was an asset and he expected to earn money from his assets. This is why Draga exacts her revenge on him.

In this fictionalized account of her childhood, Veza seems to split herself and her allegiance in two. The stepdaughter who narrates the story is horrified to discover that Draga is the widow of an evicted tenant and that she has killed her former landlord by feeding him large quantities of the food and drink that he demanded. Yet Draga is the story's heroine and the narrator readily agrees that the matter must be kept secret, which makes her complicit in the killing. Draga shares a surname with one of Frau Hatvany's four Annas in "The Canal," who stand up altogether when their name is called out, ready to take up a post as a servant in a better-off household. Whereas Anna Kozil migrates to Vienna from the Sudetenland, Draga comes from Bosnian Sarajevo, the birthplace of both Veza's mother and the heroine of *The Ogre*, another Draga. If Draga is an authorial alter ego, then by naming herself after the invisible maid who is present in every middle-class household Veza comments on herself and her own social experience when she portrays maids, though not quite in the way suggested by both Fischer and her husband.

In explaining maids' psychology, Veza begins with their way of looking out at the world, their gaze:

> Beauty among maids differs from beauty among bourgeois women only in one point. Hired and used for little money, the maids so rarely have their own way, their freedom, even a room for themselves, that their gaze darts about aimlessly, ever conscious of a restriction, a command, an exhortation — harsh reminders of their lack of possessions, lack of roots, lack of direction. The uncertainty of her gaze is the maid's mark of Cain, this unprotected soul who is unable to gloat over her mistress because she sees the master's secret wooing as a humiliation and not as a triumph. (*DF*:158–59)

The many insights into the workings of a maid's mind and the setting in Seville make "Pastora," from which the above comments come, one of her most personal stories. The Asriels told Canetti that Veza was "a wonderfully beautiful person with a Spanish face" (*VIII*:68–69); when he first saw her he merged her knowledge of Edgar Allan Poe's "The Raven" with her appearance, calling her "a raven turned into a Spanish woman" (*VIII*:70). When he gets to know her, he finds out that she is "an Andalusian who had never been to Seville, but she spoke about it as if she had been brought up there" (*VIII*:120). Her *maiden* name, Calderon, is a constant reminder of her Spanish (that is, Sephardic) heritage and marked her as Jewish, which necessitated her pseudonyms. In *The Palanquin* the Spanish refugee Senora Consuelo Gonsalez y Soto is something of a self-portrait. She is roughly the same age (fifty) and she claims it would break her heart to return to her home. The character nearest to a maid is the cleaning woman, Christina Evans, who is thirty-four, the same age as Veza when she began to publish. She is illiterate, which is surely a sign that the author senses that she is losing her ability to communicate in writing as shown by her failure to find a publisher in 1950s Britain or postwar Austria.

Maids are recurrent figures in her fiction, from the first page of *Yellow Street* where the long-serving Rosa gets run over trying to save Runkel's life, to the handful of works written in England. The number of different words for maid in her first novel shows how ubiquitous they are behind the scenes of Viennese life: *Magd, Dienstmagd, Kammermagd, Mädchen, Dienstmädchen, Kindermädchen, Stubenmädchen, Hausgehilfin, Dienerin, Bedienerin, Bonne, Servierdame* are essentially interchangeable just as the women who do the work. The list is by no means exhaustive. Maids circulate for the most part invisibly among the better-off Yellow Street households. They gain a different viewpoint on the lives of their employers, to which we become privy through their narrative. Hedi Adenberger's mother, for instance, cleans for Herr Vlk, who forbids her to move any of his furniture. Therese Schrantz confirms what we know of the Igers' family life. She worked for her previous employers for a quarter of a century until she was cast out after they died, like the dog in "A Child Rolls Gold" who finds himself without a home after his master's death. Schrantz accepts her new job at 13 Yellow Street on Frau Hatvany's personal recommendation. She enthuses that Frau Iger is "as sweet as honey! They don't make them as good as her any more. Well-known across the city" (*GS*:88–89). Yet Schrantz returns the following morning, having survived fewer hours than she did years at her previous post. Not only do the Igers row over money, the nanny disappears for an hour at a time into Herr Iger's separate bedroom. When Herr Iger demands to know how much money his wife has given her for shopping, the new maid submits her notice. What goes around comes around and on Frau Iger's advice she goes straight to Runkel's soap shop where she gets Lina's old job serving in the newsstand. Runkel is delighted to replace the beautiful young Lina with a woman in her forties. Here too the difference between the two women is expressed through their names: "The handicapped woman becomes through her name a plant, a root, while the shop assistant bears a name which expresses her femininity in the way it sounds."[12]

In writing about maids and identifying herself with them, Veza also addresses a range of social questions concerning female domestic staff that were debated by social reformers since the turn of the century in Germany. She does so with wit and understanding and challenges clichés and received opinion. These include the high suicide rate among the young unmarried women who work as maids, the link between private employment agencies and criminality, the perceived link between maids and prostitution, the illegitimate children of maids, and their repressed personality and shattered self-confidence.[13] Employers feared for their valuables, like the Prokops in "Patience Brings Roses": "Tamara would not tolerate a housemaid. A housemaid was a danger on account of the expensive jewelry, the furs and currency in the apartment, she would explain to astounded guests." The problem for the Prokops is that if they do not pay a hired hand, then there is no one to perform the multitude of women's tasks in the household. Veza recognizes the problem and her solution to it shows her understanding of the dynamics of status within a bourgeois family: "The hard work was done by Ljubka, but Tamara was not lazy either, she cooked, scrubbed, was not too proud to clean the floor, and looked after her mother" (*GbR*:10).

The German workers' movement was slow to recruit domestic servants into their ranks, the overwhelming majority of whom were women. They were suspected of identifying with their employers and even considered reactionary because very often they did not enjoy the modern status of an employee, as factory workers did. Until recently domestic staff were paid largely in kind (in the form of food and lodging and sometimes other benefits) and were therefore at the mercy of the head of the household, who also had the right to inflict physical punishment on them (his so-called *Züchtigungsrecht*). Maids were often isolated in the households where they worked and for many, the work was temporary, perhaps a steppingstone to marriage. By the first decade of the twentieth century, however, they sometimes had the opportunity of joining associations that championed their rights. They have been called the "most mobile professional group," moving from country to city, thus working at the "nodal point" of modernization as Central Europe changed from an agrarian to an urban society.[14] Veza's maids come from the Austrian provinces or the further-flung corners of the Habsburg Empire; she reflects the historical fact that women from urban areas were far less likely to take such work.[15]

The status and employment conditions of maids were a campaigning issue for the Monday women's page of the *Arbeiter-Zeitung* in the early 1930s. Some of the fiction published under the name of Veza Magd, most notably "The Canal," promotes these campaigns directly.[16] Readers who could afford the services of a maid were asked by the paper, for instance, to recruit only from the municipal agency or the trade union. Such fly-by-night outfits like Frau Hatvany's in "The Canal" were to be avoided, because only a formally registered maid stood a chance of receiving unemployment pay if she lost her job. In "The Canal" young women from the provinces present themselves to would-be employers through Hatvany's less than scrupulous agency. By the end of the story the agency has been closed down because of complaints that she sends girls directly into prostitution and encourages another to fake a suicide attempt by jumping into the Danube Canal — the only way she could be sure to be taken into a hostel for the homeless. The closure of Hatvany's agency is a sign that the action of individuals can have a beneficial effect. It is a liberal rather than a socialist solution, as the system itself has not been reformed, let alone overturned.

According to the *Arbeiter-Zeitung* on 4 July 1932, thirty per cent of Viennese maids had illegitimate children. They were not the only category of working-class single mothers. Gustl's mother in "The Poet" works in the fields during the summer and at her knitting machine in the winter: when the son of the landowner asks him what his father does for a living, he replies "I don't have one" (*DF*:19). Though they both live in the children's home, Hedi's friend Helli Wunderer is really no more an orphan than Hedi. She needs Hedi's money to go to the country to visit her mother. After her father was killed in the war, her mother works as a maid in the city so that she can see her daughter in the home "where her guardian had put her" (*GS*:161). She needed to return to the country and had not visited Helli for four Sundays in a row.

The author of the *Arbeiter-Zeitung* report on maids, who signs herself "Grete Wiesel Hausgehilfin," explains that unmarried maids' children might be the result of one-night stands and pleads for understanding. Adolescent girls living alone find love where it is offered. Grete Wiesel writes against the prejudice which suggests that unmarried mothers have low moral standards, just as Veza combats that prejudice with her representation of maids who are often frightened or disconcerted but always honest. Pastora is innocent of theft in "The Seer" and in "Hush Money"; the chambermaid is the only character to emerge with her integrity intact. In *The Tortoises* the wife of the kindhearted Felberbaum escaped Vienna and works as a maid in Manchester where she endeavors to get him a visa. The detail reinforces Felberbaum's own humanity.

Maids were popular literary figures for male writers in the 1930s, but their portrayal of them could hardly have differed more starkly from Veza's. Exiled to France after the Anschluss, Franz Werfel was persuaded by his wife, Alma Mahler-Werfel, to turn the story of her former cook into a novel.[17] *Embezzled Heaven. The Story of a Maid*, published in Sweden in 1939, fictionalizes the devout Agnes Hvizd's life of self-sacrifice and the deception practiced on her by a nephew, whose studies in theology she wrongly believed to be financing with her toil. Werfel's understanding of his heroine's psychology and motivation is entirely conventional. To be worthy of playing even "a shadowy servant's role" in his story, Teta Linek must correspond to the ideal of the perfect maid:

> She never smuggled men into the house, certainly never men in uniform, not even when she was in the bloom of youth. When she went out she never came home the worse for wear after midnight, like other maids, their hair disheveled, laughing disrespectfully in their drunkenness. She usually did without the afternoon off, to which she was entitled once a week, and spent Sunday in her little room, always ready to be of service. Her attending morning mass every day at six o'clock, disturbed the household not one jot, on the contrary, it very soon brought Teta the reputation for pious dignity, which inspired trust in her. She was visited only rarely by relatives.[18]

Teta Linek spent a total of fifty-five years in service from the age of fifteen, having moved to Vienna from Moravia. That detail about her social background is all she has in common with any of Veza's maids, however.

In turn-of-the-century Prague the student friends Franz Kafka and Max Brod took an apparently contrasting but ultimately complementary approach: both eroticized encounters with female servants in their fiction. In one of Brod's early novellas, *A Czech Serving Maid*, which he dedicated to his writer collegue Franz Blei "because he enjoyed Prague so much," a young professional man falls in love with his landlady's beautiful new maid, who turns out to be married, and succeeds in losing his virginity to her. But while he is lost in thought about her, she drowns herself after a row with her husband, apparently in the same carefree spirit in which she had given herself to her young middle-class lover. Brod's Pepi, a name that is attached to a maid character in Kafka's *The Castle*, is a pornographic male fantasy. Her objectified otherness is captured in the novel's title, as the fact that she is foreign makes her all the more desirable.[19]

Depicting domestic servants became a litmus test of political sensitivity and allegiance. Arthur Schnitzler's *Therese: The Chronicle of a Woman's Life* (1928) follows its heroine from post to post as she struggles to support an illegitimate son: she snatches moments of joy in the arms of a lover while fending off the advances from the heads of numerous households, in which she plays a succession of roles. Perhaps the greatest impression the novel leaves is how little free time Therese (!) has for herself. She does not have the freedom to lead her own life and attend to her son who ultimately kills her after having grown up in a foster family. Schnitzler too took his tale from real life but his sensitivity is very different from Werfel's. Meanwhile, Brecht's Pirate Jenny in *The Threepenny Opera* (1929), who dreams that "a ship with eight sails and fifty cannons" will sail into the harbor to avenge the slights she has suffered as a hotel kitchen maid, is an emblem of revolutionary ambition. Marieluise Fleisser, another of Brecht's girlfriend-collaborators, who was "damaged" by her involvement with him, wrote with empathy similar to Veza about a maid jilted by her widowed employer.[20]

In the five weeks after Veza Magd's name was printed for the first time in the *Arbeiter-Zeitung*, the Monday women's page carries a report of attempts to organize maids into a trade union (1 August) and an article on the prospects of eldest daughters, such as "The Victor's" Anna Seidler, who take on the role of family provider (25 July). Notices on contraception clinics compete for space with reports of the Nazi plans to use women as "industrial child-producers." Grete Wiesel favors training for the multitude of household tasks maids are expected to perform. This is available on their statutory weekday afternoon off (four hours, in addition to Sunday afternoon). The problem is that many households do not want a trained maid, preferring a "work-machine" or skivvy: *Dienstbot* designated a form of semi-bonded farm labor that postwar reforms failed to eradicate[21] and is still a common term even in the city. Wiesel describes a maid's job as one "in which young girls work from early in the morning to late at night, weighed down by feelings of inferiority, and have no opportunity to talk about themselves or find any relief."[22] The author of the article on eldest daughters reports on the issue similarly from the inside: "We all know in our circle of acquaintances older, single women who have sacrificed their own sense of self (their *Persönlichkeitsgefühl*) in order to answer the needs of their relatives."[23] Like the authors of these articles, Veza takes the feelings of these women subjects seriously. Her starting point is a feeling of inferiority or a sacrifice of self that enables her to narrate highly plausible working-class life stories. The whole narrative ethic of *Auto-da-Fé* precludes Canetti from psychologizing Therese Krumbholz's behavior in a comparable way.

Being renamed by an employer is a maid's rite of passage and symbolic of the transformation in her identity that strips her of her integrity as an autonomous individual. On becoming a writer Veza imitates this same process. One of the four Annas in "The Canal" is turned down for a post because her prospective employer has a sister who is also called Anna and who "might be offended" (*GS*:86). After the fifteen-year-old Emma Adenberger returns from one position because she was asked to massage gentlemen, she follows her next employer back to her house with high hopes. Her new mistress, who happens to be Hatvany's own sister, cuts her hair, tells her that she is now to be called "Kitty," and gives her a glass of suspiciously potent wine. The fluid distinction between prostitution and other forms of female employment is well known,[24] and when Emma-alias-Kitty wakes up from a bad dream, moments later, she finds the Banker, Herr Schleier, bending over her. He is only slightly disconcerted to hear Emma is a year older than he was told: he prefers his virginal victims to be fourteen. All the girls expect to be propositioned and have different ways of dealing with the situation. Draga Kozil's predecessor demanded extra payment from the stepfather if he wanted to get pleasure from her malnourished body. Frau Hatvany cannot understand why they complain since they all have a child by the time they get married anyway. Emma-alias-Kitty runs away to her sister Hedwig, a "Bedienerin" in Yellow Street and the single mother of the same little Hedi who found all the money in "A Child Rolls Gold" — money incidentally that a "banker" by the name of Schleier had thrown behind the lift as the police were chasing him. There is a little rich girl in "The Difference" called Schleier; the name means veil or disguise.

The importance of the degrading custom of imposing a new name on a newly appointed maid must have prompted Veza's thinking and it can be seen more clearly in Canetti's *Comedy of Vanity*. Here he treats the matter with the same seriousness as she does in "The Canal," which was published in November 1933 when he began work on his second play. In the interview between Milli Kreiss, daughter of the shopkeeper Therese Kreiss, Milli's prospective employer objects to her name: "The name makes me want to be sick. Every second skivvy [*Dienstbot*] is called Milli nowadays. I need a lady's maid [*Zofe*]" (*II*:140). He included a variation of the practice in *Auto-da-Fé* where the ex-policeman Pfaff rechristens his daughter "Poli," which "expresses her suitability for his profession. Really her name was Anna; but as the name meant nothing to him, he never used it, he was an enemy of names" (*I*:409). In *Comedy of Vanity*, they settle on the name Mary after the lady rejects Milli's own suggestion of Leonie as "too high" (*II*:141). The Lady also asks Milli whether she is pregnant, another question that Veza addressed and obsessed the employers of maids. Milli's predecessor in the household worked for them for thirteen years and they had to release her, so Milli is informed, because "she is getting too old." The real reason is that she answered them. She is a spirited woman who shocks the preacher by telling him she does not "need a husband." These female characters could not differ more sharply from the misogynist caricatures in *Auto-da-Fé*. The playwright, if not his self-portrait Heinrich Föhn, has apparently been "feminized" by the time he wrote his second play, three years after his novel.

It is possible that Canetti was influenced by Veza and that he encouraged Ibby Gordon to address the topic of housemaids in her poem "Pamela!," which was published four years before Veza's first story. Stephanie, the central character in Friedl Benedikt's *Let thy Moon Arise*, also works as a maid who moves from one employer to another. Her bed is her leitmotif. Kate, the maid in *The Monster*, also leaves her first employer to serve the monstrous Jonathan Crisp, who seduces both women. In this novel about enthrallment, domination, and subjugation, Benedikt builds on the relationship between the maid and her employer to explore the exercise of power in human relationships in general. Crisp knows how to make Kate feel guilty for her "sins," which are represented by an illegitimate child who is brought up in the country, and how, after finding a person's weakness, to inveigle himself into her confidence.

Veza's concern for maids continued after the closure of the *Arbeiter-Zeitung*. "Pastora" tells the story of a proud and beautiful young heroine who, rather than marrying the richest boy in her village, runs away to the big city of Seville that she has heard so much about. It is not economic necessity, but ambition and a sense of adventure that lead her to abandon a future at the side of Pepe Velasquez. At the outset of her picaresque progress, she works for a fruit seller in the poor district of the city, but she does not like it when he strokes her arms. The wife of the doorkeeper of the Casa de Caridad wants to recruit her to the convent, but after three days she finds herself a new job in a "very fine house" (*DF*:152). As she was not born to carry out this type of work, she wants to be the equal of her employers' daughter, the lovely Angeles. Young men often do not realize her inferiority and pay her attention when the pair walk out together, but Pastora remembers soon enough herself: "For how should she ever dare to arrange to meet a fine gentleman, she was only a maid, a maid, and she sobbed for a long time into her pillow" (*DF*:153). When Angeles' brother Don Anibal returns from America, Pastora "shrinks back to the size of the little maid who trots along next to the fruit seller's donkey, she puts away her black shawl," the same shawl she is accused of stealing in "The Seer." She catches Don Anibal's eye, as she feared she might, and hears him say to his family that she is "the best thing in your house" (*DF*:154). One night he storms into her room and showers her with kisses, which feel to her like black stains on her body after he has left the room. Don Anibal asks his mother to let Pastora work for him as his secretary, which results in Pastora losing "that maid's gaze, that shy, tolerant gaze," which Veza described in "The Canal." She became someone who writes down another's words, a man's words, rather than running errands for him, cleaning his house and bringing his food. Pastora is not the only unmarried young working-class woman associated with writing. She follows the two Annas in "The Victor" and "Three Quarters" who both work as typists and Emma Adenberger whose ungrammatical draft letter to Dr. Spanek attracts Knut Tell's attention in "Lost Property." All of them write either to or for men and they are all ultimately rejected or excluded from the domain of writing. Veza *Magd* is now writing for them, succeeding where they failed, and proclaiming her voice on their behalf.

Pastora begins to display the signs of a free person in the way that she walks and carries herself, but because her position is insecure her self-confidence is brittle. She betrays herself by getting her words mixed up when she is in the company of Angeles' friends. Even Don Anibal laughs and his father, who does not realize Pastora is a secretary and no longer a maid, snubs her more seriously when he asks her to bring food for his son's guests: "but she would have sooner died than enter that room as a servant with a tray in her hand" (*DF*:163–64). Pastora must learn that she can never be her employers' equal. After the whole family leaves for America and Angeles marries her brother's friend and business partner, a certain Mister Wooster, Pastora wastes away, and is eventually taken into a convent.

One of the last references to maids in Veza'a fiction is particularly poignant. The married couple who takes in the narrator and her husband in "Toogoods or the Light" do anything but good by their guests (Toogood sounds like "Tu gut" which means "do good"). The importunate narrator compares herself with the lowly figures that she has written about in Vienna:

> I felt like the peasant maids at home in our country who come to the city smelling of pure air and cows' milk and present themselves to the gentlewoman of the house. If she is gentle, they are taken on until their fragrance wastes away. If she is ungentle, then lie down and die, then that is what you are worth and no more. (*DF*:201–2)

Back in her home country she was not a maid but an employer of maids, a gentle mistress, who did not accuse her employees of stealing her spoons. Now as a refugee, her status is no higher than that of a family servant.

It is not only because she served others that Veza Canetti chose to call herself Veza Magd, as her husband and his friend surmised, but because she shows her allegiance with the anonymous servants in bourgeois Vienna and she wants to show what goes on in their minds. It begins as a way of adopting what she believed — "auf Umwegen" or indirectly (*PiB*:112), as he put it — he felt about her as he depicted it in Therese Krumbholz. While her views on her husband softened in the course of the 1930s, she never changed her mind on maids.

Notes

[1] Robertson, *The "Jewish Question" in German Literature*, 246–7.

[2] Dagmar C. G. Lorenz, *Keepers of the Motherland: German Texts by Jewish Women Writers* (Lincoln, NE: U of Nebraska P, 1997), 84–5.

[3] Letter to Rudolf Hartung, 5 March 1950, quoted by Göbel, "Nachwort" in *Die Gelbe Straße*, 178.

[4] Detlef Holz [Walter Benjamin], *Deutsche Menschen* (Lucerne: Vita Nova, 1936).

[5] Stefan Neuhaus, *Das verschwiegene Werk: Erich Kästners Mitarbeit an Theaterstücken unter Pseudonym* (Würzburg: Königshausen & Neumann, 2000).

[6] Elfriede Engelmeyer, "'Denn der Mensch schreitet aufrecht, die erhabenen Zeichen der Seele ins Gesicht gebrannt': Zu Veza Canettis *Die Gelbe Straße*," *Mit der Ziehharmonika: Zeitschrift für Literatur des Exils und Widerstands* 11:2 (1994), 25–33.

[7] Kröger, "Themenaffinitäten zwischen Veza und Elias Canetti," 304.

[8] Karin Walser, *Dienstmädchen, Frauenarbeit und Weiblichkeitsbilder um 1900* (Frankfurt am Main: Neue Kritik, 1986), esp. 59–80.

[9] Fischer, *An Opposing Man*, 204.

[10] "Trauer und Verlockung," ZB 226.

[11] Ibid.

[12] Vera Jost, *Fliegen und Fallen: Prostitution als Thema in Literatur von Frauen im 20. Jahrhundert* (Frankfurt am Main: Helmer, 2002), 64.

[13] Dorothee Wierling, *Mädchen für alles: Arbeitsalltag und Lebensgeschichte städtischer Dienstmädchen um die Jahrhundertwende* (Berlin/Bonn: Dietz, 1987) has sub-chapters on all these topics.

[14] Ibid., 283–87 and 67.

[15] Walser, *Dienstmädchen*, 18.

[16] Her stories featuring unscrupulous landlords and put-upon tenants did the same with respect to the question of housing, which was also addressed regularly in the *Arbeiter-Zeitung*. See Eva Meidl, "Veza Canettis Manifest: Die Kurzgeschichte *Geld Geld Geld*," in Spörk and Strohmaier, *Veza Canetti*, 57–73. A similar source in the paper has been identified for "Lost Property," see Holmes, "Elias Canetti and Red Vienna," in Donahue and Preece, eds., *The Worlds of Elias Canetti* (forthcoming).

[17] Jungk, *A Life Torn by History*, 180. Franz Werfel, *Der veruntreute Himmel: Die Geschichte einer Magd* (Stockholm: Bermann-Fischer, 1939). Other literary works contemporaneous with Veza Magd's publishing debut that feature highly conventional maid characters are Ernst Wiechert, *Die Magd des Jürgen Doskocil* (Munich: Albert Langen/Georg Müller, 1932); Walter Erich Schäfer, *Schwarzmann und die Magd* (Stuttgart: Engelhorns, 1932); and Heinrich Eduard Jacob, *Die Magd von Aachen: Eine von siebentausend* (Vienna: Zsolnay, 1931).

[18] Werfel, *Der veruntreute Himmel*, 7 and 27.

[19] Max Brod, *Ein tschechisches Dienstmädchen: Kleiner Roman* (Berlin: Juncker, 1909). See Peter André Alt, *Franz Kakfka: Der ewige Sohn. Eine Biographie* (Munich: Beck, 2005), 121.

[20] Marieluise Fleisser, "Stunde der Magd," in *Erzählungen*, ed. Günther Rühle (Frankfurt am Main: Suhrkamp, 2001), 37–42.

[21] See Therese Weber, ed. *Mägde: Lebenserinnerungen an die Dienstbotenzeit bei Bauern* (Vienna: Böhlau, 1985).

[22] *Arbeiter-Zeitung*, 1 August 1932.

[23] *Arbeiter-Zeitung*, 25 July 1932.

[24] Jost, *Fliegen und Fallen*, 85–91 (on "The Canal") and 91–102 (on Andrea Sandoval).

6: Writing under Cover, 1934–38

In the second phase of Veza's career — after the closure of the *Arbeiter-Zeitung* in February 1934 and until the Anschluss in March 1938 — she wrote two plays, *The Ogre* and *The Tiger*, and a number of short stories and novellas, which all distinguish themselves sharply from the material that appeared in the workers' press between 1932 and 1934. Canetti in contrast wrote nothing that he could present for publication. The intensified censorship meant that Veza had to change her style and subject matter if she wanted to get published in Austria, let alone Nazi Germany. Unlike Canetti, she continued to write for readers — at least there are many signs that indicate that after a period of readjustment to the new, repressive political reality, this is what she wanted to do. Success now came much harder, as there were fewer opportunities, which she seems quickly to have realized. She can hardly have dramatized the story of the Igers' marriage with the expectation that it would be published, let alone performed on stage, under either Dollfuß or Schuschnigg. Her indictment of the patriarch, the linchpin of the neo-Catholic order, for his bullying behavior, is too strong for that, regardless of whether Iger is intended to represent Dollfuß, as Angelika Schedel has proposed.[1] Dagmar Lorenz writes that "geared towards a class-conscious proletariat, *Der Oger*, with its easy-to-follow conflicts, its overt revolutionary message, and its conventional dramatic techniques, is clearly didactic."[2] This is no doubt true, but under the "catholic dictatorship" theaters were not permitted to stage plays written for "the class-conscious proletariat," that continued to be fed either the escapist vehicles Veza derided so forcefully in her critique of the German and American film industries, or patriotic historical plays glorifying Austria's national heroes.[3]

Canetti's account of this period in *The Play of the Eyes* is notoriously short on concrete historical detail, but the prominence he gives to his endless discussions with Dr. Sonne in the Café Museum and the importance he attaches to the presence of Joyce (in Zurich) or Musil (in Vienna) at his readings, show how he was starved for literary interaction in these twilight years in Vienna before the Anschluss. He seizes on what opportunities come his way and is frustrated by lack of recognition, as his efforts at artistic collaboration came to nought. Veza appears not to have ventured to the Café Museum, which limited her exposure to the public realm and there is no sign that she gave readings after her single appearance at the Leopoldstadt branch of the Volkshochschule Wien in 1933.[4]

Once again Canetti's unpublished material is more revealing:

> in the first Grinzing year came the publication of *Auto-da-Fé*, my first real
> "public" success, and directly after that, the terrible disappointment over
> our material situation, which was desperate. This is why Veza came up
> with her "system": she secretly hatched the plan of drawing attention to
> my desperate situation through suicide. Over a period of *weeks* she com-
> posed letters to people like Thomas Mann as well as to close friends and
> acquaintances, in which she explained to them what she intended to do
> and asked them to protect and look after me. She had a small blue suit-
> case in which she kept all the drafts of such letters together. She carried
> the key to it with her always. A small oval-shaped stone was placed under
> the papers, it stood for *her*, for the "little tower," as I called her mind. On
> one dreadful day the whole thing came to light, I became suspicious and
> broke open the case and read everything. In a few more days she would
> have carried out her plan. She collapsed in her tiny wood paneled room
> in Grinzing and confessed her whole plan to me. In horror I took her in
> my arms and we wept like two children.
>
> I cannot now determine the exact date of this day. It must have been
> in the autumn of 1936 — or was it already winter 1936/37? I cannot say
> now with the best will in the world whether I had held my Broch-speech
> before or after this "discovery." The situation changed at the beginning
> of 1937 in that the Czech translation of *Auto-da-Fé* came out. In April I
> read *Wedding* in public and then traveled to Prague. In June my mother
> died: an event which caused upheaval, afterwards nothing could be the
> same as it was before. It meant that I wanted to write my book about
> death. Because it was a question of writing *this* book it seemed permissi-
> ble to me to use my mother's small legacy, from which we could live for
> two years. The worst pressure on Veza was thus past. We did not know
> that Austria would be occupied in nine months. We feared it, of course,
> but did not think about it as all our thoughts were distracted by another,
> much more terrible matter: the Spanish Civil War.[5]

Veza's devotion and assumption of financial responsibility for both of them
are striking in this unpublished passage. Until his mother's death, Canetti's
sense of his own well-being depends on literary recognition: the publication of his novel in October 1935 was initially a financial and critical disappointment, contrary to his expectations, but in May 1937, his fortunes
took a turn for the better. H. G. Adler invited him to Prague to launch the
Czech translation of the novel, he had been recently interviewed in
Sonntag, where he explained his theory of drama and film, and he gave his
final public reading in Vienna. He can date his speech to commemorate
Broch's half-centenary but not his discovery of his wife's letters.

March to May 1937 was also a good period for Veza: "Clairvoyants"
came out in March in *Sonntag*, which subsequently interviewed Canetti in
April, and it was followed by "Hush Money" and "Money — Money —
Money" over the following two months in *Die Stunde*. There are signs that

she and Canetti were working as a team: in July 1936 they both agreed to contribute to a new exile journal published in Moscow under the editorship of Bertolt Brecht, Lion Feuchtwanger, and Willi Bredel, *Das Wort*, which was intended to replace the banned *Neue Deutsche Blätter* that published "Three Heroes and a Woman" in July 1934.[6] The reasons for their failure to provide material for it, however, can only be conjectured.

Canetti's own publication record after February 1934 is not dissimilar to Veza's. His success in landing *Auto-da-Fé* with a publisher is put down by some to his Italian-sounding name or to the prominence of anti-Semitism in the novel, which can be taken straight. According to his own account, he took advantage of Jean Hoepffner's offer to underwrite it. Austrian and Swiss publishers operated according to a greater financial imperative rather than political pressure after up to ninety per cent of their usual readership was cut off from them in Nazi Germany. Stefan Zweig heard of the arrangement with Hoepffner and, when he was looking for material for his new Austrian publisher, Herbert Reichner, he recommended Canetti put forward his novel.

In his interview with *Sonntag*, Canetti only mentions economic constraints when asked for his views on the state of contemporary theater. His anger may be raw but he is not specific in identifying his targets, referring instead to "most cities of culture in Europe" rather than Vienna. The paper, of course, was unlikely to have printed an explicit political critique and left its readers to interpret his comments for themselves:

> The theater business, as it exists today in most cities of culture in Europe, fills me with the greatest disgust. There is hardly another area of public life that is hopeless and ugly at the same time. You just don't know what the point is of all those pompous theater buildings. They are like enormous sweet jars with all the sweets taken out; sometimes you can still hear the paper rustling. Sometimes they really are empty, which is at least honest. Sometimes they have been taken over by sports or business people, which adds up to the same thing, since they are both just interested in breaking box office records. (*X*:135)

Canetti told his brother that *Comedy of Vanity* was to be performed in April 1934 in Vienna in a production directed by none other than Max Reinhardt but it was put off because of the "events" (2 March 1934; *BG*:191) An earlier studio production of *Wedding* that was to be directed by Canetti's friend, Hans Schlesinger, with Cilly Wang as Mariechen, had been canceled on a mixture of political and economic grounds.[7] Another production of *Comedy of Vanity* was scheduled to take place in the summer of 1937 by a celebrated avant-garde troupe, "Theater für 49" — so named because theaters with audiences under fifty were not required to have a license. Anna Mahler was engaged to design the stage set, as she did for the premiere of Ödön von Horváth's *Faith, Charity, Hope* that the same troupe performed in November 1936 (albeit under the title *Charity, Duty, Hope*, in order not to offend catholic "sensibilities"). The reasons for the abandonment of these plans are unknown, but Mathilde Canetti's death in June 1937 would certainly have prevented her son from participating.[8]

In *The Play of the Eyes*, Canetti does not give an account of February 1934, as he originally planned; instead, he presents the political developments up to the Anschluss as seamless. The cultural and moral crisis he diagnosed in his novel was far more grave than that which persuaded Dollfuß to abolish parliament. *Comedy of Vanity* was prompted as much by the book burning in Germany as the rise of clerical fascism in Austria.[9] Veza, on the other hand, was more closely connected to her native city, which makes Schedel's theory of *The Ogre* as an allegorical account of Austrian history between 1918 and 1934 not entirely implausible. For Schedel, Frau Iger stands for the state of Austria and Iger stands for Dollfuß. The other characters who represent the leading politicians and parties first join in the preparations for the marriage and then fight over the fate of the unhappy bride: Iger's father is the Social Democrat Karl Renner, a paternal figure who was the republic's first president; Stejpo Pavlovitsch is Renner's party colleague, Karl Seitz, the mayor of Vienna until February 1934 when he was imprisoned; Schwab, Iger's rival for Draga's hand, is the Christian Social Chancellor and catholic priest, Ignaz Seipel, who died in 1932. Meanwhile, Bogdan Stoitsch, who opposes the marriage from the start, represents the Communists; the medical student who (in Adler's favorite dramatic moment) rescues the wedding by not reading the real contents of the letter from Draga's other suitor, the apothecary, whom she really loves, plays the role of another Social Democrat leader, Otto Bauer. The medical student is also a portrait of Veza's beloved Georg Canetti, who was completing his medical studies as she wrote the play.

The roles do fit more or less, but it is not hard to pick holes in this reading and one is left wondering why, if Schedel is right, she is the first person to notice the allegory. Canetti did not have any reason to avoid drawing attention to it when *The Ogre* premiered in 1992. The parallels also appear to have escaped Adler's notice when he wrote his appreciation in 1950. For reasons that are not clear (might he have read a different version?), he thinks it is set at the beginning of the nineteenth century and recommends for the sake of historical consistency that Veza change the currency from schillings and dinars to guilders and crowns.

The historical events that Schedel argues are depicted are unlikely to have been rendered so precisely. She makes much of the stage direction at the beginning of act three: "After the collapse of the monarchy. The events take place nine years later in the former capital city" (*DO*:35). Nine years from 1918 is not 1934, the crisis year of the first republic, but 1927, when the

Palace of Justice was burnt to the ground by rioters protesting the acquittal of the killers of two demonstrators from the Republican Defense League. This is a key date for Canetti who, after witnessing the mayhem, became convinced that he must explore crowd behavior. Dollfuß, however, was not a significant force at this point. Furthermore, as the first act takes place in peace time, the two parts of the play are more likely to straddle the First World War.

There are two other factors, however, that speak in favor of Schedel's interpretation of *The Ogre*. All three of Veza's stories published in 1937, as well as *The Tiger*, can be read politically although the message is by no means explicit in any of them. This suggests that she realized after *The Ogre* that she had to change if she wanted to reach an audience or readers.

Had *The Ogre* been performed before a contemporary audience, the dynamic between director, actors, and audience would have resonated with the political scene. Dramatic productions under repressive regimes invariably do so and plays or stories depicting power struggles within families can easily acquire wider significance under these circumstances. "Money — Money — Money" is a typical example. In rewriting "The Ogre" chapter from *Yellow Street* that cannot be read allegorically, Veza probably came across parallels between her original plot and the fate of her country. Iger already shared his diminutive size with the Chancellor. A drama was undoubtedly being acted out in Austrian politics, the climax of which was the bloody assassination of Dollfuß on 25 July 1934, which happened to be Canetti's twenty-ninth birthday. He recognized it as such in a notebook entry that shows sympathy for the murdered leader.[10] The stage for that drama in post-1918 Austria was relatively circumscribed and the Canettis moved in circles close to key players from both the opposition and the government. Through Anna Mahler they were connected not only with Schuschnigg, since Mahler's mother, Alma, moved among the highest and, by no means, most savory echelons of Austrian politics. The day before the workers' revolt began on 12 February 1934, Otto Bauer asked Ernst Fischer if he and his wife Ruth would see a Greta Garbo film with him. Fischer replied that they had already arranged to see Elias Canetti.[11]

Both "New Boy" and "Three Heroes and a Woman" are certainly embedded in contemporary events. The "brown" newspaper seller in "New Boy," whom Seidler protects from the police out of misplaced loyalty, appears to be connected to Nazi terrorists sponsored by the Reich. The detectives investigating the case do not get very far because of his colleagues' solidarity:

> It turned out that passersby had repeatedly complained about how loud and aggressively the man in brown used to shout. It turned out that a search of the house uncovered explosives in his possession. Furthermore, the police had been looking for him for a long time. The tell-tales [the other newspaper sellers] were now questioned by the police, but they did not give him away. The two detectives now approached Seidler and looked at him in a friendlier way than usual. Now Seidler would have

enough to say about his colleague's tirades, but he just explained that he stood off to the side and didn't know anything about it. "Your colleague did not behave so well towards you, though," said one of the officers sharply, but tipped his hat politely nonetheless and went off with the other one. (*GbR*:71)

As possession of explosives in such circumstances was a capital offense at the time "New Boy" was published, Seidler has done him a great favor.[12]

The "Germans" in the so-called Austrian Legion, one of several paramilitary organizations in Austria, were waging a terror campaign against state targets since the midsummer of 1933, which reached a peak in October. Their objective was to destabilize Dollfuß, whose own campaign against Austrian Social Democracy was hardly less ruthless, so that Austria's absorption into the Reich became a practical necessity.[13] Veza addresses the question indirectly by incorporating it as a detail in her plot; her story is nothing if not topical.

In her next published story, Frau Schäfer is cleaning a tenement house that is part of the 51,000 new flats built by the Social Democrats since 1918; which was, perhaps, the single proudest achievement during their governance of "Red Vienna." Dollfuß ordered the artillery bombardment of some of the most prestigious housing complexes, such as the Ottakaring Arbeiterheim and the symbolically named Karl-Marx Hof, on 12–13 February 1934. Frau Schäfer thus works at the central location of the ill-conceived workers' revolt. Daydreaming of "a little church" in which she sank to her knees during the war to pray for her husband's safe return, her life is suddenly disrupted when "the dreadful thing happened":

> the workers who lived in the municipal tenement houses were fired on with cannons by their brothers. The big municipal tenement where Frau Schäfer worked for years had to surrender, the weapons were given up, and the workers fled through an underground passage into the little church. They thought they were safe. One after another, drunk with joy, they staggered out of the church to freedom and *every* one who stepped out of the church was shot down on the spot. (*GbR*:75–76)

The similarities between Veza's story and Fischer's factual recollection of what happened at the Ottakring Arbeiterheim are striking:

> At nine-thirty the order was given to storm the building. The gates were forced open; with bayonets fixed and sinking hearts the soldiers pressed forward into the shattered building. It was an invasion into silence. The place was empty. In one room they found a dead woman, in the next one another woman, Frau Ide Sever, at the point of death. Slumped over the window sill the body of a man. The Schutzbund defenders had escaped through the sewers. In the cellars the victorious invaders found terrified women and children upon whom they revenged themselves for the men's resistance.[14]

The frightened men who appear before Frau Schäfer (whose name means shepherd), beseeching her for aid, must rely on their fellow workers, rather than the Catholic Church, to help them. Two of the flats that the police "heroes" search house families who have lost their young men in the fighting. At number three, the son of the shoemaker, Pfeidl, whose wife is now "dying in bed," was shot outside the church the previous day. The police notice his dying mother clutching "a man's blood-stained coat in her knotted fingers" when they storm in. The scene is even worse at number four: only the grandmother is left and she has gone mad with grief after the father and two sons have been killed and the mother hanged herself. Once more, these details come over all the more powerfully because they are mentioned in passing. The focus of the story is its fast-moving plot.

Canetti's recollection, which he wrote in the months before he died, of sheltering Ernst and Ruth Fischer on the night of 12 February — an incident both Fischers recall in their memoirs — gives "Three Heroes and a Woman" a possible autobiographical twist. In contrast to his guests, who imply that they alone asked for shelter, Canetti recalls that "a group of defeated socialist warriors" knocked on the door. While Fischer says that they called at the apartment that Elias Canetti and Veza Magd shared, the apartment was in fact rented by Veza and her mother. Canetti only stayed there and he quite rightly says they came to *her* door:

> The small group of disillusioned and thoroughly exhausted warriors distributed themselves "as quietly as mice" around the various rooms of the apartment. If they made the slightest sound, Veza's seriously ill mother, who was also in the apartment, would have suffered a fatal heart attack.[15]

Similarly, the workers in Veza's story also walk on tip-toes, "as quietly as mice," and are let into a safe apartment by the inconspicuous Frau Schäfer.

Another detail concerning another mutual friend contains too much poetic truth to be taken literally. According to Canetti in 1993, Fischer needed a pillow and Veza found him a bundle of papers on which he could rest his head. The bundle belonged to Anna Mahler and contained her love letters from the future Chancellor Kurt von Schuschnigg that she had given to Veza to keep safe. Since Mahler's sympathies were with the Left, if her comrades found out about her friendship with the man who was then the Minister for Justice and was responsible for hanging a number of socialist leaders in the aftermath of February 1934, they would have denounced her as a traitor. Therefore, she handed over the letters to her friend, the future wife of her former lover. Given the bad blood between Canetti and Fischer and Fischer's very different recollection, it is difficult to know whether to believe Canetti's revised account. Perhaps his retelling was inspired by Veza's republished story. Veza's comments to Georg on Fischer are entirely positive, in contrast to Canetti's much later views. She calls him her "friend" and has high hopes for him when he briefly holds a cabinet post in the first postwar Austrian government (5 October 1945; *BG*:152).

The references to contemporary history in *The Tortoises*, where Veza balances symbolism with documentary realism, are also every bit as precise as those Schedel finds in her first play. Without giving dates or naming specific events or individuals, Veza's second novel faithfully and comprehensively chronicles the fate of Vienna's Jewish citizens from March to November 1938. An annotated edition of *The Tortoises* could show how the textual details correspond closely to the escalation of persecution after the Anschluss that culminated in the Kristallnacht. Baldur Pilz, for instance, who is so proud of his low party number because it indicates how early he joined up, belongs to the exiled Munich Legion of Austrian Nazis who return to plunder the country after the Anschluss. He shares an interest in painting with his Führer and a first name with the Hitlerjugend leader, Baldur von Schirach. Hitler's name is mentioned just once and the only event discussed is the shooting in Paris of the Nazi diplomat, Ernst vom Rath, which was followed by the burning of Jewish property throughout the Reich, which now included Austria, on what became known as the Kristallnacht. A number of other events can be inferred. The imposition of the Nuremberg Race Laws followed swiftly on the heels of the takeover and was accompanied by the first wave of terror in the second half of March 1938. This is when Felberbaum is imprisoned for the first time. A month before the Kristallnacht, during the Feast of Yom Kippur on 4 and 5 October, which Felberbaum endeavors to celebrate by fasting, and which the novel refers to pointedly as the "Day of Atonement," saw a resurgence of anti-Jewish violence in northwest Vienna, just as Felberbaum reports. Ten days later, there were attacks in the Leopoldstadt, where the second half of the novel is set. The arson, arrests, and evictions that provoked an unknown number of Jewish suicides are also depicted in the novel. They reached a climax on the night that began 9 November, when the news arrived that vom Rath had died from the shots fired by the desperate Herschel Grynszpan.[16] Grynszpan intended to assassinate the German Ambassador because his parents, whose plight mirrors that of the central characters in *The Tortoises*, found themselves in no-man's land after leaving Germany and being refused entry into Poland.

It is not known whether Veza tried to interest a theater before the Anschluss in performing *The Tiger*. She wrote it immediately after *The Ogre* and had finished it by the end of 1934, when she wrote to Georg: "I have written two plays. One of them, a comedy, will earn us some money, the other, a drama, will bring me fame" (20 December 1934; *BG*:28). *The Tiger* is very different from her first play. Unlike *The Ogre*, it was written with a view to performance, but, unlike *The Tortoises*, it was not written in freedom. While the first play is a hard-hitting critique of the use of money and male power in marriage, *The Tiger* is a mild drawing-room comedy with suspense and dénouement at the final curtain. The tone is light, the pace brisk, and the jokes come at regular intervals, all of which makes it the sort of anodyne entertainment that found its way on to the Viennese stage after February 1934. Knut Tell and Diana Sandoval provide a romantic subplot. There is more overt sexual interest located in the pretty actress Marie Schmidt, the dancer Bella Buff ("in the buff" is a colloquial English expression for naked), and the bet that Herr Tiger loses as to whether he will seduce Andrea Sandoval in the "Lusthaus" with Zierhut (or "Sir Hutt," as Smith calls him to general confusion). There is even a dance and one or two songs. The "Oriental" is a stock comic figure that serves no purpose except to extract a laugh at the expense of a foolish and uncouth foreigner, in this case, an Ottoman or East European Jew, who speaks imperfect German and wants to cook food in his room, but knows precisely how much rent he should be charged.[17] Veza's willingness to pander to a potential audience with such a stereotype, however harmless it may appear compared with the anti-Semitic propaganda pouring out of Germany, demonstrates her ambition to see the play on stage. The Oriental's poor command of German anticipates Mister Smith's difficulty with the language, which is also played for laughs. Zierhut (which means literally "ornamental hat") is also identifiable as a Jewish name and sounds distinctly comic.[18]

The main theme of *The Tiger* is the integrity of artists; this is less marked in the prose version, which she wrote earlier. *The Ogre* differs similarly from its original chapter in *Yellow Street* since both plays develop the material from the novel in unexpected or unpredictable ways. The behavior and obligations of artists preoccupied both Canettis after February 1934. The poet as the *Knecht* of his age is a concept, which Canetti elaborates in his speech on Broch's fiftieth birthday; Veza judged the first part of it to be as much about him as about the friend he was celebrating (*WK*:13). Veza develops the theme in *The Tortoises*, where Andreas Kain is endangered "in the new order" simply because "he was a writer, independent in his work" (*SK*:24). Pilz inveighs against writers because they "incite the entire foreign press against us, a scandal what they cobble together, nothing but horror stories" (*SK*:130). In Diana's first scene in *The Tiger* we learn that she has lost all her commissions: the actress does not like her portrait and wants to pay her for three hours work (Diana does not work by the hour!); the factory management wants her to cover up her naked statue of Aphrodite with a bathing costume; and the theater prefers the "court painter," Kirschl, because he is already famous. Diana stands for truth and purity. When Stuart Smith tells her she is cold and hard like her sculptures, she replies defiantly: "I can do without your judgment" (*DF*:84) and reflects his predatory gaze right back at him. Diana's high standards and uncompromising commitment to artistic truth anticipate Canetti's position in his account of the literary salons and parties of 1930s Vienna in *The Play of the Eyes*.

The American agent, Mister Stuart Smith, drives the plot of *The Tiger* with his promise to fulfill the yearnings for success felt by Vienna's entire artistic, theatrical, and literary community. Not all writers and artists are like Nick, who is prepared to put together a film script to order, but they all — even Diana and Tell — are interested in Smith's seemingly limitless offer. Through him Veza shows the artists' gullibility: they believe in him because they want to believe in him. Their willingness to believe reveals a communal wish to escape. The basic plot structure is adapted from Gogol's *The Government Inspector*, with the exception that once Gogol's false Inspector realizes the townsfolk believe that he was sent on an errand by the Czar, he milks their gullibility for all he can. In contrast, Smith genuinely believes that he is working for a wealthy boss, who turns out to be none other than Herr Tiger himself. Unfortunately, he misunderstood Herr Tiger's instructions and the play ends with Smith's exposure as an unwitting fraud and Tiger's as his unwitting patron. At the curtain, Frau Sandoval senior wants to convince Tiger that investing in art is in his best interests. He can display the paintings in his cafés: "That's what they do now in England, Herr Tiger. Still lifes on the walls. The people get quite animated. They order champagne and drink" (*DF*:149). Promulgating art to encourage drinking champagne is something of a comedown for a writer who made her debut at the *Arbeiter-Zeitung*. But evidently it was a price worth paying if it meant the play might be performed.

Had *The Tiger* found its way on to the Austrian stage in the mid-1930s, the audiences would have appreciated its gently coded messages of political criticism. The boxes of material that Smith collects to ship across the Atlantic resemble the packed bags of a community ready to leave. Frau Sandoval tells Zierhut she is interested to know what is in them in case they contain "forbidden books or papers. That happens frequently now" (*DF*:75). The willingness of Nick to sell out to commercialism recalls the political betrayal of others closer to home. The resistance of Tell and Diana to these values takes on a potentially heroic dimension. On the title page we read that it is a comedy set in "Old Vienna," a term that is usually applied to the seventeenth or eighteenth centuries. The play's superficially carefree environment is indeed centuries away from the threatening reality of Schuschnigg's Austria on the eve of the Nazi annexation.

One further intriguing possibility is opened up by the intimacy between Mahler and Schuschnigg. Mahler modeled Schuschnigg, just as Diana models Herr Tiger, who is her mother's suitor in the prose version of the story. In the world of art and power, there could be few more fascinating romances than that between the new Chancellor and the thrice-married daughter of one of Vienna's most distinguished Jewish families. If Iger is indeed intended to be Dollfuß, then Tiger, by the same token, can be understood as his successor. Messersmith (which is very close to Mister Smith) happened to be the name of the American Minister in Vienna in October 1934 and provides another possible model on the stage of politics.[19] As *The Tiger* concerns the relationship between art and power and shows how art's willingness to compromise with power results in its failure to achieve its ends, it could be said to recount its own failure to be performed. Schuschnigg's milder form of tyranny offered Vienna's artists only false hopes.

Veza's disappointment with the stage did not yet deter her from writing. All circumstantial evidence indicates that the novella "Pastora" was written in the mid- to late 1930s. She responds to anti-Semitism in a gentle and humorous fashion as if she is concerned not to endanger the chances of publication. Pastora is told by the uncouth Frau Sanchez that the Jews have "bushy beards and bushy tales," which makes her wonder whether "their tales emerged from their trousers or were hidden, but she was too ashamed to ask" (*DF*:151). She never finds out the answer as she never sees a Jew since Spain expelled or "converted" its Jewish population many centuries ago. In "Pastora," as in *The Tiger*, there is an opportunity to escape to a brighter, faraway America, but Pastora is left behind when the family who employs her emigrates. She thus fails to fulfill her youthful promise.

With the three stories that were published in 1937, we can form a clearer impression of her intentions by taking the place of publication into account. The *Wiener Tag* was a liberal paper, whose front page was filled with news from the Spanish Civil War in March 1937. On 14 March when "Clairvoyants" by Veza Magd appeared in its Sunday edition, it ran an historical essay on "Germany's first Emancipation of the Jews." Since reporting on the effects of the Nuremberg Race Laws in Hitler's Reich was difficult, an account of the affect of Prussian policy on the Jews at the time of Napoleon was used to keep the subject at the forefront of readers' attention. It was a reminder that the Nazis were undoing more than a century of progressive racial policy. Veza Magd's readers would have known how to read "Clairvoyants" as a message of anti-Nazi solidarity. Her task here was practical, as she was writing once more for a purpose with a specific readership in mind. *Sonntag*, however, presents it as an investigation into the paranormal. The headline on the supplement's cover highlights the theme, not the author's name. After nearly three and half years since her last Viennese publication, Veza must have been delighted that Ing. Robert Haas produced a series of avant-garde photographs to accompany her text. The *Arbeiter-Zeitung* never stretched to illustrations. Haas does not focus on eyes, as Veza does in the story, or an individual clairvoyant, but on the pair of hands that she describes in her second paragraph. On the front cover they stretch down from the sky above clusters of people standing still inside a circle, looking trapped or mesmerized. The story is printed beneath another photograph of the same hands in the supplement's centerfold, while an outstretched arm is raised as if in salute on the left-hand page.

The explanatory blurb indicates the editor understood very well that Veza Magd was not relating an account of an occult experience. We read:

Not all eras appear to favor to the same degree the occult and extrasensory capabilities which individuals find within themselves. In our own era once more, in which so many people despair of solving life's problems through the means of reason, we are inclined to lend our trust to those who guide our will and possess extrasensory powers. And this is why in Viennese gatherings we more than ever come across mesmerizers and clairvoyants.[20]

The literary tradition of allegorizing the fascist manipulator of the masses through a hypnotist dates to Thomas Mann's macabre story of a holiday performance in Italy, *Mario and the Magician*, published in 1929. Veza Magd's "Clairvoyants" stands somewhere in his debt.

The story's narrator, who turns out to be a writer (but a *Schriftsteller*, not a *Dichter*), encounters an eccentric group of people, a circus rider, a patron of the arts who has "fallen on hard times and lives from selling his pictures" (*DF*:24), a lady who is hard of hearing, and a waiter. They all belong to a club called "Paradise" and are under the spell of a clairvoyant, the owner of the hands, which so frighten the narrator but turn out to be made of wax. When his audience gazes upon his hands, they are said to look "as if he were Michelangelo's god the father creating the world' (*DF*:26). The clairvoyant returns their faith by making them wait for his performance. The hostess with the fanatical eyes is furious when the narrator exposes the clairvoyant as a fraud. He does this after the clairvoyant has departed by revealing that his father, to whom the clairvoyant claimed he had a special attachment, had died before he was born. The clairvoyant's last announcement was more portentous. As he took up the narrator's diary he said: "On the fifteenth of January you have made an entry. It will decide the rest of your life" (*DF*:27). Veza's stories often have a twist in their tail, the final paragraph or even final line delivering a punch line. Right at the end, we learn that the page for that particular day is blank. The clairvoyant's performance cannot have been any different for the others, yet they believe; they believe in his supernatural powers not because of evidence but because they want to have faith in him. They are then angry with the writer for trying to break the spell, not the clairvoyant for deceiving them. The charismatic performer who gazes into the future on behalf of an expectant audience is a creation of that audience's collective mind. Smith exerted a similar hold for similar reasons in *The Tiger*.

Three weeks later on 11 April in the Sunday supplement of another liberal newspaper, Veza succeeded in placing a second encoded short story. *Die Stunde* printed "Hush Money. A Story from a Luxury Sanatorium" beneath a cartoon depicting its key episodes. Opposite was an extract from Charles Sealsfield's *Austria as it is*, a book first published in 1828 in English (and not translated into German until 1919) on the lot of Austrians under Metternich: "Never, perhaps," Sealsfield wrote in his preface, "has there been exhibited an example of so complete and refined a despotism in any civilized country as in Austria."[21] The parallels between the 1820s and the 1930s would not have needed explaining to the newspaper's readers, any more than the critique contained in "Hush Money." In April 1937, the month the Condor Legion bombed the Basque town of Guernica, *Die Stunde* specialized in foreign reporting and literary extracts rather than domestic reporting. "Hush Money" appeared between stories by Luigi Pirandello and P. G. Wodehouse — whose most famous character provided the name for the American Mister Wooster in "Pastora." On 1 May, "Money — Money — Money" shared space in the same paper with Arnold Bennett and Agatha Christie. Lacking amongst this exalted literary company is other contemporary material by German or Austrian writers. This was a wide gap for Veza Magd to fill but the limits within which she wrote were narrow.

On the surface "Hush Money" is an upper-class romance with a comic twist set in an exclusive sanatorium, of the type Mathilde Canetti frequented since Canetti's childhood. The mysterious male lead, who is nicknamed the *Magnate* by the other patients, resembles the German Reichskanzler. He is "an imposing gentleman with a tiny black moustache, who, for reasons which were known only to himself, always wore riding breeches." His origins and need for treatment are unknown:

> He was the object of more speculation among the patients in the *Lilienhain* Sanatorium than even the consultant. They said he was not seriously ill at all but had reasons for hiding himself away. Politics, whispered the psychiatric cases, on account of someone's husband, averred the moderately ill. Because of his splendid appearance they called him the *Magnate*. (*TK*:12)

This Schnitzleresque sexual farce owes something to other texts by Mann, who chronicled sexual shenanigans in an Alpine spa in "Tristan," not to mention his 800-page epic *The Magic Mountain*, whose dialogues Canetti imitates in the penultimate chapter of *Auto-da-Fé*. In "Hush Money" a chambermaid unwittingly shows up the Magnate and his aristocratic onenight stand by misunderstanding why he hands her a hundred schilling banknote wrapped in a pair of the Baroness's knickers, which the chambermaid found, to the Magnate's surprised dismay, among his bedclothes. Shortly before she entered to tidy the room, the Baroness had beaten a retreat on hearing her husband's car draw up in the drive below and inadvertently left the evidence of their tryst. The Magnate reacts by seeking to buy the chambermaid's silence with the hundred schilling note — not suspecting that she would have kept her mouth shut for nothing. For Veza Magd, a maid's code of honor is different from that of a powerful man. In her innocence the maid assumes the money is intended for the knickers' owners and hands both banknote and undergarment to her, whereupon the Baroness runs off to her husband's waiting car. The chambermaid's behavior, discreet and incorruptible, is stressed in the last line: "In the sanatorium everyone was talking about the Baroness. Only the chambermaid kept her mouth shut" (*TK*:14).

In "Hush-Money," the aristocracy and haute-bourgeoisie are portrayed as otiose and mildly ridiculous and suffer from largely imaginary illnesses. The chambermaid's assumption that the Baroness took money for spending the night with a man may be naive but it is born of experience from working with them. Veza makes a point about social class: it is only the idle rich who treat illness as an excuse for romance or flirtation. If we read the story allegorically, then we see how, after jumping into bed with Hitler, the aristocracy recoils when he offers them a payback. The last laugh is on both him as well as the Baroness.

The allegorical content of this trio's most realistic story, "Money — Money — Money," whose themes are class relations and the abuse of power, is no less pronounced. The stepfather who crushes anyone weaker than himself (for instance, his son, who defies him) is called a "nabob" and compared with a "ruler" who wants nothing less than to leave money to his heirs. It is a negative desire that anticipates another aspect of the survival theme in *Crowds and Power*. The quiet determination of the household's least significant member, the maid, leads to the family's liberation from tyranny. Draga Kozil is from the lower classes, her husband fell victim to the economic downturn that followed the First World War and hanged himself because the stepfather refused to wait for his rent. The stepfather's death is Draga's carefully plotted revenge for her husband's suicide. The changes Veza made to her own childhood experience reinforce a political reading. Rather than the daughter taming the tyrant, it is the maid who outwits and defeats him. For a Viennese socialist in 1937, it is a story of hope, which must have been recognized by the paper's editors when they published it on the international day of the workers, 1 May. Given the story's defiant content and *Die Stunde*'s strategically veiled criticism, Veza might have conceived it especially for 1 May, the celebrations of which had been banned in Vienna since 1933.[22] By 1 May 1938 the Nazis governed Vienna and *Die Stunde* was closed down. "Money — Money — Money" was the last story Veza published, a little under five years after she published her first. She continued to write for nineteen years and died precisely twenty-six years later on 1 May 1963, the coincidence in the dates giving those who argue that she took her own life one of their only slender pieces of "evidence."

Notes

[1] Schedel, *Sozialismus und Psychoanalyse*, 61–73.

[2] Lorenz, *Keepers of the Motherland*, 109.

[3] John Warren, "Austrian Theatre and the Corporate State," *Austria in the Thirties: Culture and Politics*, edited by John Warren and Kenneth Segar (Riverside CA: Ariadne, 1991), 267–91.

[4] Schedel, *Sozialismus und Psychoanalyse*, 149. Schedel, however, records Veza frequenting the Café Museum, a renowned meeting place for Jewish intellectuals during the First World War. "Vita Veza Canetti." *Text und Kritik* 156 (Veza Canetti issue) (2002): 95–104; here: 97.

[5] "Allgemeines: Bedenken. Veza. Das System," ZB 60.

[6] Schedel, *Sozialismus und Psychoanalyse*, 156.

[7] Hanuschek, *Elias Canetti*, 301.

[8] Viktoria Hertling, "Theater für 49: Ein vergessenes Avantgarde-Theater in Wien (1934–1938)," *Jura Soyfer and his Time*, ed. Donald Daviau (Riverside, CA: Ariadne, 1995), 321–35.

[9] Deborah Holmes, however, has recently argued it may contain various coded references to contemporary Austrian politics. "The *Komödie* can be read as a parable of how the First Republic destroyed itself, the Christian Socials crushing the Social Democrats only to find they had undermined the bases of democracy so perilously that Austria was no longer able to resist the Anschluß." Holmes, "Elias Canetti in Red Vienna," in Donahue and Preece, eds., *The Worlds of Elias Canetti* (forthcoming).

[10] Quoted by Hanuschek, *Elias Canetti*, 219.

[11] Fischer, *An Opposing Man*, 228.

[12] Edward Timms, *Karl Kraus: Apocalyptic Satirist: The Post-War Crisis and the Rise of the Swastika* (New Haven: Yale UP, 2005), 476.

[13] Gordon Brook-Shepherd, *The Austrians: A Thousand-Year Odyssey* (London: HarperCollins, 1996), 273; Carsten, *The First Austrian Republic*, 183.

[14] Fischer, *An Opposing Man*, 239.

[15] Jungk, "Fragmente, Momente, Minuten," 97–98.

[16] Gerhard Botz, *Nationalsozialismus in Wien: Machtübernahme und Herrschaftssicherung 1938/39* (Buchloe: dvo, 1988), 93–98.

[17] Robertson, *The "Jewish Question" in German Literature*, 428–64 ("The Jew as Oriental") and 203–11 ("The Comic Jew in Drama").

[18] Dietz Bering notes Zierfisch ("ornamental fish") and Zierrat (possibly "ornamental councillor") in *The Stigma of Names: Antisemitism in German Daily Life, 1812–1933*, trans. Neville Plaice (Ann Arbor, MI: U of Michigan P, 1995), 12 and 162.

[19] Carsten, *The First Austrian Republic*, 241.

[20] *Sonntag*, 17 March 1937.

[21] Charles Sealsfield, *Austria as it is: or Sketches of Continental Courts / Österreich, wie es ist, oder Skizzen von Fürstenhöfen des Kontinents*, trans. and ed. Victor Klarwill. (Hildesheim/New York: Olms, 1972), vi.

[22] This is Meidl's view, "Veza Canettis Manifest," in Spörk and Strohmaier, *Veza Canetti*.

7: Portraits

Veza on Canetti

IT WAS CANETTI'S MOST PERSISTENT CRITIC who first suggested in a review of *Yellow Street* that "Knut Tell, Poet" was a satirical portrait of the author's future husband.[1] Being reminded of his first wife's gentle satire reportedly upset him.[2] What the reviewer could not know was that Tell appears two more times in Veza's writings, in a short story entitled "Lost Property" ("Der Fund") which first appeared in the *Arbeiter-Zeitung* in April 1933, and in *The Tiger*, which makes him her single most enduring character. What is striking in the context of the Canettis' literary marriage is that by the time of her second play Veza's attitude towards him changes dramatically. He is transformed from a well-meaning and mildly ridiculous figure to the upholder of artistic integrity in the face of commercial philistinism and worse.

Veza's literary characters often corresponded closely with people she knew. Canetti's benefactor, the Straßburg journalist Jean Hoepffner, features in one unpublished story as "Herr Hoe," which was their nickname for him. In her letters to Georg, Veza tells him that he appears as "the young doctor" in *The Ogre* (August 1946; *BG*:221) and that she has written a number of other plays or stories about people in her life. "The Tiger," for instance, "tells the story of your cousin Mathilde" (16 December 1933; *BG*:14) and her accounts of the real-life Mr. and Mrs. Milburn and the fictional couple in "Toogoods or the Light" are as good as identical. Canetti appears to have worked similarly in *Auto-da-Fé* and his two Viennese plays; indeed, when he turned to autobiography towards the end of his life and fictionalized characters he knew, sometimes changing their names, sometimes keeping them, he was adapting a practice he had developed in writing that purported to be wholly the product of his imagination.

Unlike Benedikt's Jonathan Crisp and Murdoch's enchanters, Tell was never a monster (despite the title of the first chapter of *Yellow Street*). In *Yellow Street*, where he lives alone in a book-lined flat, his love of books blinds him to life and renders him incapable of standing up to Runkel on behalf of the lovely Lina. In "Lost Property," the penniless writer is looked after by a girlfriend called Ruth who persuades him to take a job that his uncle has found for him at the Lost Property Bureau. Veza's comment on her own husband in a letter from 1947 recalls how Ruth relates to Tell in this story:

> Excuse Canetti not writing himself, he unfortunately never does and has
> let a few good chances in his life slip by. He carries on, quite carefree, a
> dreamer living in the clouds, and will certainly never have a sum of money
> worth mentioning in the bank. But he has remained quite pure, as he was,
> without making compromises. I would only confess this to you as you
> understand him properly being a pure fool yourself.[3]

Tell will never earn much money and would let his chances slip past him if
Ruth did not intervene. Ruth is furious on the evening after his first day at
work when she finds a proposal of marriage in his own hand on his writing desk. But her sleeping boyfriend, who is tired from his day's exertions
and has spent the night writing a story based on his experiences on his first
day at work, has not proposed to a real person. He has not fallen in love
with the flesh-and-blood Emma Adenberger, whom he tracked down after
finding a letter written by her in a bag handed into the Bureau. He has
proposed to his own literary heroine whom Emma's story of disappointed
love inspired him to create.

Naming the Canetti figure after the hero of Swiss liberation was ironic
and affectionately, rather than aggressively, mocking. It enabled Veza to
say numerous things about him. As William Tell is the Swiss national hero,
it ironizes Canetti's admiration of Switzerland by deflating the noble
William into the more humdrum Knut, who is distinctly unheroic in his
first two manifestations. The name also alludes to a personal memory of
their first meeting. In his version, he is captivated by Veza's exotic beauty,
her wisdom, and her literary reputation. Her first unexpected question
("Are you Swiss?") made him believe that she could see into his heart.
Canetti recalls:

> There was nothing I would rather have been. During the three years in
> Frankfurt my passion for all things Swiss had reached boiling point. I
> knew that her mother was a Sephardi, whose maiden name was Calderon,
> who lived with her third husband, a very old man called Altaras, and so
> she must have recognized my name as Spanish too. (*VIII*:73)

When he replies "unfortunately not," he feels that he reveals more about
himself than anyone at the time knew about him. She understands and
confides that she wished to have been born English and asks him to visit
her to tell her about his childhood years in England.

William Tell was one of the stories his father told him as a seven-year-
old in Manchester, along with the Grimms' *Children's and Household Tales*
and children's versions of *Robinson Crusoe*, *The Arabian Nights*, Dante,
Shakespeare, *Gulliver's Travels*, and *Don Quixote*. "It would be easy to
show that almost everything I later became was contained in these books
that I read for my father in the seventh year of my life" (*VII*:53). Only *The
Odyssey* is missing from the list of books that shaped his imagination. With
the curious exception of *William Tell*, they are all points of reference either

in *Auto-da-Fé* or in the rest of the autobiography, and sometimes in Veza's stories too. *Gulliver's Travels* is the book which Gustl wants to borrow from Jobst in "The Poet"; in *The Tortoises* she compares Werner Kain's suffering in his native city with the fate of Robinson Crusoe on his faraway island (*SK*:194), so alien and unwelcoming has his native Vienna become to him. Even Veza appeared to Canetti like a character from *The Arabian Nights*, while he calls her stepfather a character from Dante's Hell. But he recalls that he plucked up the courage to pay his first visit to the Ferdinandstraße with the excuse of asking her about *King Lear*, which John Bayley recalls he compared with his own novel on account of the texts' shared relentless bleakness.[4]

In *The Tongue Set Free*, father and son read *William Tell* directly after finishing Dante:

> This was the occasion that I heard the word "freedom" for the first time. He told me something about it that I cannot remember. But he added something about England: that was why we moved to England because people are free. (*VII*:53)

Jacques Canetti freed himself by defying his own father and moving to Manchester against his wishes. His revolt was overdue and he impressed on his son that he should not follow in his footsteps by bowing to family pressure and becoming a businessman like him. Instead he should "become what he would like to become" (*VII*:55), words that the young Canetti takes as his father's testament. After *William Tell* the next book the pair read is a biography of a contrasting historical character, Napoleon, who, in this British account, stands for the tyrannical misuse of power. As far as Canetti is concerned, since his father suddenly dies before they finish the book, he is for ever associated with death. Since power and death become two of Canetti's life-long preoccupations, the story of the freedom-loving Tell is not only an antidote to the power-driven Napoleon, who anticipates yet more dangerous figures in the twentieth century, but also a foundational literary experience. It is inconceivable that Veza did not hear of his personal tie with this central figure in Swiss national mythology. We must surely imagine her hearing the story in similar terms to those he uses in *The Tongue Set Free*.

Knut Tell is the most tangible evidence of Veza's critical reaction to *Auto-da-Fé*. Through him she criticizes both the novel's thematic content, including its depiction of women, and Canetti's method of collecting linguistic material by listening to the Viennese public for "acoustic masks." She also elides Canetti the writer with his novel's hero, Peter Kien. At issue with Tell is an attitude to reality and in particular to the people who can serve him as models for his fiction. This relationship between the mind and the world, which breeds confusion between fiction and experience, is the epistemological problem at the heart of *Auto-da-Fé*. Tell is obsessed with text and sees the world through books. Like Kien, he gives script primacy over people. In "The Monster," Tell immediately incorporates the thief who bangs on his door looking for shelter into his own imaginary world. He makes him into a character in a story that he is imagining. Kien's reaction to Fischerle is not dissimilar. In "Lost Property," Tell is a thief who steals other people's stories.

"Lost Property" is a story of a young working-class woman exploited in different ways by two professional men: the doctor who treats her for free in the expectation of sexual favors; and the poet who has ambitions of writing her story. Canetti would have had no difficulty in recognizing the personal reference. Fräulein Adenberger's letter that fascinates Tell is a written "acoustic mask" like those he recorded on his nocturnal peregrinations through Vienna. Adenberger's poor command of language expresses the emotional hurt Dr. Spanek inflicted on her more forcefully than carefully formulated grammatical sentences could have done. She is from the same working-class stock as her namesakes in *Yellow Street*, but while Veza as a novelist dignifies their experiences, Tell is interested in her story only if it is detached from her as a person. He finds the text she wrote more fascinating than her:

> To Dr. Spanek
>
> Once you said to me be delicate towards women, but you have caused me pain. Coming to Teschen was my downfall. In my soul and in my body and only because I love you, never forgetting it. Nevertheless you did not see a refined woman from the city in front of you but a country girl, who you however shamed like she walked the streets. My cheeks go red from shame and tears come into my eyes when I think of it and when do I not do that. I wish to go mad and not to have to think for once but that is not granted to me, you tell me yourself what life can still be to me. I now say farewell and send best wishes, Your . . . (*DF*:13)

Her deficient linguistic skills exclude her from the society of "Bürger" to which the doctor belongs.

Veza tells the story of a love that never could be from the point of view of the lower-class would-be mistress. Adenberger knew at the beginning there could be no love across the classes and originally turned him down because "the difference between us is too great" (*DF*:14). Once Dr. Spanek has left the hospital without saying goodbye, she regrets her rejection of him and sets off to seek him out, still believing that he did not charge for his medical treatment out of kindness rather than for any other motive. When she finds him at his country retreat, she is confronted by his fiancée and the scene is set for her humiliation. Spanek demands that she explain herself:

> "I find it bizarre," he said, "that you have come here, young woman, where is your sense of tact, you come here and darken the pure air of a lady, do

you not know what you owe to your station, and anyway, what do you want, Miss, nothing whatsoever happened between us, I would like to make that clear, I demand that you make that clear to my fiancée" (*DF*:15).

Back in Vienna Adenberger stammers to Tell that this woman is not right for her former suitor. She has "mean eyes," ever the sign of a villain in Veza's fictional world, and will make the doctor unhappy. The spurned young woman is so used to serving those above her that she subordinates her own desires to wanting the best for the man she cannot have.[5]

Even though Tell is not concerned with Adenberger, he still blushes when she opens the door to him after he went in search of her ostensibly to return her handbag. He sees her beauty and has been found out, though his real motive is scriptural rather than sexual curiosity. After first offering to punch Dr. Spanek in the face on her behalf (as he offers to stand up to Runkel on Lina's behalf in *Yellow Street*), he races home to commit his version of her story to paper, feeling like a thief because he still has her letter in his hand. After doing this he "fell so much in love with his character that he began a letter to her and made a proposal of marriage" (*DF*:16). He thus uses Adenberger no less selfishly than Dr. Spanek hoped to: writing her story becomes sublimated sexual activity.

Veza varies this theme in *Yellow Street*, where he lives behind a door with a plaque bearing the words "Knut Tell, Poet." He is intrigued when an opportunistic thief clutching a bunch of bananas appears on his threshold, announces he is being "pursued," and asks for shelter: "You are a quite fine fellow, you have come to the right place, you have experienced something, you must tell your story, please, take a seat" (*GS*:25). Tell announces himself to be a book thief — as we already know, he also pinches other people's stories. He tells a good story himself and wants the thief, who goes by the unlikely name of Graf (Count), to steal something more valuable than a bunch of bananas, perhaps the crown jewels, because then he could travel, to somewhere remote and exotic, perhaps to Bali. "I will lend you a book about Bali," he promises, "and you can buy yourself a library, a much bigger one, ten times as many books" (*GS*:25–26). This is a humorous reference to Kien's academic specialism in Oriental languages and his defining possession, which is his library of twenty-five thousand volumes. Unfortunately the aristocrat of action disappoints the light-fingered poet, replying that he would rather have "a rabbit farm." Their encounter ends with Graf giving Tell the bananas, calling him "young man," and explaining that he only took them for a joke. After Tell explains his plan for the crown jewels, Graf calls out "but that is theft," and makes the poet the prospective thief. Their roles are reversed. Graf himself has an evening job as a hotel porter.

Tell's confusion of fiction and reality recalls Kien, just as Tell's attractiveness to women recalls Canetti's own, notwithstanding their physical differences. The effect on women of Tell's blond locks, tall figure, and fine manners is said to be devastating. When Tell admits Graf into his apartment, all the female neighbors are said to be looking at him "with delight." In the next episode when he offers to intervene on behalf of Lina: "The nurse looked at him in delight, the coal woman with lust, the Fine Lady so that he could see the outline of her face from its most advantageous angle" (*GS*:32–33). Once more Tell is enchanted by the idea of doing something but three days pass before nurse Leopoldine knocks at his door and asks for his signature on a petition demanding Lina's reinstatement. His signature is one thing that — as a writer — he can give easily.

In *The Tortoises* Andreas Kain's similarly imposing physique has a different purpose. He embodies a nobility and generosity of spirit that contrasts with the squalid justifications for violence and persecution pronounced by those who surround him. His looks also contradict the Nazi theories of racial characteristics, according to which Jews are small, dark, and hook-nosed. Canetti was neither blond nor tall. According to von Mayenburg he was "wide-hipped, small and squat" and had "a little mustache over the tautest mouth I have ever observed on any human being, and the sharpest eyes behind an enormous pair of glasses."[6] Like other women von Mayenburg found him attractive because he was exciting to talk to. Thus whether Veza satirizes or idealizes her fiancé-husband, she transforms him physically.

"Lost Property" was not republished until 2001 and was not among the stories that Canetti could potentially consult when he was writing his autobiography. *Yellow Street*, of course, was available. His account of his own behavior in *The Torch in the Ear*, however, shows numerous similarities with Tell's in both stories, but especially "Lost Property." He is attracted in one episode to criminals who frequent a pub in Grinzing. In preparation for writing his novel, he too "hunted" material, but it was not the written versions of people's stories, which are rarer and more difficult to collect, but their verbal presentations of themselves that he coveted. After finding the Berlin culture of celebrity oppressive, he liked to bathe himself in the speech of ordinary city folk in Vienna, closing his eyes in public places to listen to them. He began in night-cafés, on park benches, or on public transport. "I wanted to see *each one*, listen to each one for a long time, again and again, even in their endless repetitiveness." The variety astounds him "even in the poverty, the banality, the misuse of words" (*VIII*:337). His choice is entirely democratic. Indeed, the more ordinary the speaking subjects, the more interested he is, since, as in the case of Veza's Fräulein Adenberger, their struggle with language reveals the fissures in their identity and the contradictions in their desires. But he still sees his speaking subjects, which are his raw material, from the outside, they are objects he observes, and their use of their own mother tongue is imperfect, clumsy, distorted, however great its variety. Language can be an imprecise medium for self-expression: "They betrayed themselves when they appealed for understanding, they blamed each other so inappropriately that insults sounded like praise and praise like insults" (*VIII*:337). Their lack of facility with speech encapsulates their lack of power (their *Ohnmacht*): speech keeps them apart rather than binding them together. This imperious, illiberal linguistic opinion informs the comic presentation of speech in his novel and first two plays.

Von Mayenburg published a remarkably similar account of Canetti's linguistic collecting. Like her husband, Ernst Fischer, she recalls discussions of *Auto-da-Fé*, which Canetti had just finished, and the work in progress, *Crowds and Power*, and she says that she "learnt to love him" during them. They were an intellectual adventure because he illuminated the world from a unique angle, and advanced as far as the "mysteries of existence." Yet there was something threatening and not altogether wholesome about his pursuit of live subject-matter as his interest was not only linguistic. She calls him a *Menschenfresser*, a predator, a cannibal or — yes — an ogre, someone who consumes his fellow human beings:

> The city was his hunting territory. (I do not know to this day whether he ever set foot in a real forest). He spent the whole day and half the nights hunting for people and sometimes trusted chance to bring the most varied victims across his path, he always had something to chew on. In order to approximate the plenitude of human types which Canetti consumed, I would have to enumerate the most bizarre professions, all age groups, social classes, and levels of educational attainment, from people who could not read at all to those who had read everything, and go through all physical diseases and psychiatric complaints from the everyday to the most rare. He often managed to uncover the heart and the kidneys with a single bite and then regaled himself on both the bone marrow and the brains of his victim. He also possessed the unique ability to make everyone believe that they had never been so completely understood, right into the most secret caverns of their soul, the last fiber of their body, as by this hunter of people. More than that: Canetti knew how to get things out of people, talents, experiences, memories, thoughts and secret wishes, which they did not even know they had within them. Thus they not only felt themselves elevated by his greedy attention but lifted out of themselves, up into the heady thin air where only a unique being could breathe, capable of such flights into the stratosphere no other earthly creature could accomplish. Thus they did not even notice that they had just been eaten up, that they had leapt into the insatiable stomach of the people eater Canetti, who had only swallowed them for the sake of resurrecting them — in notebooks which grew into books, plays, academic treatises.[7]

This ability to give himself to whomsoever he was talking and make them believe they were the center of his world was a gift he shared with Iris Murdoch. He chided her for doing too much listening, but her motivation was exactly the same as his: she needed material. Von Mayenburg continues in the above vein for another rapturous page. However lurid her description of his techniques of emotional dismemberment, however completely she understood the ways he exploited his interlocutors, she was fascinated by him and described herself as "a friend of similar insatiability and curiosity." Veza too appears to have had moral reservations, but her Knut Tell is a model of restraint in comparison with the *Menschenfresser* in their mutual friend's memoir.

In Tell's third and final appearance in *The Tiger* he cuts a very different figure. Here his behavior contrasts with that of the opportunistic Nick, the would-be author of a film-scenario. *The Tiger* ends with Tell holding hands with fellow artist Diana Sandoval after the exposure of the American agent, Mister Smith, as a fraud. When Diana and Tell meet for the first time, they bond in opposition to Smith and the commercialization of art. If this is a comment on Mahler's affair with Canetti, then there is satisfaction in Diana's rejection of men in the first prose version written as chapter four of *Yellow Street*, which is followed by this gesture of reconciliation with her husband when the story is transferred to the stage. The difference between the two versions can be attributed to the change in Canetti's personal attitudes signaled by *Comedy of Vanity*. It was also an expression of wish-fulfillment. Veza nursed him through his disappointment with Mahler that cast him down for at least four years. It appears that the sculptor's refusal to take him seriously as an intellectual and artist upset him, in other words, her failure to respond as a creative partner or collaborator. In his notes for *The Play of the Eyes*, he recalls suffering from her disdain up to the summer of 1937:

> The same time stands were marked by a defeat which had no end, my squandering of myself to Anna. She got the best from me, I took it to her straight away. I kept nothing from her that had any significance for me: she consumed it eagerly and straight away *forgot* it [his emphasis]. This abjection lasted four years.[8]

In Veza's play, in contrast, Diana responds to his bon mots and confidences.

The Tiger appears to mark the happy end of Veza's literary reaction to Canetti as a *Dichter*. Characters who have been associated with him continue to appear in her fiction, however. Perhaps we should recognize him as the artist called Bent in "Three Quarters," as Sibylle Mulot does?[9] In this story, which appears to have been written in the second half of the 1930s, three young women, the disfigured Anna, the hunchbacked Maria, and the tall beautiful Britta, who constitute the "three quarters" of the title, are united in their fascination for the tall, blond artist with blue eyes and the unusual English name. They all pose for him and he becomes the center of their world; their interest in each other is predicated only on their interest for him. Bent has the same number of syllables as Tell and Kain and Canetti calls his heroine Therese *Krumb*holz (crooked or bent). Unfortunately, "Three Quarters" ends weakly, it seems that Veza was unsure where she intended to take it.

The autobiographical background to *The Tortoises*, on the other hand, is not disputed, but the treatment of the main characters (Andreas and Werner Kain, Eva and Hilde) tells us little about their real-life models (Canetti and Fritz Wotruba, Veza and the young Friedl Benedikt). Yet it is striking that Eva is not a writer and that Hilde has no literary ambitions. Only Andreas Kain is associated with books, which he reads in a study described as a monk's or hermit's cell. He is also an author of novels and currently "is writing a big book about everything" (*SK*:102). Andreas Kain's humanity is predicated on his poetic vocation and illustrated in his treatment of others. He once rescues Werner from a beating by two SA-men in a pub after Werner starts an argument on the subject of racial purity. He also tells stories, in which good always triumphs over evil in order to reassure his wife and others. He even argues that the Kristallnacht will make the people turn away from the Nazis. Andreas refuses to leave without Werner and his wife, passing up the opportunity to flee because he does not believe that Eva could cope with a journey over the mountains. The gifts which Veza gives him as a poet are formidable:

> he thinks ahead, and what he does not know he can divine. That is surely the way with all writers; they have this way of looking so they can see through your head as if your eyes were made of glass. It hypnotizes you, you can feel it, right into your heart. (*SK*:18)

Were it not for Canetti's (unpublished) account of this period in which he claims to owe his life to Veza's steadfastness and courage, one would be tempted to conclude that Veza projects her loss of emotional equilibrium on to Eva and contrasts her mental disintegration with her husband's serenity. In their written versions, whether fictionalized in Veza's case or autobiographical in Canetti's, they each make the other into the stronger character.

Anna Mitgutsch's suggestion that Andreas Kain is the bad husband who is responsible for the arrest and consequent death of Werner in Buchenwald is untenable on a number of counts.[10] It is true that Werner would not have been taken away had Andreas not left the flat to watch the fires of Kristallnacht. But Andreas had no way of knowing that the knock on the door would come when it did or that staying at home would prove more dangerous than going out. The episode shows the arbitrariness of terror, the luck which the survivors need to get out, and the Nazis' refusal to listen to Werner's reasoned argument that he is not the Kain they are looking for.

Veza's last portrait of her husband, her introduction to the selection of his writings that presented him to a new post-war German readership, is very different and was published under a different pseudonym, in fact, under someone else's name entirely. By introducing Veza's first two books in the early 1990s, Canetti was returning the favor she did for him shortly before her death. Her words are panegyric. She sticks very close to the texts, his novel, plays, jottings, *Crowds and Power*, and the still unpublished travelogue, *Voices from Marrakesh*. It is still the most lucid introduction to his early work that exists. The details on his parents and childhood in Bulgaria, the significance of the Danube river and the Burgtheater in his family's mythology, how he first spoke Spanish, and how his mother taught him German, are all now familiar to readers of his autobiography. She begins with praise for *Auto-da-Fé* from a British academic critic, Jack Isaacs, and quotes from the handful of authoritative sources in pre-war Germany and Austria, such as the *Frankfurter Zeitung*, which reviewed *Auto-da-Fé* on Easter 1936 ("one of its last free literary statements," *WK:*9) and the *Sonntag* interview from April 1937. This information is at her fingertips — one imagines the carefully kept, dog-eared press cuttings from a quarter of a century ago. Knowledge of her husband's life and the tiny number of public comments his novel had hitherto provoked is one thing, a detailed understanding of his published and unpublished writings, which was necessary for her first to make her selection and then to discuss it, is another. She died one year after the book was published, not living to see him enjoy the recognition that eluded both of them during her lifetime.

Canetti on Veza

It is possible that one reason for Veza to invent Knut Tell was that she felt Canetti had expressed his deeper, perhaps unspoken feelings for her and their relationship in his depiction of Peter Kien's disastrous encounter with his housekeeper. He portrayed Veza more directly in *Comedy of Vanity* and *The Numbered*, as well as the last two volumes of the autobiography. His approach changed dramatically between 1932 and 1934, which is the time between *Auto-da-Fé* and *Comedy of Vanity* and when Veza started to write. His comments in the autobiography also differ considerably from those written in the last four years of his life after her writings had come to light. First in person in 1932, then from the grave in 1990, she reminded him of her independent point of view by getting into print. The greatest disjunction, however, is between what he considered putting in *The Torch in the Ear* and *The Play of the Eyes* (or possibly wrote for his own private record), and what he actually published.

He mentions Veza on one other occasion during the interview for Swiss radio in 1968 when he discussed his life and writing in public for the first time. In response to the interviewer's clearly scripted enquiry about his private life, he replies:

I am pleased that you ask me this question because by far the most important thing that there would be to say about my private life would be about
my relationship with my wife who has been dead for four years now. I got
to know her as a student in Vienna and she straightaway began to help
me and inspire me. She was a writer herself and understood something
about the métier. It was she who took me to the first reading by Karl
Kraus, which in itself meant that she had a great influence on my life.
What was beautiful later on was that she was the only person to whom I
read every chapter of a book, I only read them to her. She was the
sharpest critic, but did not discourage me. Perhaps it was particularly fortunate that she preferred other novelists. Not the same ones that I preferred, her models were Tolstoy and Flaubert, mine were Gogol and
Stendhal, which meant there were always two standpoints and it was very
good and useful to discuss things from two points of view. But I think her
greatest quality was her strength of belief and her patience. I do think that
women are the only people capable of showing such patience. You must
imagine living with a person who was working for twenty years on the
same book. As emigrants the material circumstances were of course also
not the best. A book which does not make any progress, which is always
being interrupted, whose end is never in sight and then to stay with it and
keep going, to support you, that seems to me to an incredible quality.
And what I feel is miraculous, a miracle in fact, is that such a woman really
succeeded in bringing this book to an end and to experience this end. I
am convinced that the first volume of *Crowds and Power* would still not
exist today had it not been for her. (*X*:217)

By contemporary standards Canetti was not an enthusiastic interviewee
and disliked answering questions from an audience after readings. But in
the interviews he gave, he related many episodes from his earlier life that
are now familiar from his autobiography: at first Veza as independent
writer and literary collaborator evidently belonged to the narrative of his
life that he decided to divulge. Very quickly he expunged her.

The only critic to explore the autobiographical background to *Auto-
da-Fé*, the book he read chapter by chapter to Veza, concludes that
Canetti was exploring potential aspects of his own interaction with the
world through both Kien brothers, Peter and Georg, as well as the hunchback Fischerle. Peter Kien's battle with Therese is thus based on Canetti's
years of struggle with his mother, as narrated in *The Torch in the Ear*.
Mathilde Canetti's insistence that her son leave the cloistered "paradise"
of the Villa Yalta in order to experience something of the world is paral-
leled by Therese hauling Kien down from his ivory tower by marrying
him. Notwithstanding the differences between Therese and Mathilde
(one has never read a book, whereas the other loved nothing more), both
value money and the ability to earn it higher than intellectual or artistic
activity.[11] These parallels are striking, but now that so much more is
known about Veza, the part her relationship with the author played in the

novel's genesis seems more significant. Marrying and starting a family would have entailed earning money and reducing the time available for intellectual work. As Veza proposed to alter radically the nature of their relationship shortly after reading *Auto-da-Fé*, it is reasonable to assume that until then they had not ruled out a conventional marriage, or that it at least was what *she* wanted. Canetti articulated his response to her plans through his novel.

Canetti makes no secret that his writing *Auto-da-Fé* put their relationship under great strain. Veza had followed his progress from close-up as he read out each chapter to her and listened to her responses. She was most concerned with the effect the mental effort and emotional journey of literary creation had on him and his psychic health:

> She breathed a sigh of relief when the ascetic year of the novel was over and no reader subsequently can have been as relieved as she was when the gaunt sinologist went up in flames [. . .] Much of what went into the third part of the novel touched her to the quick and she was convinced that my never-ending probing into the sinologist's persecution mania would have dangerous consequences for my own mental state. It was thus hardly surprising that she breathed a sigh of relief after I read out the last chapter to her. (*IX*:15)

The Play of the Eyes begins with his bursting in on Veza in the Ferdinandstraße after he has finally finished. For the first time he uses the key to her flat that she has given should he ever need her in an emergency. He wants her advice, which he has been ignoring for as long as he has been writing on the opposite side of the city. It is a sign of his return to her after finishing the project that caused dissension between them.

Shortly before his death he explained with greater candor what the source of friction between them was. Veza "had never been able to free herself from the suspicion that Kien's hatred of women somehow, indirectly, applied to her too" (*PiB*:112). In an unpublished passage from *The Play of the Eyes* he concludes his explanation of their open marriage by recalling her horrified reaction to what he had written: "She spoke about it in such a way as to suggest that this freedom which she wished me to have was a matter of her own dignity. Her pride could not recover from the terrifying image of Therese in the novel."[12] In order to prove herself the opposite of the quintessential narrow-minded hausfrau, Veza insisted on the bohemian liaison that British readers at the beginning of the twenty-first century would find so shocking. In the published version, Canetti reveals first that "she was not certain" about *Auto-da-Fé* (*IX*:196) and then, in the last paragraph in which he mentions Veza, that she "made her peace" with the novel shortly after the time it was published. What is interesting here is that he is telling the story of how the nineteen-year-old Friedl Benedikt became his literary pupil. It was Veza who persuaded him to take seriously their importunate neighbor who borrowed her style from Dostoyevsky by saying that she has progressed intellectually and artistically, "as we all did," from Gogol's story, *The Overcoat*. By "we" she appears to mean not only she and husband but Dostoyevsky, too. Canetti realizes that *Auto-da-Fé* made a similar overwhelming impact on Benedikt as it once did on Veza. Both women, he implies, came to writing as a result of reading his novel:

> There was nothing that I would not have done for the greater glory of Gogol. I noticed too that in this way Veza tactfully made her peace with *Auto-da-Fé*, as it too came "as we all did from *The Overcoat*." She was — to my relief — no longer so concerned about the fate of the book. She recognized what happened to the girl when she read it, took the matter seriously and called for my help. (*IX*:239)

Veza's quoted use of the first person plural ("as we all did") is perhaps the most explicit reference to their shared literary vocation. As his next partnership with a new pupil begins, his old one peters out. His depiction of Therese Krumbholz was his original crime against Veza; her revenge was to start writing and to insist that they put their relationship on a different footing.

In her letters to Georg, Veza is always enthusiastic on the subject of promoting her husband's novel, but says remarkably little about what she thinks of its contents. She twice mentions Therese, but both times with unmistakable irony (24 October 1946; *BG*:242 and 27 August 1947; *BG*:284). She makes no bones over preferring his plays, even rehearsing the plot of *Wedding* to Georg after the war, forgetting that he had the opportunity of reading it when it was published in 1932 (5 October 1945; *BG*:150). It is not the least bizarre facet of this literary marriage that they both, though for different reasons, rated the other's dramas higher than their prose fiction, for which they are both more likely to be remembered. She says that she prefers *Comedy of Vanity* and *Wedding* to *Auto-da-fé* because they both anticipate everything that happened later in the decade in which they were written (2 June 1946; *BG*:212), but his novel surely does that even more forcefully. She also criticizes his choice of *Die Blendung* as its German title (15–16 October 1945; *BG*:155).

She had numerous reasons for believing that he was communicating a message to her which only she could understand. "Veza" and "Therese" share a number of syllables (like "Leda" and "Veza" or "Knut Tell" and "Kanetti Elias"). Therese, who is initially called Hermine, is sixteen years older than Kien, precisely double the difference between Veza and Canetti. Pfaff, however, is said to be eight years older than his wife, whom he beats to death before turning his violent and amorous attentions to their daughter. Therese has worked for Kien for eight years before Kien discovers what he believes is her reverence for books and decides to marry her. When she objects to Pfaff describing her as a "serving maid" (*Dienstmädchen*), she mentions another significant number: "She wouldn't let him get away with serving maid. She had been running a household for thirty-four years. It would soon be a year since she became a respectable woman" (*I*:353). Veza was thirty-four in 1931, the year *Auto-da-Fé* was finished. Only Veza and their closest mutual friends could have noticed the wounding significance of these numbers.

Die Blendung can be taken to refer to the characters' fatal blindness to the world, which in turn mirrors the blindness of an entire society edging towards destruction. In his autobiography Canetti claims that he took his title from a Rembrandt painting that shows Delila hastening away from the scene of her treachery, scissors in hand, at the moment her lover's tormentors prepare to put out his second eye. Rembrandt called it *The Triumph of Delila*, but Canetti sees only the male hero's defeat and alludes to it as *Die Blendung Samsons*. This image of female betrayal taught him about hatred: that special hatred a member of one sex can feel for a member of the other (*VIII*:114). The first time he felt like that was when his cousin Laurica in Rustchuk withdrew her books from him and refused to teach him to read and he, at age five, pursued her around the house with an axe and shouted that he wanted to kill her. In revenge she had pushed him into the vat of boiling water, which very nearly killed him. His own novel's title refers to men's hatred of women and in particular the male's fear of his mate taking away his powers. Relationships between the sexes are characterized from the beginning by high emotions and competition for script.

When Veza listened to what her boyfriend was reading to her, she realized that her pupil for the last six years had produced a female monster whose monstrosity was a consequence of her femininity. That he did so in order to mock contemporary Austrian misogyny, as he mocked anti-Semitism through Fischerle, may not have been an adequate explanation:[13] his men, however egregious each specimen may be, are varied in tone and bearing, while his women are all defined only by their sex. *Auto-da-Fé* not only prompted Veza to write, it gave her grounds for wanting to get her revenge, to display her own "Geist" and creativity. Her first step was to assume the identity that was apparently assigned to her: as Therese began work as a maid at the age of fifteen, what more appropriate name could Veza choose other than *Magd*? *Therese* Schrantz is the name she gives to the middle-aged maid who works briefly with the Iger family in *Yellow Street*.

There are several outward similarities between Therese's recollection of her abusive childhood in the chapter "Dazzling Furniture," Pfaff's abuse of his wife and daughter in "The Kind Father," and Veza's experience of her stepfather, as related by both her and Canetti. Kristie Foell, writing before the re-publication of "Money — Money — Money," speculated that Pfaff's rape and murder of his daughter Anna was inspired by Veza's own experience, as Canetti related it in *The Torch in the Ear*:

> the objects of Veza's struggle are similar to Anna's: a superhumanly strong father figure who insists on copious meals of steak on demand, who controls his money with the utmost selfishness, and who seeks to control the space in which the members of his family live by bursting into their rooms unexpectedly.[14]

Therese's mother found herself another man after "the father had been dead for barely six years," which is roughly the same gap between the death of Veza's father and the arrival of Menachem Alkaley. Therese deals with her stepfather rather differently than the narrator of "Money — Money — Money" and Pfaff's daughter Anna. While Anna behaves courageously before she is brutally killed, Therese is a willing victim of abuse at her father's hands:

> He was a fine sort, a butcher, he hit her and chased after the girls the whole time. I gave his face a good scratch. He wanted me, I thought he was repellent. I only let him so that the mother would be annoyed. She was always: everything for the children. My god, the look on her face when she comes back home from work and finds the bloke with the daughter! He had not even done it. The butcher wants to jump off. I hold him tight so he can't get free until the old girl is in the room, by the bed. Then what screaming. With her bare fists the mother chases the man out of the room. She grabs hold of me, cries and even wants to kiss me. I have none of it and scratch. (*I*:65–66)

Therese is not a portrait of Veza in the way that Knut Tell is a portrait of Canetti. But there is ample evidence that her biography supplied him with some valuable source material.

Parts of *Comedy of Vanity* read as if she were looking over his shoulder as he wrote, as she well might have since he wrote it after moving out of his lodgings in Hacking's Hagenberggasse:

> Since then I had been with Veza in the Ferdinandstraße, in her "yellow street," as she called it in her stories, it was the street of the leather merchants. I had returned once more to the Leopoldstadt. This is where I finished the "Comedy of Vanity," the greater part of which was written there in her apartment.[15]

He shows awareness of social injustice for the first time and sensitivity on a subject very close to his wife's heart: the position of housemaids. Dr. Leda Frisch is no maid but a qualified medic in psychiatry and is engaged and then married to Dr. Heinrich Föhn, who is an ironic self-portrait.[16] The choice of mythological name is playful within the context of the play: as Leda was impregnated by Zeus in the shape of a beautiful swan, Canetti casts himself in the role of king of the Gods. Föhn, however, is the name of an Alpine wind.

Until the end of the play Heinrich and Leda appear on stage together as a couple, putting their relationship and differing views on show each time. On their first entrance, as the bonfire of images grows brighter and fiercer in the background, she prompts a discussion of gender. Parodying Weininger's *Sex and Character*, Heinrich claims that the prohibition of images has become necessary because "we have become feminized. That is our misfortune." Leda tells him that she likes listening to him "when you speak like that. You have then something really masculine." She goes further:

> LEDA: Yes, really war-like. Victor.
> FÖHN: Do you think so? Victor? (*II*:88)

Through the pompous Heinrich, Canetti satirizes his own intellectual pretensions and mockingly identifies himself with Veza's first predatory villain, Siegfried Salzman.[17] At the end of the play, the joyous townsfolk build a monument to Föhn for inspiring them to liberate themselves from the ban on images and individual identity. A little earlier in the "sanatorium" where people go to gaze at themselves in mirrors, he delivers a speech into a clapping machine, the accidental recording of which is the catalyst for a revolt. Canetti's satire of Veza in the figure of Leda and his own relationship with her in Leda's obeisance to Heinrich must be judged in this context of self-mockery.

Canetti's third and last play, *The Numbered*, a metaphysical comedy on the subject of death, was written in 1952, the same year as Veza's third and last play, *The Palanquin*. He again portrays himself and his wife. As each character is named after a number that is their age at death, it is easy to identify him as Dr. Forty-Six, his age at the time of writing. Veza is "the lady in the front row" (*II*:190), the position she took at the Karl Kraus readings she attended so faithfully.[18] There is no longer any satire or even gentle teasing on his part, just as her portraits of him after 1934 contrast with her first two accounts of the exploits of "Knut Tell, Poet" (*GS*:25). "The lady in the front row" distinguishes herself from other women by not running after men with high numbers because of the long lives they have ahead of them. She instead wants to find a man who will die at the same moment she does:

> MAN: You are an unusual woman.
> WOMAN: Perhaps I am. I do not want to survive the man whom I love. But I also don't want him to survive me. That is not just jealousy, as you are perhaps thinking.
> MAN: No, it is a very healthy feeling. (*II*:192)

She does not get her wish, as becomes evident when they appear again in the second act on what she reveals to be her last birthday, her forty-third.

In this second scene together, he gushes: "We love each other," "I cannot live if I don't know when you are coming back. I have to know. I want to know," "I can't live without you," "I have never been as fond as another person as I am of you," "I will do anything to see you again" (*II*:206–7).

Veza Canetti was fifty-four when *The Numbered* was written. Forty-three had been her age in November 1940, the point when she realized she would never again see her beloved Vienna. Within the scheme of thought in *Crowds and Power*, which he interrupted to write *The Numbered*, Forty-Three's wish to die at the same moment as her lover shows humility and the absence of any sentiment of power because surviving the death of another is a demonstration of power over him. The selfless Forty-Three wants no power over her lover and in return demands that he have none over her.

Canetti did not write publicly about Veza again until *The Torch in the Ear*, which was published seventeen years after her death, but her presence is certainly felt in his notebooks. Those from the year of her death stand out. Several express his grief, rehearse the circumstances of her death, reflect on their life together, express his debt and gratitude over and over again, and address her as if in prayer. There are suffused with the feeling that she suffered because of him. On 4 June 1963: "People say to me: you are fortunate to have lived thirty-eight years with her. How many people were that fortunate? I was, I, I was, but her, her, her?" His grief is greater than that of the hero of the first great work of Western literature, *Gilgamesh*, who travels to the center of the earth to conquer death after his beloved friend Enkidu is taken from him. Canetti always admired his refusal to accept death and now exclaims on 6 October: "Gilgamesh, Gilgamesh, for you it was only Enkidu." A notebook for 6 August to 20 August is entitled "In Veza's Name." He begins it with an invocation and a vow:

> If your love is not to have been in vain, my sweet, dear Veza, I have to honor you. What I have failed to do up to now, I will make good. Bless me, give me the strength of being worthy of you. If I have not been able to keep you myself, then I want to make come true what you believed in. I did not deserve to have you with me and you have gone. Now I want to deserve to think of you and to keep you in me with all strength and purity. I love you more than the whole of the rest of the world. I look for traces of you everywhere and I have found them all, you will smile at me again.

Seventeen years later, a published paragraph on Veza states that "Veza's secret was her smile" (*VIII*:154). In 1963 he wanted friends to write down their memories and appreciations of her for a book that he would publish. He wants to establish a "Veza-Canetti Prize" and a "Veza-Canetti Foundation." By dedicating his books to her, he will make her name be remembered, as Dante immortalized his Beatrice. On 19 September he writes: "Now I know what my homeland is, Veza is my homeland." Many entries begin with the number of weeks it has been since her death.[19]

As Veza was an all but constant presence in his adult life, his portrait of her in his autobiography has puzzled many readers on account of his failure to bring her to life with the same conviction he shows for so many far less significant characters. The reason is that he was unsure how to do her justice, which is evident from the unusually large amounts of draft material that he ultimately discarded. There are substantial portions of three such chapters, provisionally called "Veza: What she Read," "First Visit," and "Mourning and Enticement." The section of *The Torch in the Ear* called "The School of Hearing" was originally entitled "Tolstoy or Gogol," which would have drawn more attention to their literary quarrels. For *The Play of the Eyes*, there are drafts, albeit somewhat shorter in length, with the following titles: "General: Misgivings. Veza. The System"; "Friendship of Veza and Anna"; "Marriage (late marriage)"; and "Veza and Georg," all of which are written in code. It was in order to keep his writings secret from Veza, who sometimes went through his notebooks as if she were a teacher marking his homework, that he adopted his schoolboy shorthand for this purpose in the first place.[20] Now he reverts to it as if he still fears that another pair of eyes will pry into what he has written or that the information is too private even to be expressed in terms which another could understand.

Canetti worries that Veza might suffer the same fate in his narrative as his mother:

> I still do not know what direction the new book should take. How should it have a direction before I know how it ends. Since I have been reading in the letters from that time, *the death of my mother* [Canetti's emphasis] seems the natural ending. But even if I decide on this ending, how much of the time in Grinzing should come in? Anna has turned out to take up a great deal of space, and Scherchen even more. Veza features at the beginning, in connection with Büchner and later, of course, as soon as the subject turns to the events of February 1934. But otherwise Anna pushes her into the background. As soon as she befriends her and becomes her lady-in-waiting and confidante, Veza loses out. What could happen then is what happened with my mother's character, whose "decline" from the first to the second volume of the autobiography, was felt by many, and by me too, as painful. That must not on any account happen to Veza. She is at her weakest in relation to Sonne. I cannot pass over how much she disliked him. She feared two things: the terrible effect which the torment over Anna had on me, and my prostration (as she felt it to be) under Sonne.[21]

These words were written when he first sat down to begin *The Play of the Eyes*. They are fascinating because they show how he transforms memories into text: much of what he mentions does not find its way into any of the finished chapters. What ultimately happened with Veza's character is precisely what he said must not on any account occur. She declined — more than that — she disappeared into the background completely. It was none other than Mahler who claimed that his portrait of Veza made her "unrecognizable."[22]

Canetti wrestled with the problem for another year and a half, writing in November 1983: "You must give up something of Veza, otherwise she won't come alive. You don't want to give up anything. And you don't want to add anything either. How is she supposed to become something?"[23] Six months later he was fretting over a more specific question, the answer to which would return to haunt him: "I don't know how I should deal with Veza's writing. It played a big role, but one which became very unhappy later in England."[24] He had tried already to broach the topic in *The Torch in the Ear*, where he initially gave a fuller account of her giving nature in a passage, which, together with a paragraph from "Marriage (late marriage)," is transplanted into the Foreword to *Yellow Street*. He already had the words he needed to introduce Veza's writing on paper. What made him change his mind about alluding to it?

Hanuschek notes a similar discrepancy between his account of the riots on 15 July 1927, when Vienna's Palace of Justice burnt to the ground and the police shot ninety unarmed workers, and the importance that Canetti always assigned to the events for his intellectual development. This epochal day and its aftermath do not warrant many pages. His biographer gives two reasons for the discrepancy. Fischer had already published his detailed memoir, which is colored with terms from *Crowds and Power* that reflect the former friends' detailed discussions of the crowd's actions with one another. What would have been the point of Canetti going over the same ground from his point of view? *Crowds and Power* already gave his account of 15 July, albeit indirectly.[25] Regarding Veza, perhaps he felt he had already memorialized her in his jottings or in the dedications to his books. There was also much that was too personal, too painful, or even plain embarrassing: Veza's miscarriages, followed by her proposal to curtail their sexual relationship; his own subsequent "polygamy" and the accepting role she played in that; their shared bouts of depression and thoughts of suicide, in Vienna after 1934/35, in London after 1939; and his overwhelming grief when she died. He had also been married for the previous ten years to Hera Buschor, to whom he dedicates *The Play of the Eyes*.

There are a number of discrepancies between the drafts and the published chapters concerning Veza. In each instance the final version is a depletion of the earlier draft. His very first impression of her was that she was an aesthete with little experience of practical life. He even told her that she reminded him of a certain sort of woman he had encountered in Frankfurt who "turned up their nose at politics as they did at uneducated people." She told him to read Molière's *Les Précieuses ridicules* — and for once he gives the impression of following her recommendation — where he would find a far better example of her "type":

in later years whenever we had differences of opinion, especially if they were of a literary nature, I would just say to her: "You are a précieuse!" "Of course," would be her answer, "and if you hadn't met me, you wouldn't know what it was."[26]

As well as sharing a trait for secretiveness, they were competitive and prepared for their encounters, which, even in *The Torch in the Ear*, sound rather like tutorials. He still feels the shame of recommending a book to her that she dismissed as unworthy of discussion, a judgment he was forced privately to acknowledge as justified. When it came to politics, even if he was wrong that she was dismissive of the subject, he felt that "she was at any rate not sure of herself in this field and when it came up in conversation she diverted it to the physical expressions of politicians. Physiognomy was one of her main interests."[27] Then one day she surprised him with detailed knowledge of Machiavelli and Lenin, which he assumed she had read on one of her secretive visits to the Vienna University Library. Given her later political commitment, which is clearly attested from the early 1930s onwards, her relative lack of political interests in the mid-1920s is a significant revelation. Canetti does not even present it as surprising, let alone explore it.

In stark contrast to the impression he gave readers of his published text, at first, there was no hostility between Veza and Mathilde. Veza had come to the flat in the Radetzkystraße, the same one they share with "Johnnie Ring" in *The Torch in the Ear*, to collect their rent on behalf of her aunt, who was in Belgrade. Neither had any interest in frequenting the association for Ladino-speaking Jews in the Leopoldstadt. They were interested in books and concerts, not gambling at cards. The nineteen-year-old Canetti had not seen his mother so animated for years as she was when talking to their landlady's beautiful niece. His feelings were entirely new. On the first of each month, rent collection day, he made sure he was at home, though they rarely spoke during her brief visits:

> I opened the door when the bell rang and there she stood in a gigantic straw hat, finely dressed, beaming and alluring. I led her into the sitting room, what sort of room was it when she was inside it, the oak furniture shrunk in size and lost its heaviness. It was as if one could fly with her from one apartment to another, which is how she suddenly appeared, she flew over the Danube-Canal, none of the arid words that poisoned life here was uttered from her lips, every one of her words originated from the freedom that I desperately longed for.[28]

Once again, in the published version he reins in his emotion: *The Torch in the Ear* contains no comparably effusive descriptions of first love.

After he finally decides to accept her invitation and pay a visit to her home, he finds himself telling her about his father; in the twelve years since he died, it is the first time he has confided his feelings and memories to anyone. Then there is the discovery that she not only also had family in Manchester but her uncle also lived in Burton Road in West Didsbury. He no longer has to keep these names to himself, he can share them with Veza, who can even recall hearing about his father's death. Their encounter is also marked by argument, which he subsequently both softened and schematized for publication. Immediately, he felt antipathy to her favorite poem, Poe's "The Raven," which she recited on his first visit. What he does not reveal is that he refuses to read the books that she mentions and admits that he hesitated for years before reading the books which meant the most to her. Even at this point he felt that he was encroaching on her territory. Her favorite authors were "weapons" in their arguments: "When she wanted to argue with me, because she was annoyed by my lack of trust or my jealousy, which knew no bounds (and which she savored in small doses), then she would attack me with Tolstoy."[29]

In the published version he marvels that her taste in reading was independent of Kraus, unlike his own, and that she had absorbed so many literary characters into her own being and personality. The Veza in the autobiography is more idealized:

> There were battles, but never a victor. The battles dragged on over months and, as it would turn out later, over years: but it never came to a surrender. We each expected the other to have an opinion but did not anticipate what it would be. If what had to be said was pronounced in bad faith, it would be nipped in the bud. That was precisely what Veza made an effort to avoid; her secret carefulness was part of her delicate concern, but it was not like that of a mother, since we were equal to each other. In spite of the severity of her words, she never gave herself an air of superiority. But, she would never submit, and she would never forgive herself, if, for the sake of making peace or out of weakness, she kept her views to herself. Perhaps "battle" is the wrong word for our disputes because a complete understanding of the other was part of it and not merely an estimation of his or her strengths and quickwittedness. She found it impossible to wound me with malicious intent. (*VIII*:207)

His use of the word "victor" is significant given the way they both deploy the term in their literary writings. The autobiography is about the overcoming of power relationships, about reaching a state of communication with another where power plays no role. His exemplary figures are Broch, whose breathing denotes his interaction with the world, Musil, Merkel, and Sonne. In spite of their arguments, his partnership with Veza fits the same pattern. The passage above continues:

> I learnt how to interact intimately with a thinking person, and it depended on not only on hearing each of the other's words but on attempting to understand them as well, and, on demonstrating this understanding by responding precisely and without distorting anything. Respect for other people begins by not ignoring their words. I would like

> to call it the *quiet* apprenticeship of this time, although it was conveyed in so many words, for the other, opposite apprenticeship, which I attended simultaneously, was loud and spectacular. (*VIII*:207)

That other apprenticeship was served with Kraus; that with Veza could not have contrasted with it more.

A year after their first meeting when he entered the flat in the Ferdinandstraße, he quickly learned the most significant fact in Veza's autobiography, her self-assertion at the age of eighteen against her stepfather, that same "ogre" who leaves his mark on their early fiction. Until Veza "tamed" him, it was his habit to stand in the doorway to her room, cursing in Spanish, waving and banging his stick to demand roast meat and wine, which was all he lived on until he died at an advanced age in 1929. Again, this is in part a literary story, and Veza published her own fictionalized account of it. Locking her door proved ineffective because the stepfather found and disposed of the keys. Veza's solution was to teach him that he would only be given what he wanted if he stayed in his own room and did not disturb her. When he obeyed, she rewarded him with meat and wine of the best quality. Henceforth Veza's room was her own territory, her refuge, and soon it became her young admirer's refuge too. The emphasis is on a victory, which secured that precious commodity: freedom.

After his mother left the Radetzkystraße for Paris with the two younger brothers, Canetti moved into a room in the Haidgasse, a ten minute walk from where Veza lived. He stayed here until May 1927 when he moved to the Hagenberggasse in Hacking where he wrote *Auto-da-Fé*. This second move signals his first attempt at distancing himself from Veza, since he must travel the breadth of the city to see her. He gives an account of their first argument, which resulted from a difference of views on gender and his initial questioning of his teacher's opinions. Their real arguments, it appears from the discarded material, were on a variety of themes. Selecting gender, as he did for the discussion between Heinrich Föhn and Leda Frisch in *Comedy of Vanity*, covertly draws attention to their shared writing project and their major dispute over his novel. He recalls: "On some other matters I opposed her, for instance, I soon noticed that she had a sort of chauvinism for all things female. She submitted to women-worshippers without any resistance" (*VIII*:204). He cites the Viennese poet and scion of the Leopoldstadt, Peter Altenberg. In the course of an argument over the moral and literary merits of their respective favorite Russians, Veza calls him "an inveterate misogynist" (*VIII*:205), a label often applied after *Auto-da-Fé* is published. She is for Tolstoy because of *Anna Karenina*'s supreme expression of empathy for the female soul, he is for Gogol, the author of the grotesque *The Overcoat* and the satirical masterpiece, *Dead Souls*. Their quarrel ends when he gives her a present of Max Gorki's memoir of the elderly Tolstoy, "the best thing that he ever wrote, loose jottings [*Aufzeichnungen*], which he left untouched for a long time before he published them, without destroying them by unifying them into a fake system" (*VIII*:206).[30] This argument anticipates, or in this account, displaces the one over his novel, and the reconciliation that follows also appears emblematic of their larger relationship. The term *Aufzeichnungen*, which can cover aperçus and pensées, diary jottings, aphorisms, as well as memoirs or notes, is what he uses for his own daily writing that he began in earnest in 1942 as a creative counterweight to his research for *Crowds and Power*. Veza calls the book by Gorki the best present he has ever given her and adds: "This is what I wish for myself more than anything else in the world: that you one day will write like that" (*VIII*:206). Is this another of his coded hints? Does it mean that he is writing his autobiography for Veza now, fifty years after he upset her with *Auto-da-Fé*? If so, then in his own attempt at "loose jottings," his published autobiography, he falsified his material because he imposed a unifying system of interpretation, which is largely undeveloped in the discarded fragments.

Canetti includes nothing about his adult sex life in his autobiographical trilogy, a discretion he abandons only in his account of his affair with Iris Murdoch in *Party in the Blitz*. He mentions two affairs after he meets Veza that occur on either side of writing his novel. The first is with Gordon in 1927–28 and the second, briefer and more passionate in the summer of 1933, with Mahler. Even though he devotes as much time to Friedl Benedikt towards the end of *The Play of the Eyes*, he does not divulge that they became lovers — or that she was to become a published writer. Despite this coyness on his behalf, the autobiography has its fair share of sex. It just takes place off-stage, in an adjoining apartment at the Pension Charlotte (where Fräulein Rahm subjects her lover to masochistic love rituals), or in the next room at the family flat in the Radetzkystraße (where Johnnie entertains a male friend), or in his very own room in the Haidgasse before he took over the tenancy between the buxom Ruzena and his predecessor as tenant.

In *Party in the Blitz*, she remains a peripheral figure among his collection of character portraits from English life in the 1940s and 1950s. This in part reflects her unwillingness to play a public role in exile. She either hides in the background because she preferred not to accompany him to parties or, when she does make an exception to attend the launch of the English translation of *Auto-da-Fé*, she is worsted in argument by one his closest friends, who is the only man in England to have read his novel in the original, Arthur Waley. Mr. and Mrs. Milburn, their English hosts in Chesham Bois, who are thinly disguised as Mr. and Mrs. Toogood in Veza's own story, believe her to be drunk when they first meet her, leaving Canetti to reassure them on her behalf. These are signs that she is losing her ability to interact successfully with others in social situations.

In all the autobiographical texts written over two decades, Veza is either isolated or idealized, but she does not fully come to life. He wanted at all costs "to do her justice" but seems not to have been able to devise a satisfactory way of doing so. Canetti loved her all through his life but never knew what he should do with her in his writing when that life became its subject. This indecision was evident in his literary portraits of her, partially in Therese, then in Leda Frisch and Forty-Three. His many pictures of Veza are frustrating, puzzling, and contradictory. Yet had it been otherwise, there would have been less for him to write about. His reactions to her writings, rather than her presence in his life, are more extensive and give greater insights into his own literary work, which she helped to create.

Notes

[1] Sibylle Mulot writes: "She for her part attached a couple of substantively malicious characteristics to Knut Tell, the charming young poet in *Yellow Street*, whose name has quite a few of the letters of Kanetti Elias. No, the relationship between the two kindred spirits cannot have been easy." Mulot, "Das Leben vor der Haustür." The hypothesis that Tell is a portrait of Canetti is also supported by Meidl, *Veza Canettis Sozialkritik*, 61 and Hanuschek, *Elias Canetti*, 274.

[2] Göbel, "Zur Wiederentdeckung Veza Canettis," 4.

[3] Veza Canetti to Theodor Sapper, 22 May [either 1947 or 1948], quoted by Schedel, *Sozialismus und Pyschoanalyse*, 191.

[4] Bayley, *Elegy for Iris*, 164–65.

[5] See Ingrid Spörk, "'Ich sammelte Ketten. Ich bekam Ketten. Sie sind mir geblieben . . .' Zu Liebe und Ehe im Werk Veza Canettis," in Spörk and Strohmaier, *Veza Canetti*, 91–120.

[6] Von Mayenburg, *Blaues Blut und rote Fahnen*, 109–10.

[7] Ibid., 110–11.

[8] 21 August 1982, ZB 60.

[9] See Mulot, "Das Leben vor der Haustür" and "Befreundet mit den Geliebten."

[10] Mitgutsch, "Veza Canetti," 107.

[11] Barbara Meili, *Erinnerung und Vision: Der lebensgeschichtliche Hintergrund von Elias Canettis Roman Die Blendung* (Bonn: Bouvier, 1985).

[12] "Heirat (späte Heirat)," ZB 60.

[13] See Donahue, *The End of Modernism*, 43–75 ("'The truth is you're a woman. You live for sensations': Misogyny as Cultural Critique").

[14] She also makes a case for linking Anna and Benedikt Pfaff with Anna Mahler and her second husband, Ernst Krenek. Foell, *Blind Reflections*, 159–60.

[15] "Heirat (späte Heirat)," ZB 60.

[16] See Czurda, "Veza Canetti," 127 and Schedel, *Sozialismus und Psychoanalyse*, 19.

[17] On Elias Canetti as "victor" (*Sieger*), see Melzer, "Der einzige Satz," 98.

[18] See Schedel, *Sozialismus und Psychoanalyse*, 201–2.

[19] ZB 22.

[20] Hanuschek, *Elias Canetti*, 266.

[21] "Allgemeines: Bedenken. Veza. Das System," ZB 60.

[22] Herta Blaukopf, "Das überlebensgroße Bild des Vaters. Erinnerungen an Anna Mahler," in *Anna Mahler: Ich bin in mir selbst zu Hause*, Barbara Weidle and Ursula Seeber, eds. (Bonn: Weidle, 2004), 144–52; here: 145.

[23] 6 November 1983, ZB 60.

[24] 6 May 1984, ZB 60.

[25] Hanuschek, *Elias Canetti*, 146–48.

[26] "Veza: Ihre Lektüre," ZB 226.

[27] Ibid.

[28] Ibid.

[29] "Tolstoy oder Gogol," ZB 226.

[30] Presumably Max Gorki, *Erinnerungen an Lew Nikolajawitsch Tolstoi* (Munich: Der neue Merkur, 1920). Gorki was closely associated with the Bolshevik Revolution. In 1928, Malik published a collection of Gorki's recollections of his contemporaries, including Tolstoy. Max Gorki, *Erinnerungen an Zeitgenossen* (Berlin: Malik, 1928). The choice of literary gift to seal their reconciliation indicates their shared political allegiances.

8: Rivalry and Partnership

FAR MORE THAN Friedl Benedikt or Iris Murdoch, let alone Kathleen Raine, Veza reacted not only to her husband's personality but also to his writing and ideas. In turn she exerted a more profound influence on him than any of his literary girlfriends or pupil/mistresses. While he put her into his fiction and drama before he made her a major character in his autobiography, her ideas (on the psychology and ethics of sight, ogres, the hunt, physical disability, the life of animals, cinema, even sexual equality) fed into his work. Their relationship went through phases of partnership, conflict, reconciliation, and renewed partnership. In Vienna they responded to the same set of cultural and political circumstances and worked in parallel and as equals on their independent projects. Their writings also constitute part of a remarkable private dialogue.

Canetti's creative partnerships with other writers or artists took numerous forms. If Murdoch and Benedikt were literary girlfriends, then Veza was his literary mother. In her letters to Georg, she calls both Elias and the younger Georg Canetti her "sons"; and she mothers both of them in terms of their physical well-being and their professional ambitions. A good mother traditionally puts the interests of her children before her own, and Veza appears to have been a very good mother in this respect. In both her prewar letters to Georg and her more numerous postwar ones, she devotes at least twenty times more attention to Canetti's literary aspirations than to her own, which often appear as afterthoughts when she mentions them at all. The correspondence also gives a sharper sense of Georg's own professional writing as a medical researcher than it does of Veza's writing. The only one of Canetti's projects that he and Veza discuss with each other, and which both present to Georg, are his three lectures on Kafka, Proust, and Joyce, which he was invited to deliver in return for a handsome fee in the summer of 1948 at Bryanston School in Dorset. Over a period of months we get an insight into the way Veza badgered him to get down to work and fretted that he would let the opportunity pass him by. She nagged Georg too to ensure that Canetti concentrated on the lectures when he came to France to visit him. One reason for Veza's concern is that Canetti had barely read anything by the trio of famous contemporary authors (28 March 1948; *BG*:322). In a letter from him to her, Canetti appears reliant on her to get the lectures written in numerous ways, thanking her for her help in reading Proust, for instance, without which he would be "lost" (3 May 1948; *BG*:335). This interaction looks to have set the tone for their collaboration on *Crowds and Power* over the next decade. She shared the task of preparatory reading, suggested ideas, and inserted motifs that she had first used in her own writing. This is, however, only one aspect of their work together, albeit now the most visible thanks to the publication of their letters. What goes on between the lines of their writings is more fascinating and more complex.

With the exception of Canetti's jottings, there is little that either he or Veza wrote that does not relate to something in the oeuvre of the other. Usually the relationship is characterized by contrast and contradiction rather than amplification: creative and personal tension drove them to their careers as writers. For instance, her novella "Patience Brings Roses" is set in a large Viennese townhouse, like his play *Wedding*, which he finished a few months before her work was published. In each text social structures are reflected in the demographic composition of the distinctive Viennese houses, as to some extent they were in *Auto-da-Fé*. Veza blames the crass inequalities in wealth and power for the tragic outcome, while his characters are all equally venal. His judgement is moral rather than directly political like hers.

Canetti's writings were an immediate point of reference for critics discussing Veza's work when it was first republished. Helmut Göbel and Eva Meidl note a shared interest in disabled figures, such as Fischerle, Runkel, and the Mäusles' son, and the correspondences between Vlk, who ends his days in Steinhof psychiatric hospital, and Kien, whose character developed out of Canetti's view of the same hospital from the window of his lodgings in the Hagenberggasse. Meidl compares Kien with Iger: Kien marries Therese in the belief that she is an heiress just as Iger marries his wife for her inheritance; Frau Iger is locked up in the family flat like mother and daughter in the chapter "The Kind Father" from his novel.[1] Ritchie Robertson saw Veza's prose version of "The Ogre" as a direct response to Canetti's account of domestic violence in *Auto-da-Fé*: her harrowing depiction of patriarchal brutality favors psychological and social realism at the expense of grotesque but aesthetically pleasing stylization because her narrative voice inhabits the dulled sensibility of the female victim.[2] "The Kind Father" was a chapter Canetti often read in public, to small circles of friends, or to larger groups. Veza includes it in *The World in the Head* and calls it "that monstrous story" (*WK*:10) in her introduction. As I have already argued, it contains traces of her own experiences at the hands of her stepfather, which she turns into another more directly autobiographical literary story, "Money — Money — Money."

Like many writers from the interwar period, both Canettis were fascinated by the cinema for related but ultimately different reasons. Through the 1930s Veza was a relentless critic of the world of film ("Die Welt des Films" was the weekly section in the *Arbeiter-Zeitung* that reviewed new releases). In *Yellow Street*, cinema is associated with immorality and sexual coercion. Andrea Sandoval recognizes the "separées" in the *Lusthaus* where Herr Tiger wants to seduce her "from the cinema" (*GS*:136). In *The Tiger*, the cinema industry's artistic banality is contrasted with Diana Sandoval's creative integrity and Knut Tell's cleverness. Veza appears to have no more respect for Marlene Dietrich, by then in exile from Nazi Germany, than for Hans Albers: when the singer Pasta claims Dietrich uses the same perfume as she, Herr Tiger replies contemptuously with a disrespectful pun on her name, "Marlene Sperrhaken" (*DF*:94). A plot line for a film requires action, excitement, sex, crime, or murder, not "lessons" or "points," as writers for the *Arbeiter-Zeitung* were more likely to cultivate. Instead of the moral truth or aesthetic beauty that guides Diana Sandoval's artistic production, what the audience wants to see is paramount for the filmmaker. Nick pitches his initial idea to Pasta, who encourages him in his efforts to sell it to the American agent, Mister Smith:

> The artist X-Y goes on a journey with his bride to Italy. There he experiences the eruption of a volcano and saves the life of a young girl. Her wildness delights his artistic eye and he takes her back with him. (*DF*:99)

Pasta points out that the introduction of the "young girl" has led Nick to forget the artist's wife before introducing her. Tell supplies the pair with an ending that they like, which involves the artist in a Jekyll-and-Hyde type of double existence. ". . . is that banal enough?" (*DF*:102) he inquires.

With Tell's involvement in this discussion, Veza might suggest her husband's own interest — or lack of it — in the medium. Canetti reports to Georg in March 1934 that he is assisting a Viennese writer, whom he "deeply despised," with a film script under the condition that his name is not mentioned (2 March 1934; *BG*:19). Money was the sole motivation: if the film were accepted, he would have no financial worries for two years. Two-and-a-half years later, Veza reports to Georg that Canetti's film (whether the same one or a different one is not clear) will be made with seventy percent certainty. If it is made, their financial position will be improved significantly (16 September 1936; *BG*:63). Two lectures that Canetti was invited to give in March 1938 to the Austrian Werkbund deal at some length with cinema, as indicated by notes in the *Nachlaß*. He calls Hollywood the modern Olympus and the star system a "mystery cult," but he is less engaged than Veza with contemporary theoretical or political debates.[3] He seems fascinated with the idea of the film image as shadow, which is perhaps an original and certainly an eccentric preoccupation. In the interview with *Sonntag* from April 1937, he calls the disembodied shadows in the Greek underworld the first films and compared the magic that emanates from film stars with the feelings that cave painters had towards their subjects, the larger-than-life images of bears and mammoths.

When asked for his film idea in *The Tiger*, Tell promptly describes a plausibly Canettiesque situation:

> Two villages . . . whose clocks on account of ancient caprice tell the time an hour apart. And all the incidents which come about because of the whimsical, tragic, completely delightful and completely awful confusions that result from it being quarter past eleven in one village and one step away in the other village it is already quarter past twelve. (*DF*:100)

Canetti's first collection of jottings begins with a more metaphysical time experiment in which people from a certain age start to grow smaller. One book of jottings refers to time in its title: *The Secret Heart of the Clock*. He notices too how Kafka set his watch an hour fast to indicate his sense of non-belonging. Nick dismisses the idea by saying "that is novel material, dear fellow."

Tell's dismissive attitude to contemporary film seems like Canetti's. There is no indication that he pursued his cinematic interests after the abandoned lecture project. That is not true of Veza, who makes many references to her regular visits to the cinema in her letters. H. G. Adler finds that *The Ogre* would make a good film, and comments:

> You have, dear Veza, looked into the hearts of everyday folk and this makes me understand what draws you so often into the cinema, where everyday aspirations, everyday deceptions, everyday joys etc. are revealed almost effortlessly in hurried changes of scene, in the same way as you succeed in depicting everything.[4]

Yet *Yellow Street*, which does have "hurried changes of scene," is surely the most filmic of Veza's texts. In *The Tortoises*, Felberbaum runs a cinema until he is imprisoned in the wave of arrests following the Anschluss. Pilz offers to get him released if he signs away his property and that is why the Nazi sits in the Jewish-owned cinema. Felberbaum neither loves films nor understands them: his cinema is a business that he runs because "it is profitable today" (*SK*:161). He can only tell whether he will make money from showing a film, not if the film is any good. When he decides to make the new lady feel more welcome in the flat where they are both billeted by brightening up the kitchen, in which she is to sleep, he gets out his box of souvenirs and looks for a suitable poster to put on the wall. His pinups of the stars are images of commodities in poses of domination. Greta Garbo as a courtesan is talking to someone "in a far corner whom you could not see but who judging by her triumphant expression must have been completely crushed" (*SK*:161). The very same Albers who stard in *The Victor* is pictured "in riding breeches, with his horse whip over his knees" (*SK*:162), attire similar to that worn by the Hitler look-alike in "Hush-Money" and the hypnotist Cipolla in Mann's *Mario and the Magician*. Both stars are depicted as disdainful or aggressive; their physical perfection is alienating. What's more, they are dominators of the kind who appear in *Crowds and Power*. The kindhearted Felberbaum does not notice their poses but, later in the novel when he meets the vivacious young Hilde, he is struck by her superior beauty that is apparent through her physical presence as a real human being:

> He found the girl magnificent, she was a beauty, far more beautiful than the faded stars he knew from films, her voice sounded warm and full, her look, her shape, and every movement she made were warm and full too. (*SK*:213)

The difference between the real-life Hilde and these pictures of film stars is that Hilde inhabits her own image: in Canetti's terms she is made of flesh and blood rather than shadow.

Felberbaum expresses an unease with film as art or medium that transcends a socialist critique of its exploitation for commercial or propagandistic purposes:

> It was not that he was a great fan of films. Rather the opposite was true; it made him nervous to see figures flickering by whom you could not hold, who no longer exist at the end of the piece, as if they dissolved, like dreams that annoy you when you wake up because nothing was real. Of course he knew that the figures were alive, that they came all the way from America and presented themselves in person. He had seen such a film-star with his own eyes, but that merely increased his suspicion when this famous lady, who arrived from across the sea, had nothing in common with her appearance on the stage, nothing at all, which quite horrified him. (*SK*:160–61)

Again, the similarity to Canetti's ideas on image and shadow is plain. Veza's socialist analysis of an individual film's content gives way to an aesthetic critique that is by nature conservative. However, she limits herself to the star-based film studios of Hollywood or Babelsberg and appears to be aware of no other form of cinema. It belongs to the melancholy aspect of *The Tortoises* that even "these days are over" when money can be made with cinematic products by someone as cinematically illiterate as Felberbaum.

In both of Veza's novels, there are themes, motifs, and assumptions that are found in Canetti's. In *Yellow Street*, which is in some ways a corrective to *Auto-da-Fé*, they are the marriage, gender roles, and the portrayal of the poor. It is evident that both novels are set firmly in the fractured environment of the interwar Austrian capital, a bubbling cauldron of resentments, even though Vienna is not mentioned by name in either. Both give an account of Viennese mentalities on the eve of Nazism. The real-life counterparts of Iger, Pfaff, and Therese will all be in the crowds cheering Hitler after the Anschluss on Vienna's main square, the Heldenplatz. Their anti-heroes, Runkel and Fischerle, are also cut from the same cloth: their disfigurement alienates them from their fellow human beings and determines their behavior, it also expresses their Jewishness (openly with Fischerle, unacknowledged with Runkel). In *The Tortoises*, Veza reinscribes the rapacious Fischerle as the kindhearted Felberbaum, and Therese as the Kains' landlady whose "verbal signature" — her obsession with the restitution of South Tyrolia that she believes the Nazis promise — corresponds with Therese's obsessive catchphrases. She also rewrites the relationship between the Kien brothers in the relationship between Andreas and Werner Kain. Werner is arrested and killed after a long discussion with Andreas, just as Peter sets fire to his library after a discussion with Georges when they too lay out their diverging world views.

For Veza, *Auto-da-Fé* is both a model and a countermodel. There are even correspondences in apparently inconsequential details. "On Furniture" in *The Tortoises* relates to "Dazzling Furniture" in *Auto-da-Fé*: Therese rearranges Kien's spartan furnishings and expels him from sections of his library apartment that she takes over for herself.[5] The various pieces of furniture are heavy, solidly built, and cannot be moved easily. They belong to a bourgeois matrimonial convention of establishing a household and a family. As a writer committed to a life of the mind, Kien has no need for them; Therese's purchase of furniture is a sign of her ensnaring him in conventional domesticity that will kill off — per his misogynist fear — his intellectual life. In Veza's novel, moving the furniture is an indication of their eviction, first from their house, then from their country.

The Tortoises is Veza's response to National Socialism, Canetti's response is *Crowds and Power*; the Kristallnacht of 9 and 10 November 1938 is for her what 15 July 1927 was for him. It reflects their different working styles, genres, and personalities that her novel was finished within a year of the Nazi pogrom, whereas it took him thirty-three to finish his grander work. Its completion also underlines that Canetti recovered, by all accounts with Veza's help, from the bouts of self-doubt and depression that befell him in Vienna in the second part of the 1930s and periodically in London to continue his writing career, whereas she let herself be defeated by her disappointment.

From the mid-1930s the disjunction in the development of their literary careers makes their parallel progress more difficult to reconstruct. While Canetti stopped writing after he had finished *Comedy of Vanity* in the aftermath of February 1934, the rest of this decade was Veza's most productive period. Sometimes she reacted to him and what he had already written, sometimes she anticipated what he addresses decades in the future, perhaps an indication that he was posthumously responding to her. By early 1934, their literary and political views appeared to converge and it is Canetti who moved in her direction. *Comedy of Vanity* and *The Ogre*, both completed around the time Dollfuß secured his grip on the Austrian state, are twin diagnoses of political ills. Both end with the cure of a mentally disturbed patient that has a wider significance and more general applicability. After Veza's death, he wrote in his notebook that "we influenced each other. I owe her the Comedy, she owes me the Ogre."[6] H. G. Adler's reference to Veza's and Canetti's shared misgivings regarding the length of

Act 4 in *The Ogre* shows both how the couple discussed it with him and how Canetti's views on the chapter were significant to him.[7] Her husband evidently still took an interest in her first play in 1950.

Veza's scramble to finish *The Tortoises* upon their arrival in Britain testifies to her eagerness to reconnect with a reading public, as well as a need to earn money and perhaps justify her visa. After her failure to find publishers her trail slowly goes cold. Judging from *The Palanquin*, she stopped interacting with her husband: there is nothing in this uncharacteristically inert social comedy that corresponds with Canetti's *The Numbered*, written the same year. His own silence may have played no small part in her decline: he had given her no further written stimulus, his jottings, like his encoded diary, were for his eyes only — except the collection he presented to Motesiczky, who, along with Benedikt, competed with Veza for his creative and intellectual attention since settling in England. The literary marriage that existed through the 1930s appeared to be dead well before 1952. From then on, she was his assistant, amanuensis, even coach, the same role that she played before either had published a word. She lived her literary life by assuring the continuation of his.

This pattern can be observed after Veza's death, when Canetti belatedly deals with figures and themes that they discussed in the 1920s and 1930s and Veza often wrote about *first*. However, it is already apparent with respect to *Crowds and Power*. Several of the book's key concepts already appeared in her fiction: the survivor triumphing over the death of others ("The Victor"; *III*:267–329); the related concept of the ruler thwarting his heirs' expectation of inheritance ("Money — Money — Money"; *III*:286–90); the "sting" contained in commands that the commanded person carries until he passes it on to another in a new command (Runkel's personality is built on this idea; *III*:357–96); and the mentality of the "pack," which, as is clear from *The Tortoises*, they had studied on the Viennese streets after the Nazi invasion (*III*:109–46). By devoting herself to his project, she worked towards a book that she already helped shape; the ideas were formed in conversations between the two of them.

At the outset there was more likely to have been conflict. Their divergent approach to the destitute, including maids and prostitutes, and the working classes generally, is encapsulated in their differing portrayals of the blind, in particular blind beggars, namely, Canetti's Knopfhannes and Veza's Diego. Knopfhannes makes his living by pretending to be blind; two passersby in "The Seer," the first an Englishman, the second a Turk, suspect that Diego is faking in the same way. The Turk even calls a policeman who points out that Diego's eyes do not have any color: "Can't you see the white stripe under his eyelids?" (*GbR*:86). Theft and ownership are constant preoccupations for all the characters in the middle book of *Auto-da-Fé*, which is set among Vienna's thieving, pimping underclass. Their motives are invariably vulgar or base. One of the novel's most famous chapters, "Private Property," takes place in a police station. Whereas Canetti's intellectuals are deluded frauds, he presents women through the eyes of misogynists, Jews from the perspective of anti-Semites, and the proletariat from that of the frightened bourgeoisie, Veza sees the same figures from the inside. While his novels are populated by types, hers have more individuals. As we have seen, there is something clinical and detached about the way he collects "acoustic masks." As a novelist or dramatist, he exhibits neither warmth nor understanding for his characters, whose grotesque venality he exposes. What separates him from Veza is her empathy for her figures who are based no less than his on living beings. This difference in approach is perhaps what he alludes to when he writes in the foreword to *Yellow Street* that she "was not interested in invention," in contrast to him (*GS*:8), a distinction which so rankled with Anna Mitgutsch.[8]

Canetti noted the difference in an unused chapter for *The Play of the Eyes*. The connection is personal, existential even, as well as literary, as she reacted with dread to his enthusiasm for eccentric, marginalized individuals. Like his self-obsessed fictional characters, such people whom he encountered in real life remained enclosed in their own private worlds. Veza's fear was that he would turn into one of his literary subjects. In part, however, she shared his fascination, but she made different use of it in her fiction:

> Perhaps she knew more about me than I did myself. The violence of my disinclination to habits and ingrained rituals between human beings filled her with fear. She had observed my fascination for everything on the *margins*. When I would tell her excitedly about human beings who were quite different from all others, who had no way of communicating any more to any other person, who had turned their backs on the world and remained that way, she suspected a profound inclination in that direction in my own nature. I could, which happened frequently in spite of my admiration, condemn the self-absorption of such characters, — she did not take that part of my story seriously. What she did take seriously was the enthusiasm for the bizarreness of such a being, for his particular form of boldness which made him want to remain himself, for his obstinate rejection of any falsification of his character, any concession to others who would have made his life easier.
>
> Veza herself admired extraordinary characters. In the stories which she had been writing for some years such people often featured. But they were always victims, people who had suffered injustice, they were helpless, crippled, disrespected, but most of all she liked writing about women who ruined themselves in the service of others or in a bad marriage.[9]

He never wrote at greater length about her writing or her attitude to his work than here. His comments confirm my general conclusions drawn from a close comparison of their fiction and drama. Veza was more inclined to enclose these unusual characters in a clear moral framework. He was aware of how she reacted to him and took account of it, but judging from his remarks in the above passage, he had an ultimately limited appreciation of her achievements.

One illustrative example of their respective treatments of marginal figures can be found in *Yellow Street*'s Frieda Runkel and Thomas Marek from *The Torch in the Ear*. Marek, whose real name was Herbert Patek, was paralyzed from the neck downwards and, like Runkel, was dependent on others to push him about in a pram or wheelchair. Both he and Runkel devise ways of exerting psychological power over their environment to compensate for their lack of physical strength. Their use of power defines both of them. In the first paragraph of *Yellow Street* Runkel decides to end her "miserable life" (*GS*:15) by getting herself run over. As she cannot control her own movements, she fails to kill herself but her actions result in the death of her maid. Marek had tried to commit suicide on three separate occasions either by eating a whole newspaper, or swallowing fragments of glass or mercury from a thermometer. He fails each time but does not cause harm to anyone else. For Canetti, one of the most remarkable features of Marek's condition is that he does not have the freedom to end his life. Marek's lack of body contrasts with his prodigious intellectual capacity signaled by his voracious reading, which he can accomplish for himself, turning the pages with his tongue. It also leads to his unusual powers of perception that give him a unique perspective on other people: he can judge others, for instance, by the sound they make when they walk. Meeting Marek enabled Canetti to begin his own novel because his condition makes Marek the prototype for his obsessive fictional characters. This is why he merits more attention than any of the famous individuals from the world of art and literature who cross Canetti's path in Berlin and Vienna. He is a foundational figure in a different, more fundamental sense than the ogreish Menachem Alkaley because he enabled Canetti to begin writing.

If Marek is the godfather of the deluded characters in *Auto-da-Fé*, Runkel is the evil genius at the center of Veza's first novel. For the first and only time, Veza's character is more grotesque, more twisted, and more closed to the world and the interests of others than Canetti's. Since she was disabled herself, some readers have argued that she projected her own physical limitations on to Runkel without, however, explaining why the character's selfish behavior should contrast so starkly with Veza's own.[10] The problem with Runkel is that she is a victim who is a villain, indeed her victimhood determines her villainy, whereas Veza Canetti is said to write only about victims. Runkel uses her power as employer and property owner to avenge the slights she suffers on account of her appearance. After she dismisses the beautiful Lina, she is delighted by the attention Lina's supporters pay her in their unsuccessful attempts to get her reinstated. Her refusal to give in to them is a consequence of her narcissism, which results in muted sympathy for her at best. Is this Veza's response to her boyfriend's idealization of his disabled neighbor or is she exploring anti-Semitic stereotypes, as he did through Fischerle? Since she does not mention Jewishness explicitly, the former seems more likely.

Marek too has power over his family, in particular over his parents (his sister has escaped him by getting married), because he receives a scholarship of 400 schillings a month from a benefactress that they depend on. Although he is dismissive of his father, who he insists "failed" in life, he uses this power more benignly than Runkel. He is also more vulnerable: his aversion to hearing accounts of physical activities from which he will always be excluded does not result in revenge but in great sadness.

Whether Canetti remembered Runkel when he was writing *The Torch in the Ear* is impossible to determine (unlike some of her stories, the manuscript for *Yellow Street* was in his hands), but Veza would have heard reports of the real-life Marek before she wrote her first novel. In this case, the original oral version of the story was told by Canetti to Veza, some time after May 1930 when he and Herbert Patek began their friendship. Veza then used it in her novel in 1933–34 and he published his recollection in 1980. The pattern is similar with Veza's meat-devouring, liquor-swilling ogre-stepfather, except that Canetti also had his own memories of tyrannical Jewish patriarchs: she told him her story when they first met (1925), which he partially incorporated into his novel (1931), before she wrote her very different account ("Money — Money — Money," 1937), and he finally gave his version of her original story in *The Torch in the Ear* (1980).

When Canetti wrote his own version of the story about Veza's stepfather, it seems certain that he forgot her "Money — Money — Money." It was not among the stories he held on to and it was not discovered until 2001, when it was too late to be included in *Der Fund*. This makes the detailed correspondences between her and his accounts all the more remarkable. He alters the stepfather's real name from Menachem Alkaley to Mento Altaras, as he alters many other names, and adds a decade or so to his age, but the similarities are more significant.[11] Altaras also has precisely "forty-seven houses," he too leaves the house in such shabby clothes that he is taken for a beggar and is proud to return with fruit he has been given, he too wields a stick, lives on meat and alcohol, and burns his money so that neither wife nor stepdaughter will inherit it. By destroying his wealth to thwart his heirs, he enacts a pattern of behavior that Canetti identifies in *Crowds and Power* as something common among autocrats. Since the wielder of power cannot countenance an heir inheriting that power after his death, he will bring down his empire in order to prevent it passing into the heir's hands. He devotes a whole chapter to this phenomenon: "The Despot's Hostility to Survivors Rulers and Their Successors" (*III*:286–90). Veza's stepfather cut her out of his will and provided only for her mother after his death, which Canetti calls "his delayed revenge" for her taming of his behavior. The story of his burning his money, however, appears to be a fiction, since in one of the discarded chapters for *The Play of the Eyes*, he reveals that the money, which Alkaley arranges in piles in his room, simply disappeared by his death.[12] Veza and Canetti both prefer the literary version of the story, which one or the other of them presumably made up.

Veza's stepfather became a type for both of them. "Her rescue of her own atmosphere, safe from the stick-banging, the threats and curses of this uncanny man, which she managed to achieve at the age of eighteen, formed Veza's character" (*VIII*:130). Neither of them calls him an ogre or a monster but his appetite, his hostility to children, and his love of money are all distinctly monstrous, ogre-like qualities. Herr Iger is associated with all of them. While Iger does not eat any children like ogres in folktales, he is associated with orality in the opening paragraph when "a fat gentleman," who is an old acquaintance, joins the newly weds in the railway carriage that is taking Maya to "the big, unknown city." Maya's new husband invites him to share their provisions: "The confectionery and the refreshing fruits, the homemade marzipan, the cakes and pastries, everything disappeared into his gaping mouth" (*GS*:47). In one of the most disturbing episodes Iger forces his own child to eat until he breaks down in tears. By portraying the ogre as force-feeder rather than eater of his own offspring, Veza inverts the traditional motif, which would hardly be convincing in a modern realist setting. In "Money — Money — Money" the stepfather denies the children food while eating large amounts himself. Family meal times are unhappy affairs:

> At lunchtime we would all sit at the table and my mother would pile up my plate. But if she placed that tiny piece of meat on top that a child of twelve needs, he would fix his colorless eyes on the tiny piece and say:
> "She's getting meat!"
> However kindly my mother would now look at me, I could not get the meat down and that is what he seems to have anticipated. He would skewer it onto his fork and place it with satisfaction onto his plate. Pudding had to be consumed secretly in the kitchen, as he did not tolerate pudding. He himself ate great amounts of meat, drank liquor and wine from the bottle, and defied the predictions of the doctors. (*TK*:16)

Benedikt Pfaff shares the propensity for violence and, in particular, a violent hostility to children. He also demands similarly large and regular helpings of meat that his daughter must provide.

The title of Veza's story anticipates another important chapter in the autobiography, where Canetti scribbled the word "money" repeatedly over sheet after sheet of paper in disgust at his mother's refusal to let him take part in a walking holiday on the grounds that they could not afford it. Money, which is the ogre-like Uncle Salomon's obsession, is the essence of all things that Canetti hated. In Veza's last two published stories, which both have the word money in their titles, the magnate and the stepfather are both associated with money while the penniless maids embody humanity and decency. With a reference that only her husband would understand, Veza aligns her struggle against her money-obsessed stepfather with Canetti's against his mother. Their shared view of the links between money and ogres was remarkably consistent.

There are traces of the stepfather in one of *Yellow Street*'s two "monsters," Herr Vlk, who also lives off the rent from his properties, is self-obsessed, has problems with his sight, and goes quite mad. While the stepfather burns his rolls of banknotes in his stove, Herr Vlk paints the walls of his Steinhof cell with his own excrement. In Veza's English works, an obsession with saving money leads to both Mr. and Mrs. Toogood in "Toogoods or the Light" and Mr. and Mrs. Spinks in *The Palanquin* saving their faeces to use as fertilizer on their garden. For both Canettis, property ownership debases the moral character. In *Wedding*, Frau Gilz is similar in age to Veza's stepfather, the house that she owns and all her tenants and relatives want to inherit defines her mean character. The landlady in *The Tortoises* convinces herself that her tenants' misery should be countenanced because "it is better that a tiny number should suffer than the whole of the German people" (*SK*:35). The stepfather's "forty-seven houses" are mentioned numerous times in a dozen pages. His only friend is a compatriot who has similar wealth:

> He was very satisfied with her visits. But then she lost her money. When she reappeared after a while looking rather crestfallen, he would not look up.
> "You are a beggar now," he said, and with that she was dismissed.
> She crept past my mother and did not come again. (*TK*:18)

Meanness is the stepfather's defining characteristic: on the day he arrives he gives a single sweet to his waiting stepdaughter in a manner that indicates he is demonstrating generosity and expects gratitude. He also hits her on her leg with his stick as a way of "showing affection," as Herr Iger also strikes his children in *Yellow Street*. When the first person narrator takes the advice of her relatives and buys him a present, he at first enjoys playing with it, but then reflects that it must have cost her money and announces he will cut her mother's allowance, as she must be getting too much if her daughter can afford to buy presents.

Canetti depicts Veza as winning the game of competing wills in *The Torch in the Ear*; since it involves power, it is the type of situation that fascinated him in his life and work and we encounter it, albeit in altered guise, in Benedikt and Murdoch's fiction. Her account diverges most markedly from his in this respect since she (the author Veza *Magd*) projects a revenge fantasy on to the maid. This makes her story closer to the folk-tale tradition, one of the functions of which was to reassure because the ogres were either rendered harmless or killed.[13] Frau Iger also stands up for herself by the end of both the narrative and dramatic versions of *The Ogre*, though more demonstrably in the play. It belongs to the modern German tradition of the Bluebeard story. Like Mrs. Bluebeard, Maya Iger expressly disobeys her husband after he leaves the house. While Bluebeard's wife uses the special key he leaves her to enter the forbidden chamber, Maya spends his money on extra food. Both wives are rescued at the end by representatives of their families. In emphasizing the barbarity of the husband's behavior and the wife's innocence, Veza breaks the taboo imposed by the brothers Grimm, who brought Charles Perrault's seventeenth-century tale of Bluebeard to Germany, "on depicting irrational, human, male evil." For both Canettis, as for Perrault, the ogre is "fully human (rather than supernatural) and socially integrated."[14] Pfaff has three roles, policeman, father, and husband, and he kills both his "wives." The fairy-tale tradition is obvious to Anna who dreams in vain of a knight dressed in black to take her away in a carriage. Then she is killed. She is the only female character in the novel to rebel against her condition and she pays a heavy price in contrast to Veza's more optimistic treatment of Frau Iger.

Pfaff is commemorated implicitly in *The Tortoises* when Werner reports that his house caretaker was "the greatest enthusiast for the National Socialists" (*SK*:205) but that he has become disillusioned by the time of the Kristallnacht. All the caretakers in the Leopoldstadt desert the Nazis for two reasons: the SA challenges their authority and the Jews no longer have money to give tips. One theme of this novel concerns clinging to hopes while the city is engulfed in the flames of the burning Jewish properties. Faith in the disillusionment of caretakers, who often work as police informers, is one such example. Pfaff is based on a real house caretaker. When Fischer discussed his recollection of 12 February 1934 with Canetti in the late 1960s, he claimed the reason he and Veza fretted for his and Ruth's safety and knocked at his door was due to their fear that their caretaker would denounce them to the police: "You're familiar with that caretaker; he comes into my novel *Auto-da-Fé*."[15] For Fischer, Canetti was writing about real people and politics. A comparison with Veza's fiction brings this point home too.

In *The Tongue Set Free* there are two other autocratic patriarchs whose behavior anticipates the stepfather Veza creates. The first is Canetti's paternal grandfather, who curses his own son when he takes his family from Rustchuk to Manchester. Jacques Canetti wins that battle of wills but dies very suddenly a year later at the age of thirty. The penitent grandfather is convinced that his curse, the worst curse that can be made, caused his death. But for Canetti, it is Uncle Salomon, his mother's brother and father's business partner whom the family joins in Manchester, who earns the title "ogre" through his exclusive association with money, the pursuit of which he believes should be everyone's primary aim in life. While

Jacques Canetti rebels against his controlling father and succeeds temporarily, his son ultimately overcomes Uncle Salomon. By the time he is an adolescent, he has other plans for his future rather than following his father into business. These are already causing conflict with his mother. Towards the end of *The Tongue Set Free*, Uncle Salomon visits the family in Zurich:

> I considered him no less a monster than I always had, the embodiment of all things reprehensible, and my mind had formed an image of him which was appropriately brutal and dreadful — but I no longer thought of him as dangerous. I would get the better of him all right. (*VII*:245)

After a lecture on becoming a businessman instead of studying at university, he attends a Christmas concert at his school. At night he dreams of punishing his uncle by tying him to a chair and making him listen to the music. Thus the uncle-ogre is vanquished in his imagination, just as he was in Veza's autobiographical story.

Ways of seeing fascinated both Canettis. The failure of men in "The Victor" to see Anna's beauty until she is dead belongs to a pattern present elsewhere. As there is a correct and an incorrect way of using one's eyes, how an individual looks out at the world and his fellow human beings reveals a great deal about his character, his status, his appreciation of his own importance, and his sense of comradeship or lack of it. A person's life story can be summed up in his visual expression. The narrator of "Clairvoyants," who is a writer, denounces the charlatan who pretends to see into his past and future as a "*Falsch*seher" (the neologistic antonym of the story's title, "*Hell*seher") because his predictions are plain wrong. His followers, who show no sign of believing the evidence in front of their eyes, have eyes that are said to be either "weak" or "fanatical." Veza's villains can never see properly. Herr Iger has "no eyes at all, nothing but tumors in his face" (*GS*:102). The stepfather's "eyes were not large and dark," as the narrator had wished in hopeful anticipation of a kindly new pater familias, "but rather small and colorless, as if he were blind" (*TK*:15). In *The Tortoises*, Pilz has "deep cavities" "where otherwise eyes would have been" (*SK*:39), while the eyes of the "finely dressed and powdered lady" who identifies Andreas Kain as Jewish to the waiter in a café are "cold" (*SK*:42). The jaundiced Herr Vlk wears yellow-tinted glasses at the end of *Yellow Street* so that everyone else appears as yellow as he does. In his final delirium in Steinhof, Vlk has the glasses taken away from him which is why he needs to smear his own excrement on to the walls to make them yellow. Herr Vlk, who one reader described as "so mean he cannot afford a vowel for his name," sees only what he wants to see. Even before his illness he fails to notice that Lina no longer works at Runkel's newsstand, even though it is his complaint that helps get her dismissed.

All these myopic characters are concerned only with themselves, which is why they cannot perceive others, or if they do perceive them, do so with the eyes of the powerful. The powerless look at the world quite differently. In "The Canal" we read that

> what gives the maids away is their gaze. Its truth has been submerged, their ambition whipped out of them. They do not know that it is not *they* who debase themselves. And only occasionally do they suspect it. (*GS*:97)

When Anna Seidler first arrives at Salzman's factory and sees her colleagues with brightly painted faces, "she did not look at them critically but with that reserve which poverty and a sense of duty impose" (*GbR*:49). Such humility and lack of power can also foster a correct way of seeing. In "The Seer," the blind Diego lives by begging at the side of the street and has no power over anyone. His fellow citizens nevertheless call upon him to judge a dispute between the maid Pastora and the glamorous Blanca over the ownership of a silk shawl, which, as we know from Veza's other Seville story, Pastora's mother gave her before she set off for the big city. All circumstantial evidence speaks in favor of Blanca, but Diego can tell from the smells on the shawl what no one can tell by looking. The humble Pastora had indeed worn it that very morning and she lost it at the market, just as she claimed, when Manilito picked it up and immediately presented it to Blanca. Diego thus demonstrates that he can "see" more with his nose than others with their eyes. They let their vision be clouded by their prejudice that tells them that a maid from the country is too poor to possess such a splendid garment.

Whereas Veza treated the subject of seeing ethically, Canetti's approach is more often philosophical or epistemological. *Auto-da-Fé* (or *The Blinding*, as the German title should be translated) begins with a man asking Peter Kien for directions to Mutstraße and becoming more and more impatient with him for not answering. Kien regards his question as a typical example of human folly: the man is standing beneath a sign with the name of that very street written on it. The man cannot see what is in front of his own eyes, which makes him typical of all the characters in the novel, including most emphatically Kien himself because he has no self-awareness. Knopfhannes is obsessed with passersby swindling him by dropping buttons instead of coins into his hat, but it is he who is cheating them by pretending to be blind in the first place. Canetti adapts the stereotype of the professional mendicant cheat, drawing perhaps on the false beggars in Brecht and Weill's *The Threepenny Opera*, which he had seen premiered in Berlin in 1928. In contrast Diego's blindness is both genuine and ennobling.

Canetti continues with the theme of sight in *The Play of the Eyes*, where he draws attention to "the spaciousness and depth" of Anna Mahler's eyes, which captivate him completely when he first meets her and do not let him in peace after she has ended their affair. They say to him: "jump into me with all that you can think and say, say the word, and drown" (*IX*:70). In

The Tongue Set Free and *The Torch in the Ear*, he is concerned with speech and hearing in all their varieties, but, in contrast to Veza and in spite of its title, he does not fully develop an aesthetic of sight in volume three. Because Mahler's eyes only flash across a small segment of it, which covers Veza's most productive years between 1931 and 1937, it has been suggested that his title was inspired by his wife's memory.[16] He was certainly well aware of how Veza used her own eyes. In *The Numbered*, "the lady in the front row" is said to have remarkable eyes, as Forty-Six notices:

MAN: I remember your eyes. You are always look at me in such a
         remarkable way. I don't know what it is, but one does not
         forget your look.
WOMAN: I thought you hadn't noticed me at all. You always seemed to
         be concentrating so hard on what you were doing.
MAN: I was doing that too. But I noticed your look a long while
         ago. There is something different about it. (*II*:190)

Anna Mahler and Fritz Wotruba are two mutual friends about whom they both wrote. He calls Wotruba his "twin" in *The Play of the Eyes* and portrays him as Wenzel Wondrak in *Comedy of Vanity*, where Mahler's character is named Francois Fant, the rebellious son of the brothel madame, Emilie Fant, who is modeled less flatteringly on Alma Mahler-Werfel.[17] According to Canetti, Veza bases Werner Kain on Wotruba and Diana Sandoval on his sculpting pupil, for whom Veza acted as a "lady in waiting," which suggests an unequal relationship.[18] Mahler was not quite thirty when Canetti first met her in her workshop on Vienna's Operngasse with a message from Hermann Scherchen. She had already been married three times and since she grew up among poets, painters, and publishers, she had even served as a model for a literary character (in Oskar Kokoschka's *Orpheus and Eurydice*). Her independence of spirit was made manifest in such sculptures as "Standing Woman" and her self-assertion as wife and lover is reflected in Veza's choice of a name for her. The editor of an exhibition catalogue to mark her centenary in 2004 writes:

Famous men lay at her feet and she happily tolerated their admiration as long as it did not lead to restrictions of her freedom. Through her behaviour she showed herself to be inwardly independent and only answerable to herself.[19]

The contrast with Veza Magd is striking. While Diana is a name for a woman with a sense of self regard, the opposite seems to be true of one who names herself after a maid. There are signs of Veza's admiration for her in *The Tiger*, where Mahler is named after the goddess of hunting and chastity possibly in reaction to Canetti's experience of her: chastity because Mahler retains her personal and sexual independence; hunting because Canetti was for once the prey. In classical mythology Diana not only kills the hunter-giant Orion (Benedikt's nickname for Canetti), she transforms one male admirer into a stag before setting her dogs on him after catching him spying on her and her maidens as they bathed naked. The story is told by Ovid in *Metamorphoses*, a book especially dear to Canetti as the twentieth-century writer of transformations. For a woman writer interested in the sexual politics of seeing, Diana's action is the ultimate revenge fantasy of the objectified female.

Given the accounts of his pursuit of his human prey through the Viennese streets, it seems likely that Canetti acquired a hunting nickname before he met Benedikt. As Wilhelm Tell is renowned as an archer — and by extension hunter —, he is linked to this rich source of imagery, ideas, and metaphor in both *The Tortoises* and *Crowds and Power*. The metaphysics of hunting fascinated both of them before they were chased out of their country. Canetti's association with hunting is certainly long-lived: in Murdoch's *The Flight from the Enchanter* resistance to Mischa Fox is coordinated around an old suffragette journal called *Artemis*, the Greek name for Diana. Fox's Machiavellian alter ego goes by the name of Calvin Blick (which means gaze or look in German). In the mid-1950s Murdoch used both seeing and hunting as imagery for her Canetti-inspired figures. When Canetti first entered Mahler's sights, he found her eyes predatory:

> There are eyes which one fears because they are set on disembowelment, they serve to track down their prey, which once identified, has no choice; even if it succeeds in escaping it remains branded as prey. The petrification of the merciless gaze is terrible. It never alters, no victim has influence over it, it stays true to its image for ever. Who ever falls into its sights has become a victim, there is nothing that he might say and he can only save himself through complete transformation. As that in reality is not possible, myths and people have come into being in its stead. (*IX*:70)

He might well recall the experience in these terms since she soon spits him out and sends him back to Veza, who married him six months later. He drew a connection between hunting and desire when he watched Gerda Müller play the title role in Kleist's *Penthesilea*, which he calls his adolescent initiation into sex. When the young Canetti saw Müller play Kleist's heroine, he had recently been reading *The Bacchae*:

> The wildness of the warring Amazons was like that of the maenads, instead of the Furies who tear the king's live body to pieces, it was Penthesilea, who set her pack of dogs on Achilles and bit her teeth as one of them into his flesh. (*VIII*:51)

There is a link with Mahler because Müller's husband at this time, the conductor Hermann Scherchen, befriended Canetti ten years later and brought about his first meeting with Mahler by sending him to her with his *billet doux*. His and Veza's portraits of Mahler parallel each other closely:

she is the only woman who appears to have been in control of her dealings with Canetti.

In one instance it appears that Veza picked up an idea Canetti discarded and wrote in story form what he had planned to develop in a volume for his *Comédie Humaine of Madmen*. "The Flight from the Earth" is her account of one of these "madmen," namely, the dreamer or fantasist who wants to fly into space, whom Canetti describes at the end of *The Torch in the Ear*:

> F. was the fantasist: he wanted to get away from the earth, up into space; all his thoughts were focused on how to get away from the earth; his immense love of discovery was steeped in his dislike of everything that he could see around him down here. His yearning for the new and the undiscovered was fed by his disgust for what was in front of him. (*VIII*:299)

As a Canetti critic has recently pointed out, none of the other madmen are described in such detail; most only get a title and an abbreviation (such as "R., a religious *fanatic*, C. the *collector*"), which gives the *Phantast* a special status.[20] Canetti calls all his figures, who are ultimately aspects of the same phenomenon, "living one-man rockets" (*VIII*:300) because of their single-minded obsessions, which give the fantasist greater metaphorical centrality. Veza's hero is a "fantastical person" (*DF*:38) who suffers from an "illusion" (passim), who hates existence, and undertakes making a machine to remove his human remains into space so that he can escape the cycle of life. The coincidence of vocabulary between her fictional and his autobiographical narrative is too great to be fortuitous.

"The Flight from the Earth" stands out among Veza's stories for its all but complete lack of realism. It is a literary *jeu d'esprit* but it also includes the first full account of what Canetti later calls "transformation":

> This unhappy man not only tortured himself with his own existence, his sick mind forced him to place himself inside every form of existence, from the smallest sea creature to the human being, and to bear all the suffering that every being endured. He saw a piece of himself as the smallest sea creature swallowed up by a larger sea creature, and it made him suffer. (*DF*:45)

This first account of his central conceit is also the first critique of it in the form of a satirical exaggeration. It tallies precisely with what Kathleen Raine recalls Canetti saying:

> Once he said to me that it would be his wish, if that were possible, to experience the being of every creature in creation; for one whole day he said, he would like to be a worm — to know what it is to be that worm, so limited and inexpressive.[21]

Veza's fantasist inventor returns from his first ecstatic flight into space to live among the working classes, but his suffering and loneliness petrify him so he could not communicate his love for them. Instead he wrote "an embittered and grotesque description of the earth" (*DF*:44). Not for the first or last time Veza wrote about both Canetti the man, her husband, lover, and literary confidant, as well as his ideas and did so in a mildly critical mood.

On other occasions, Veza's parodic reaction to her husband's writing could be entirely uncritical. This is the case in "Hush Money" from 1937 where the consultant recalls the gynecologist turned psychiatrist, Georges Kien. Doctors feature frequently in both their oeuvres, but they are as likely to be charlatans, like Dr. Spanek, as devoted medical practitioners. Their attitude to their patients is a test of their ethical character, because they can use their knowledge and status as easily for ill as for good.

Georges Kien's similarity with the Lilienhain consultant in "Hush Money" is plain. First *Auto-da-Fé*:

> Georges Kien began as a gynecologist. His youth and beauty made him immensely popular. In that period, which only lasted a few years, he surrendered himself to French novels; they made an essential contribution to his success. Without wanting to, he treated the ladies as if he loved them. They each confirmed his taste and drew the right conclusion. The fashion for being ill spread among the little monkeys. He took whatever fell into his lap and had difficulty keeping up with his conquests. Surrounded and spoiled by numerous women ready to serve him, he was rich and well-bred and lived like Prince Guatama before he became Buddha. (*I*:436)

And now "Hush Money":

> The consultant sighs as he enters the room of the patient in number eight. Her bare arms lie wide apart on her pillows.
>
> "How is your digestion?" the consultant asks and sits down in front of her. He usually begins with the appetite but this patient is too beside herself today. She does not answer and looks at him with damp eyes.
>
> "What a rude question, doctor!"
>
> "Do you have a temperature?" He takes hold of her wrist.
>
> "When you touch me!"
>
> The consultant pulls out his watch and looks into space for a minute. Then he checks a graph.
>
> "How is your appetite?"
>
> "Abnormal," she says and devours him.
>
> This makes the consultant smile his glassy smile and he takes her hand in both of his as he gets up, gets up in such a way as to suggest it costs a great act of will not to tear the sick woman away with him. And then he goes. (*TK*:11)

Both doctors are very clearly inspired by Georg or Georges Canetti, whose physical attractiveness is mentioned by both his brother and sister-in-law in their letters to him. Veza even begins a letter to him "Dear Georges Kien"

(1946; *BG*:169). When Georges Kien treats a banker's wife who is desperate to get him into her bed, he meets the banker's deranged brother who lives sequestered as a gorilla with a submissive, scantily-clad "secretary." The banker-husband could return at any minute like the Baron in "Hush Money" who arrives to rescue his errant wife. This confirms the pattern identified elsewhere regarding Veza's reactions to her husband's writing: in 1934 it is a corrective, in 1937 a homage.

The thematic and stylistic parallels continue into the first years of British exile with her trio of wartime stories. Fifty years later, writing in the manuscripts that were posthumously published as *Party in the Blitz* he is more charitable to their vegetarian, teetotalist hosts in Amersham and at greater pains to understand the British than she is in "Toogoods or the Light" because Mr. Milburn shared his passion for books. Veza's satire is withering. While they continue to eat well, their houseguests are given half-rotten vegetables cooked in nothing but water, a culinary failing that seems to offend the story's narrator nearly as much as the black worms she finds sharing her meal one day:

> The principle of this retired clergyman was that if the empire admits these god-forsaken people and if I even take them into my house, then these refugees are to show gratitude to me for England's generosity, and they to bring me as much benefit as possible (*DF*:197).

This lightly fictionalized story is the closest Veza comes to memoir and a rare example of her reacting more severely to circumstances than Canetti. His more gentle account is surely tempered by the passage of time, but his superior ability to adapt to his new surroundings is clear from both accounts.[22] The title episode from *Party in the Blitz* has its corollary in Veza's "Air Raid." Her old lady carries on reading her detective novel as if the bombs are not falling, just as his partygoers continue with their party, apparently oblivious to the danger tumbling from the skies. Both admired this peculiarly British phlegmatic reaction.

In November 1936 Canetti elaborated Veza's notion of the poet as the *Knecht* of his age. Knecht, the nom de plume she used to publish "Three Heroes and a Woman," is the male equivalent of Magd, which means servant, even vassal. He changes her meaning, because for him the poet is beholden to the times, that is, the historical epoch he lives in since he is obliged to confront them.[23] Veza's concerns are more localized and more immediately practical in "The Poet," where poetry is allied to justice and the practice of justice in education. The source of poetry is experience. "The Poet" shifts attention away from the poet's material, which was her focus in "Lost Property," to the person of the poet. The impecunious, fatherless Gustl is discovered as a young man to have poetic gifts and he returns to his hometown to write his life story. Unlike Tell, he has no need to look for material: he feeds off his own experiences that he counts on a stick by carving a notch each time something significant happens to him. A series of antitheses show the differences between Gustl and his contemporaries, including the apostrophized readers:

> The earliest memory we have is that the ceiling above us is made of green leaves, which lie as if on top of our eyes, because we are pushed in prams through parks and down avenues. But Gustl's first impressions were vertical. He was carried around on his mother's her arm, carted about one could almost say, like a sheaf of corn, and he saw colors, posts, brightness, and took such fright that his face soon was no more expressive than a baby monkey's. (*DF*:18)

Gustl plays in the dirt, which the landowner's children Jobst and Nelli are forbidden to do by their governess. They have toys but Gustl has none. Once at school, however, Gustl is praised above his classmates for the way he writes his letters. When he learns to read "it appeared to him as if he had only just come into the world. Everything before was in a haze. But a book is soon read and now began his hunger for new books. Gustl started to debase himself" (*DF*:20). He does this first by collecting tennis balls for Jobst who promises that he can borrow *Gulliver's Travels* in return. Nothing comes of the promise because his governess does not let him lend out his books.

At school Gustl continues to stand out. While the other boys like him, they think of themselves as better than him. Unlike Gustl, they all know what they want to do when they grow up. Another teacher spots his talent for creative writing and he eventually gets a job teaching, before studying in the capital. Afterwards he teaches at a state school and wins over his pupils "through the fanatical enthusiasm in his practice of justice" (*DF*:21). As a boy he suffered the injustice of poverty and the disdain of children who were better-off. Now that he is in a position of authority, he does not compensate for the slights he suffered. On the contrary, he practices justice so that others do not suffer the way he did. When his superiors recommend that he write down the secrets of his methods, they discover that he has the talent of a poet and they call on him to write his autobiography. His successful teaching was inspired by his experience, which is in turn the subject of his writing and is connected to his teaching: both are founded in his memory of imperfect social interaction as a child. When he returns to his hometown, he finds Jobst and Nelli have lost their family property and with one exception, his classmates have not fulfilled their ambitions. "They were all prematurely aged and desiccated" (*DF*:22). He feels no joy in their failure compared with his success in life. His return is a return to the community. Angelika Schedel is right to contrast the conclusion of Gustl's experiences with Käthi's in "The Difference."[24] Tell is another contrastive figure.

Baldur Pilz is the antithesis of another poet, Andreas Kain, whose temperament is no less noble than Gustl's. As a painter of hunting scenes, Pilz is the only artist in *The Tortoises*. His picture, which Felberbaum has been obliged to buy from him, shows a hunter bending over a stag that he has shot, a position of superiority and power that stresses his conquest over the animal. It is impossible to argue with Pilz because he is so ill-informed and badly educated. What he says is not true and does not make sense, but that does not matter to him. The poet is no match for the Nazi because the Nazi has "the fist," the synecdoche that denotes Pfaff in *Auto-da-Fé*. In a discussion with Werner, Andreas argues that thinkers have lost the battle because they are not in power and those in power "do not get as far as thought" (*SK*:226). Canetti echoes this sentiment: in *The Play of the Eyes* he remarks on National Socialism apropos of the circumstances under which he wrote *Comedy of Vanity* that "the paucity of its thought content, which served as its motor, stood in incomprehensible contrast to its effect" (*IX*:87).

Another area of shared interest was animals, whether as literary "characters" whose behavior contrasts with that of human beings, as sources of imagery and metaphor, or as fellow creatures subjected to human cruelty. In 2002 Hanser published an anthology of Canetti's scattered writings on animals, collecting examples from across his entire oeuvre, especially *Crowds and Power*. The anthology's editor promptly accepted another commission and became his biographer. According to Brigitte Kronauer in the afterword, Canetti explores the workings of power with reference to the relationships between animals and humans and questions the boundaries between species, especially human and non-human animal life.[25] Taking her cue from Kronauer, Dagmar Lorenz notes that in Veza's *Yellow Street* there are "numerous animal characters" and that in *The Tortoises* "sensitivity and concern for the most common animals set the persecuted Jews apart from the Nazis" and "the fate of the animals and that of Jews follow a parallel course under Nazism."[26] While this is true, she overstates Canetti's affinities with contemporary animal rights campaigners. He refers to animals to pose a series of questions rather than formulate a coherent set of views. Veza essentially does the same.

In *Yellow Street*, the only "animal character" is a dog called Grimm who looks after little Hedi Adenberger when she finds a wallet full of money. He is loyal to her because she encouraged him to eat after he had been abandoned by the heirs of his original owner. By sharing a bowl of porridge with him she created a bond between herself and the dog, whereas his new owners could only think how much feeding such a large creature would cost. It was the original owner's *maid*, Hedi's own mother, who took "the refined hound" home with her after the death of Grimm's owner, who was her employer. She was initially worried that he would find her home too modest and look down on her: "But then she noticed that it does not make any difference to a dog, which made her pleased" (*GS*:144). Unlike human beings dogs do not notice the *difference* that divides the social classes. Unlike the child, Hedi, and her working-class mother, the bourgeois inheritors of Grimm consider him as a piece of property and do not realize his value as a living creature. Hedi, however, could not have hung on to that wallet without Grimm.

Veza's "Herr Hoe at the Zoo" is a fable on the folly of expecting wolves, monkeys, and lions to behave better than human beings. It partly reprises the man-gorilla motif from Canetti's novel. He too did not necessarily intend his comments on animals to be taken literally, as Gerald Stieg discovered after serving him rabbit on a visit to his Paris home: both Canettis were happy to eat animals.[27] Herr Hoe becomes so "indignant over the wars which are now raging in the world" that for the first time in his life he raised his voice to the other regulars in the pub and shouted: "There are no predatory animals, only predatory human beings" (*DF*:33). Hoe's belief in the non-predatory nature of lions is as illusory as the belief in possibility of predicting the future proves to be in "Clairvoyants." "Herr Hoe at the Zoo" lays bare an illusion through reason and deduction. The wolf, whose cage Herr Hoe first shares, does not attack him because he just had his lunch and was not hungry. The lion leaves him because the keeper pushes in a large piece of meat just in time to distract him. The narrator also wonders if the smell of Herr Hoe's lavender soap does not help put him off. Unlike the clairvoyant, Herr Hoe is treated with respect, even though he is exposed. The story's narrator, like the crowd that gathers at the zoo to witness Herr Hoe's bravery, would like to believe that the world is in fact the way Hoe thinks. He is left triumphant and happily unenlightened at the end:

> The three cheers that greeted Herr Hoe sounded as if they were uttered by ten thousand sets of vocal chords. You should not think though that he has been arrogant since then. On the contrary, he blames himself for doubting the lion. And he blames me on account of my genuinely human interpretation with the lavender. (*DF*:37)

Thanks to an encoded half-chapter found among the drafts for *The Play of the Eyes*, Veza's "Herr Hoe at the Zoo" can be dated with some confidence to 1935. Canetti reveals Herr Hoe to be Veza's name for his Strasbourg benefactor Jean Hoepffner, whom he met in the early part of that year:

> I call him by the abbreviated name that Veza gave him in her fairy tales. You could not in fact write about him in any other way. It was not just the role that he played for us, an unexpected saviour, who brought a change in my life; it was his essential character, which Veza recognized much more clearly than I did since I had met him in Strasbourg where his profession had nothing whatsoever to do with fairy tales.[28]

This is the only time he refers with such precision to the subject of one of Veza's stories. His use of the first-person plural ("that he played for *us*,"

my emphasis) shows solidarity with her. The plural ("fairy tales" —
Märchengeschichten) suggests that other stories featuring Herr Hoe may
have been among the material she destroyed or left behind in Vienna. That
his own fictionalized, highly literary portrait of Hoepffner in *The Play of
the Eyes* is a variation on Veza's theme in "Herr Hoe at the Zoo" shows
either that he recalls her literary treatment from half a century ago or that
he refreshed his memory by rereading it, since "Herr Hoe at the Zoo" was
in his possession.

Hoepffner shared with Veza a reverence for Adalbert Stifter, whose
books he read each day, and with Canetti a passion for Stendhal, in particular for *The Charterhouse of Parma*, which he took to be the opposite of
everything written by Stifter. This makes Hoepffner in Canetti's account
an integrative, harmonizing figure for the Canettis, though he could not
transcend the contradiction between the French and the Austrian writers
in his own life. Hoepffner's love of Stifter was intimately entwined with his
character and view of the world:

> He could not abide modern stuff, where everything was shown to be dark
> and hopeless, where there was not a single good person. That simply was
> not right, he had some experience in life, he had met many people in his
> job, he never encountered a single bad person among them, there were
> only good people. You just had to see them as they are and not impute
> any false opinions to them. (*IX*:172–73)

Veza's own love of Stifter is shown in her depiction of the innate innocence
of children; it was so profound that Canetti avoids mentioning him in his
autobiography, as he avoided reading Stifter himself for many years after
meeting Veza. What Canetti writes of Hoepffner and the great nineteenth-
century exponent of "the gentle law" could equally apply to Veza, however.
When it comes to what links Stendhal and his own work, he does not leave
his readers to make their own deductions. Hoepffner reads *The Charterhouse
of Parma* because it shows "how the world would look if there were bad
people. One needed this experience but only as an illusion." In Hoepffner's
view, Stendhal's novel should serve humanity as a deterrence. After hearing
about Canetti's own novel, Hoepffner asserts that he will never read it himself (though he did read and praise Veza's stories). Other people should have
the opportunity to read it, however, for the same reason that they should
read Stendhal: "It would have a good effect. The people who read it would
wake up as if from a nightmare and be thankful that reality is different, not
like this dream" (*IX*:173). This is why Hoepffner offers to underwrite it.

In *The Tortoises* it is not, as Lorenz says, "the persecuted Jews" in general who are concerned for animals, but in particular Andreas Kain. The
numerous references to animals in the novel are not all positive: Frau Pilz,
who is inclined to show friendliness to Eva, is said to become like "an obe-
dient dog" (*SK*:116) when her husband reprimands her. When Eva speaks

of "the laws against dogs and Jews," Hilde corrects her: "You mean the laws in favour of dogs and against Jews" (*SK*:68). In another passage the Jews are below dogs in the new hierarchy, which only the goodnatured Felberbaum has not apprehended: "His face assumed an expression of even greater contentment and whoever saw it could not have imagined that he found himself in a city in which those like him counted for less than dogs" (*SK*:155). In contrast Odysseus's dog is more faithful than the returning king's subjects when at the end of his long life he recognizes his long-absent master and promptly expires. Like the people of Ithaca at the end of *The Odyssey* when confronted with their disguised King, the people of Vienna no longer recognize their Jewish acquaintances. But unlike Odysseus they have not left their homes or put on a disguise (*SK*:123).

Andreas Kain rescues a basketful of tortoises from a Nazi who was etching swastikas on to their shells. When he offers to buy all the drinkers in the winery a glass of wine if they take home one of the animals, the owner accepts them all and from then on they roam freely in his garden. Kain also helps a local farmer buy his cow so that the local children will have a supply of milk. Pilz, in contrast, wants the cow to be killed because the tenant made it ill and it no longer gives enough milk. Pilz first kills a sparrow because it eats the cherries in the garden and then the landlady's elderly dog because they are — in his misunderstood Darwinist terms — burdens on the rest of the community: "a poorly sparrow is like a cripple. A parasite. A parasite is the same as a sponger" (*SK*:46). He carries out both killings as demonstrations of this morality to a group of children. What applies to sparrows and dogs applies to all living creatures: "If you die easily, you belong where you have just gone so easily yourself. If you die you do not deserve to live. That's how you cleanse the world" (*SK*:58). In the First World War, Pilz treated human beings with the same lack of respect and shot Russian prisoners of war because there was not enough food for them:

> War is war and in peace time the brave hunter steals up on his prey. I once painted a picture of a stag which had been shot by a hunter. What plea-sure that is. The hunter bends over the noble beast as if he is intoxicated. The hunt is beautiful. (*SK*:50)

In contrast, Felberbaum's description of the painting that he bought from Pilz and hangs on the wall of Werner's kitchen concentrates on the "bleed-ing deer" (*SK*:154). Pilz is the predator, Felberbaum the prey. Their dif-ferent perspectives are determined by their respective roles. Suddenly, Veza's novel lands on the thematic territory of Canetti's *Crowds and Power*.

The Tortoises anticipates Canetti's next big book in numerous ways just as it reacts to *Auto-da-Fé*. In pursuit of the Jews the Nazis are described as "a pack of hungry hyenas" (*SK*:205). When the news comes that Andreas,

Eva, and Felberbaum do not have to leave Werner's flat as they had originally been told, it is said that the hyenas have temporarily spared them
because other victims have sated their lust for blood: "Quiet can now be
expected, the storm has abated, and the hyena too is tired, the pack has got
its victim, and before they can digest it, we will depart" (*SK*:197). There
are frequent references to the hunt: Pilz calls the persecution of Jews on
Kristallnacht a "rabbit hunt" (*SK*:252); the narrator comments on Kain's
perilous walk through the city: "We are in the twentieth century and are
experiencing a peculiar hunt. The hunt practiced by the head hunters
among the savages? No, we are among Germans" (*SK*:40–41). Canetti
makes similar comparisons across the centuries and between civilization
and the "native peoples" from remote parts of the world in order to show
the barbarism of modern man. Andreas Kain tells Werner: "I have come
from the shoot. They have hunted me, hounded me, I have saved myself
by coming up here and I am still being hounded" (*SK*:44). Canetti distinguishes between numerous types of hunting "pack" and the variety of ways
they have of sharing their prey, but in the sections on "packs" and hunting he concentrates on tribal practices and historical examples. The references in Veza's novel make plain that the original hunt took place on the
streets of modern Europe.

The hunt is related to the topic of Jewish identity, which the Canettis
explore through the contrasting figures of Fischerle and Felberbaum.
Veza's benevolent character, who naively attempts to observe Jewish feasts
and rituals as his persecutors line up against him, seems designed to contradict each of the stereotypes that Fischerle embodies. Where Fischerle is
rational and quick witted, Felberbaum's intelligence borders on the
simpleminded; while Fischerle is incurably suspicious of others and out for
what he can get for himself, Felberbaum believes the best of everyone, is
hopelessly optimistic, and instinctively shows hospitality to others and
solidarity with his persecuted fellows. Fischerle wants riches, Felberbaum is
content with little and has never made more than a modest living. All they
have in common is the goal of emigrating: Fischerle is murdered by the
"blind" man as he returns to his lodging for the last time before heading
for the boat that is to take him to America; Felberbaum is waiting for the
visa to allow him to join his wife in Manchester, where she has found work
as a maid.

While Canetti challenges anti-Semitism through Fischerle by showing
how ridiculous the caricatures appear when concentrated on one figure,
Veza attacks the propaganda by attaching the generalized accusations
against the Jews to individuals. Neither Andreas Kain nor the Kains' vivacious young neighbor Hilde fit the Nazi description of Jewish physical features. Felberbaum fought in the war, as did his friend who lost "half his
head" defending Austria. Twenty years later on Kristallnacht this former
soldier is made to pay for the use of the brush and paint when he writes

Jud (Jew) on his property at the insistence of the mob. Veza's account of the brutality is all the more forceful for its narration from Felberbaum's well-meaning and naive perspective: he reports what he sees without offering any explanation; he has none. The answers would be worked out over the next two decades in *Crowds and Power*.

The "case of Veza Magd" and her relationship with her more famous, more determined, and perhaps more gifted husband confused literary critics, who made a series of assumptions that turned out to be wrong. Feminists initially assumed that there could only be one model of a literary marriage in which the more powerful husband crushed and exploited his subservient wife. Traditionalists were inclined to dismiss her writing and to conclude that she had only been published because she shared his name. Others, who had all come to write on Veza after publishing first on Canetti, assumed that the literary traffic went in one direction, that there was only one sort of collaboration: her reactions to him. This gave Veza more credit but not her just deserts. I hope to have shown in this book that their literary relationship was dynamic and that influence was mutual because each inhabited the imagination of the other.

Canetti had other literary partnerships, whereas Veza had no others on her own account. He worked not only with mistresses and girlfriends but with male literary friends, such as Franz Baermann Steiner, Rudi Nassauer and Erich Fried, as well as Ernst Fischer, who all helped substantially with *Crowds and Power*. None of these contributed to Canetti's first three Viennese works and none are major characters in the autobiography. Veza worked with him from the start and nearly all her writing relates to his in some way. She often reacted to him and his thought critically, which in turn adds to an understanding of his achievement, and she remained a presence in his imagination until his death thirty-one years after her own. Two years before he died he wrote to Armin Ayren on his effort to compensate for Veza's inability to witness the world's rediscovery of her work. He said that he would tell himself "that Veza is inside me and so she has heard about it after all. Even though I see through the degree of this self-deception completely, it does me good. What I would give for it to do her good too!"[29]

Notes

[1] Göbel, "Bemerkungen zum verdeckten Judentum"; Eva Meidl, "Die gelbe Straße, Parallelstraße zur 'Ehrlichstraße'? — Außenseiter in Veza Canettis Roman *Die gelbe Straße* und Elias Canettis Roman *Die Blendung*," *Modern Austrian Literature* 28:2 (1995), 31–51.

[2] Ritchie Robertson, "Häusliche Gewalt in der Wiener Moderne. Zu Veza Canettis Erzählung 'Der Oger'" *Text und Kritik* 156 (Veza Canetti issue) (2002), 48–64.

[3] Hanuschek, *Elias Canetti*, 307.

[4] H. G. Adler, "Brief über Oger," in Spörk and Strohmaier, *Veza Canetti*, 214.

[5] Stieg, "Antwort auf Anna Mitgutsch," 39.

[6] Quoted by Hanuschek, *Elias Canetti*, 484.

[7] Adler, "Brief über Oger," in Spörk and Strohmaier, *Veza Canetti*, 212.

[8] Mitgutsch, "Veza Canetti," 99.

[9] "Heirat (späte Heirat)," ZB 60.

[10] Franziska Schößler, "Masse, Musik und Narzissismus: Zu den Dramen von Elias und Veza Canetti," *Text und Kritik* 28 (Elias Canetti issue)(2005), 76–91; here: 79.

[11] Hackermüller, "Begegnungen mit Elias Canettis Wirklichkeit."

[12] "Heirat (späte Heirat)," ZB 60.

[13] Peter France, *Politeness and its Discontents: Problems in French Classical Culture* (Cambridge: Cambridge UP, 1992), 27–39 ("Ogres"); here: 39.

[14] Mererid Puw Davies, *The Tale of Bluebeard in German Literature: From the Eighteenth Century to the Present* (Oxford: Oxford UP, 2001), 67.

[15] Fischer, *An Opposing Man*, 237.

[16] Kröger makes this suggestion, "Themenaffinitäten zwischen Veza und Elias Canetti," 287.

[17] Hanuschek, *Elias Canetti*, 304–5.

[18] "Allgemeines: Bedenken. Veza. Das System," ZB 60.

[19] Barbara Weidle, "Ich bin in mir selbst zu Hause," in Weidle and Seeber *Anna Mahler*, 47–71; here: 61.

[20] Stefanie Wieprecht-Roth, *"Die Freiheit in der Zeit ist die Überwindung des Todes": Überleben in der Welt und im unsterblichen Werk. Eine Annäherung an Elias Canetti* (Würzburg: Königshausen & Neumann, 2004), 61–62.

[21] Raine, *The Lion's Mouth*, 55.

[22] Dagmar C. G. Lorenz, "The Millburns and the Toogoods: Veza and Elias Canetti's Experience of Exile," in Donahue and Preece *The Worlds of Elias Canetti* (forthcoming).

[23] Elias Canetti, "Hermann Broch. Rede zum 50. Geburtstag. Wien, November 1936," *Das Gewissen der Worte. Essays* (Frankfurt am Main: Fischer, 1981), 10–24; esp.: 12–13.

[24] For a more complete reading of "The Poet," see Schedel, *Sozialismus und Psychoanalyse*, 73–83.

[25] Brigitte Kronauer, "Tierlos," in Elias Canetti, *Über Tiere* (Munich: Hanser, 2002), 107–15.

[26] Dagmar C. G. Lorenz, "Canetti's Final Frontier: The Animal," in Lorenz, *A Companion to the Works of Elias Canetti*, 239–57; here: 252.

[27] Hanuschek, *Elias Canetti*, 574.

[28] "Herr Hoe," 4 April 1983, ZB 60.

[29] Ayren, "Vom Toten und vom Tod," 151.

Works Cited

Primary Sources

Veza and Elias Canetti

Brief an Georges. Edited by Karen Lauer and Kristian Wachinger. Munich: Hanser, 2006.

Veza Canetti

Introduction to *Welt im Kopf.* Vienna: Stiasny, 1962.

Die gelbe Strasse. Munich: Hanser, 1990.

Der Oger. Munich: Hanser, 1991.

Geduld bringt Rosen. Munich: Hanser, 1992.

Die Schildkröten. Munich: Hanser, 1999.

Der Fund. Munich: Hanser, 2001.

"Schweigegeld" and "Geld — Geld — Geld." In *Text und Kritik* 156 (Veza Canetti issue; 2002): 11–27.

Elias Canetti

Werke, vols. I–X. Munich: Hanser, 1992–2005.

Individual texts with date of first publication

Hochzeit. 1932.

Die Blendung. Written 1930–31, published 1935.

Komödie der Eitelkeit. Written 1933–34, published 1950.

Die Befristeten. Written 1952, published 1964.

Masse und Macht. 1960.

Aufzeichnungen 1942–1948. 1965.

Der andere Prozess: Kafkas Briefe an Felice. 1969.

Alle vergeudete Verehrung. Aufzeichnungen 1949–1960. 1970.

Die Provinz des Menschen. Aufzeichnungen 1942–1972. 1973.

Die gerettete Zunge: Geschichte einer Jugend. 1977.

Die Fackel im Ohr: Lebensgeschichte 1921–1931. 1980.

Das Augenspiel: Lebensgeschichte 1931–1937. 1985.

Das Geheimherz der Uhr: Aufzeichnungen 1973–1985. 1987.

Separate volumes

Aufzeichnungen 1992–1993. Frankfurt am Main: Fischer, 1996.

Party im Blitz: Die englischen Jahre. Munich: Hanser, 2003.

Aufzeichnungen für Marie-Louise. Munich: Hanser, 2005.

Other Authors

Abse, Dannie. *Goodbye, Twentieth Century: An Autobiography.* London: Pimlico, 2001.

Adler, H. G. *Eine Reise: Erzählung.* Bonn: bibliotheca christina, 1962.

Bachmann, Ingeborg. *Malina.* Frankfurt am Main: Suhrkamp, 1971.

Bayley, John. *Elegy for Iris.* New York: Picador, 1999. British title: *Iris: A Memoir of Iris Murdoch.*

Brod, Max. *Ein tschechisches Dienstmädchen: Kleiner Roman.* Berlin: Juncker, 1909.

Dickens, Charles. *Oliver Twist.* Edited by Kathleen Tillotson. Oxford: Oxford UP, 1999.

Fischer, Ernst. *An Opposing Man.* Translated by Peter and Betty Ross. London: Allen Lane, 1974.

Fleisser, Marieluise. "Stunde der Magd." In *Erzählungen,* edited by Günther Rühle, 37–42. Frankfurt am Main: Suhrkamp, 2001.

Fried, Erich. *Ein Soldat und ein Mädchen: Roman.* Hamburg: Claasen, 1960.

Gordon, Ibby. "Pamela!" *Die literarische Welt,* 28 September 1928.

Gorki, Max. *Erinnerungen an Lew Nikolajawitsch Tolstoi.* Munich: Der neue Merkur, 1920.

———. *Erinnerungen an Zeitgenossen.* Berlin: Malik, 1928.

Honigmann, Barbara. *Ein Kapitel aus meinem Leben.* Vienna: Hanser, 2004.

Jacob, Heinrich Eduard. *Die Magd von Aachen: Eine von siebentausend.* Vienna: Zsolnay, 1931.

von Mayenburg, Ruth. *Blaues Blut und rote Fahnen: Revolutionäres Frauenleben zwischen Wien, Berlin und Moskau.* Vienna: Promedia, 1993.

Murdoch, Iris. *The Flight from the Enchanter.* London: Chatto and Windus, 1956.

———. *A Severed Head.* London: Chatto and Windus, 1961.

———. *A Fairly Honourable Defeat.* London: Chatto and Windus, 1970.

———. *The Black Prince.* London: Chatto and Windus, 1973.

———. *The Sea, the Sea.* London: Chatto and Windus, 1978.

Nassauer, Rudolf. *The Hooligan.* London: Peter Owen, 1960.

———. *The Cuckoo.* London: Peter Owen, 1962.

Raine, Kathleen. *The Lion's Mouth: Concluding Chapters of Autobiography.* London: Hamish Hamilton, 1977.

Reichart, Elisabeth. *Februarschatten*. Salzburg: Müller, 1985.

Rubens, Bernice. *Set on Edge* London: Eyre & Spottiswoode, 1960.

———. *When I Grow Up: A Memoir*. London: Little Brown, 2005.

Schäfer, Walter Erich. *Schwarzmann und die Magd*. Stuttgart: Engelhorns, 1932.

Schnitzler, Arthur. *Therese: Chronik eines Frauenlebens*. Berlin: Fischer, 1928.

Sealsfield, Charles. *Austria as It Is: Or Sketches of Continental Courts/ Österreich, wie es ist, oder Skizzen von Fürstenhöfen des Kontinents*. Translated and edited by Victor Klarwill. Hildesheim/New York: Olms, 1972.

Sebastian, Anna [Benedikt, Friedl]. "Das armselige Werk einer vernarrten und faulen Schülerin," 1942–44, ZB 217.

———. *Let thy Moon Arise*. London: Cape, 1944.

———. *The Monster*. London: Cape, 1944.

———. *The Dreams*. London: Cape, 1950.

Sinclair, Upton. *Money Writes!* New York: Albert and Charles Boni, 1927.

Werfel, Franz. *Der veruntreute Himmel: Die Geschichte einer Magd*. Stockholm: Bermann-Fischer, 1939.

Wiechert, Ernst. *Die Magd des Jürgen Doskocil*. Munich: Albert Langen/Georg Müller, 1932.

Secondary Sources

Aaronavitch, David. "The Iris Troubles." *The Observer*, 7 September 2003.

Adler, H. G. "Brief an Veza Canetti v. 5.6.1950." In Spörk and Strohmaier, *Veza Canetti*.

Adler, Jeremy. "J. as in Jew." 28 February 2003, *Times Literary Supplement*.

———. "Nachwort." In *Party im Blitz*, by Elias Canetti, 211–28. Munich/ Vienna: Hanser, 2003.

———. "Introduction." In *Party in the Blitz: The English Years*, by Elias Canetti, 1–41. Translated by Michael Hofmann. London: Harvill, 2005.

———. "Nachwort." *Aufzeichnungen für Marie-Louise*, by Elias Canetti, 67–113. Munich: Hanser, 2005.

Alt, Peter André. *Franz Kafka: Der ewige Sohn. Ein Biographie*. Munich: Beck, 2005.

Angelova, Penka, and Emilia Staitschev, eds. *Autobiographie zwischen Fiktion und Wirklichkeit, Schriftenreihe der Elias Canetti Gesellschaft*. Vol. 1. St. Ingbert: Röhrig, 1997.

Atze, Marcel, ed. *"Ortlose Botschaft": Der Freundeskreis HG Adler, Elias Canetti und Franz Baermann Steiner im englischen Exil*. Stuttgart: Marbach, 1998.

Ayren, Armin. "Vom Toten und vom Tod. Erinnerung an Elias Canetti." *Allmende* 46/47 (1995): 146–57.

Bayley, John. "Canetti and Power." In *Essays in Honour of Elias Canetti*, translated by Michael Hulse, 129–45. London: André Deutsch, 1987.

Beckermann, Ruth. *Die Mazzeinsel: Juden in der Wiener Leopoldstadt 1918–1938*. Vienna: Löcker, 1984.

Bering, Dietz. *The Stigma of Names: Antisemitism in German Daily Life, 1812–1933*. Translated by Neville Plaice. Ann Arbor: U of Michigan P, 1995.

Blaukopf, Herta. "Das überlebensgroße Bild des Vaters. Erinnerungen an Anna Mahler." In Weidle and Seeber, *Anna Mahler*, 144–52.

Botz, Gerhard. *Nationalsozialismus in Wien: Machtübernahme und Herrschaftssicherung 1938/39*. Buchloe: dvo, 1988.

Breitenstein, Andreas. "Nationalismus für Anfänger." *Neue Zürcher Zeitung*, 8/9 May 1999.

Brook-Shepherd, Gordon. *The Austrians: A Thousand-Year Odyssey*. London: HarperCollins, 1996.

Carsten, F. L. *The First Austrian Republic 1918–1938: A Study Based on British and Austrian Documents*. Aldershot: Gower, 1986.

Conradi, Peter J. *Iris Murdoch: A Life*. London: HarperCollins, 2001.

Czurda, Elfriede. "Veza Canetti: Ein ferner Stern, unleserlich." In *Buchstäblich: Unmenschen*. Graz: Droschl, 1995, 112–35, esp. 122. First published as "Veza Canetti — Dichtung und Wahrheit." *manuskripte* 117 (1992): 114–20.

Davies, Mererid Puw. *The Tale of Bluebeard in German Literature: From the Eighteenth Century to the Present*. Oxford: Oxford UP, 2001.

Donahue, William Collins. *The End of Modernism: Elias Canetti's Auto-da-Fé*. Chapel Hill: U of North Carolina P, 2001.

Donahue, William Collins, and Julian Preece, eds. *The Worlds of Elias Canetti: Centenary Essays*. Newcastle: Cambridge Scholars Publishing, Forthcoming.

Eigler, Frederike. *Das autobiographische Werk Elias Canettis: Verwandlung, Identität, Machtausübung*. Tübingen: Stauffenberg, 1988.

Engelmeyer, Elfriede. "'Denn der Mensch schreitet aufrecht, die erhabenen Zeichen der Seele ins Gesicht gebrannt.' Zu Veza Canettis *Die Gelbe Straße*." *Mit der Ziehharmonika: Zeitschrift für Literatur des Exils und Widerstands* 11:2 (1994): 25–33.

Fischer, Ernst. "Bemerkungen zu Elias Canettis *Masse und Macht*." *Literatur und Kritik* 7 (1966): 12–20.

Foell, Kristie A. *Blind Reflections: Gender in Elias Canetti's Die Blendung*. Riverside, CA: Ariadne, 1994.

France, Peter. *Politeness and its Discontents: Problems in French Classical Culture*. Cambridge: Cambridge UP, 1992.

Fuchs, Anne. "'The Deeper Nature of My German': Mother Tongue, Subjectivity, and the Voice of the Other in Elias Canetti's Autobiography." In *A Companion to the Works of Elias Canetti*, edited by Dagmar C. G. Lorenz, 45–60.

Göbel, Helmut. "Bemerkungen zum verdeckten Judentum in Veza Canettis *Die gelbe Straße*." In *"Ein Dichter braucht Ahnen": Elias Canetti und die europäische Tradition*, edited by Gerald Stieg. Akten des Pariser Symposiums, 16–18.11.1995. Bern: Lang, 1997.

———. "Zur Wiederentdeckung Veza Canettis als Schriftstellerin. Einige persönliche Bemerkungen." *Text und Kritik* 156 (Veza Canetti issue) (2002): 3–10.

———. "Nachwort." In *Die gelbe Straße*, by Veza Canetti, 169–81. Munich: Hanser, 1990.

Goebel, Rolf J. *Constructing China: Kafka's Orientalist Discourse*. Columbia, SC: Camden House, 1997.

Hackermüller, Rotraut. "Begegnungen mit Elias Canettis Wirklichkeit. Eine Spurensuche in Wien." In Angelova and Staitschev, *Autobiographie zwischen Fiktion und Wirklichkeit*, 141–52.

Hanuschek, Sven. *Elias Canetti: Eine Biographie*. Vienna/Munich: Hanser, 2005.

———. " 'Alle grossen Beziehungen sind mir ein Rätsel.' Paarverweigerungsstrategien bei Elias Canetti." *Text und Kritk* 28 (Elias Canetti issue) (2005): 110–17.

Hermann, Frank. *Der Malik-Verlag, 1916–1947: Eine Bibliographie*. Kiel: Neuer Malik, 1989.

Hertling, Viktoria. "Theater für 49: Ein vergessenes Avantgarde-Theater in Wien (1934–1938)." In *Jura Soyfer and his Time*, edited by Donald Daviau, 321–35. Riverside, CA: Ariadne, 1995.

Herzfelde, Wieland, ed. *Dreissig neue Erzähler des neuen Deutschland: Junge deutsche Prosa*. Berlin: Malik, 1932. New edition with an introduction by Bärbel Schrader. Leipzig: Reclam, 1983.

Hochhuth, Rolf. "Nur ein bißchen tot." *Die Welt*, 5 June 1992. Reprinted in Spörk and Strohmaier, *Veza Canetti*, 164–66.

Holmes, Deborah. "Elias Canetti and Red Vienna." In Donahue and Preece, *The Worlds of Elias Canetti*. (forthcoming).

Holz, Detlef [Walter Benjamin]. *Deutsche Menschen*. Lucerne: Vita Nova, 1936.

Isaacs, Jack. *An Assessment of Twentieth-Century Literature: Six Lectures Delivered in the BBC Third Programme*. London: Secker & Warburg, 1951.

Jarka, Horst. *Jura Soyfer. Leben, Werk, Zeit*. Mit einem Vorwort von Hans Weigel. Vienna: Löcker, 1987, 19–23.

Jelavich, Barbara. *Modern Austria: Empire and Republic 1815–1986*. Cambridge: Cambridge UP, 1987.

Jost, Vera. *Fliegen und Fallen: Prostitution als Thema in Literatur von Frauen im 20. Jahrhundert*. Frankfurt am Main: Helmer, 2002.

Jungk, Peter Stephan. *A Life Torn by History: Franz Werfel 1890–1945*. Translated by Anselm Hollo. London: Weidenfeld & Nicolson, 1990.

Jungk, Peter Stephan. "Fragmente, Momente, Minuten. Ein Besuch bei Elias Canetti." *Neue Rundschau* 106:1 (1995): 95–104.

———. "Elias Canetti und Ernst Fischer." *Neue Rundschau* 106:3 (1995): 154–55.

Kebir, Sabine. *Ein akzeptabler Mann? Brecht und die Frauen.* Berlin: Aufbau, 1998.

Korino, Karl. *Robert Musil: Eine Biographie.* Reinbek bei Hamburg: Rowohlt, 2003.

Kosenina, Alexander. "Veza Canetti, *Die Gelbe Straße* (1932–1933/1990)." *Meisterwerke: Deutschsprachige Autorinnen im 20. Jahrhundert,* 52–71. Cologne: Böhlau, 2005.

Kracauer, Siegfried. *Von Caligari zu Hitler: Eine psychologische Geschichte des deutschen Films.* Frankfurt am Main: Suhrkamp, 1984.

Kröger, Marianne. "Themenaffinitäten zwischen Veza und Elias Canetti in den 30er Jahren und im Exil. Eine Spurensuche in den Romanen *Die Schildkröten* von Veza Canetti und *Die Blendung* von Elias Canetti." In *Das literarische Paar: Intertextualität der Geschlechterdiskurse,* edited by Gislinde Seybert, 279–308. Bielefeld: Aisthesis, 2003.

Kronauer, Brigitte. Afterword "Tierlos." In Elias Canetti, *Über Tiere,* 107–15. Munich: Hanser, 2002.

Krützen, Michaela. *Hans Albers: Eine deutsche Karriere.* Berlin: Quadriga, 1995.

Lorenz, Dagmar C. G. *Keepers of the Motherland: German Texts by Jewish Women Writers.* Lincoln, NE: U of Nebraska P, 1997.

———, ed. *A Companion to the Works of Elias Canetti.* Rochester, NY: Camden House, 2004.

———. "Canetti's Final Frontier: The Animal." In Lorenz, *A Companion to the Works of Elias Canetti,* 239–57.

———. "The Millburns and the Toogoods: Veza and Elias Canetti's Experience of Exile." In Donahue and Preece, *The Worlds of Elias Canetti.* (forthcoming).

Marko, Gerda. *Schreibende Paare: Liebe, Freundschaft, Konkurrenz.* Zurich: Artemis and Winkler, 1995.

März, Eduard. *Wiener Zeitung,* 23 January 1987.

Meidl, Eva. "Die gelbe Straße, Parallelstraße zur 'Ehrlichstraße'? — Außenseiter in Veza Canettis Roman *Die gelbe Straße* und Elias Canettis Roman *Die Blendung.*" *Modern Austrian Literature* 28:2 (1995): 31–51.

———. *Veza Canettis Sozialkritik in der revolutionären Nachkriegszeit: Sozialkritische, feministische und postkoloniale Aspekte in ihrem Werk.* Frankfurt am Main: Lang, 1998.

———. "Veza Canettis Manifest: Die Kurzgeschichte *Geld Geld Geld.*" In Spörk and Strohmaier, *Veza Canetti,* 57–73.

Meili, Barbara. *Erinnerung und Vision: Der lebensgeschichtliche Hintergrund von Elias Canettis Roman Die Blendung.* Bonn: Bouvier, 1985.

Melzer, Gerhard. "Der einzige Satz und sein Eigentümer. Versuch über den symbolischen Machthaber Elias Canetti." In *Die verschwiegenen Engel: Aufsätze zur österreichischen Literatur*, 83–100. Graz: Droschl, 1998.

Mitgutsch, Anna. "Veza Canetti (1897–1963)." *Literatur und Kritik* 335/336 (1999): 99–109.

Mulot, Sibylle. "Das Leben vor der Haustür. Nach mehr als einem halben Jahrhundert erschienen: der unbekannte Roman einer unbekannten Dichterin — *Die gelbe Straße* der Veza Canetti." *Die Zeit*, 6 April 1990.

———. "Leben mit dem Monster." *Facts* 5 (1999): 122–25.

———. "Befreundet mit den Geliebten." *Der Spiegel*, 22 December 2001, 190–92.

Neuhaus, Stefan. *Das verschwiegene Werk: Erich Kästners Mitarbeit an Theaterstücken unter Pseudonym*. Würzburg: Königshausen & Neumann, 2000.

Pauley, Bruce F. "Political Antisemitism in Interwar Vienna." In *Jews, Antisemitism and Culture in Vienna*, edited by Ivar Oxaal, Michael Pollak, and Gerhard Botz, 152–73. London/New York: Routledge and Kegan Paul, 1987.

Pfoser, Alfred. *Literatur und Austromarxismus*. Vienna: Löcker, 1980.

Praesent, Angela. *Die Zeit*, 17 April 1992.

Robertson, Ritchie. *The "Jewish Question" in German Literature 1749–1939: Emancipation and its Discontents*. Oxford: Oxford UP, 1999.

———. "Häusliche Gewalt in der Wiener Moderne. Zu Veza Canettis Erzählung 'Der Oger.'" *Text und Kritik* 156 (Veza Canetti issue) (2002): 48–64.

Rotschild, Thomas. "Offener Brief an Peter Stephan Jungk." *Neue Rundschau* 106:2 (1995): 177–79.

Schaber, Suzanne. "Wer ist Veza Magd?" *Die Presse*, 10 April 1999. Reprinted in Spörk and Strohmaier, *Veza Canetti*, 171–75.

Schedel, Angelika. *Sozialismus und Psychoanalyse: Quellen von Veza Canettis literarischen Utopien*. Würzburg: Königshausen & Neumann, 2002.

———. "Vita Veza Canetti." *Text und Kritik* 156 (Veza Canetti issue) (2002): 95–104.

Schlenker, Ines. "'So grüss ich vom Herzen meinen Hofmaler Mulo und küss ihn auf die Palette': Die Freundschaft zwischen Elias Canetti und Marie-Louise Motesiczky." *Text und Kritik* 28 (Elias Canetti issue) (2005): 126–39.

———. "Painting Authors: The Portraits of Elias Canetti, Iris Murdoch, and Franz Baermann Steiner by Marie-Louise von Motescizky." In *Franz Baermann Steiner Celebrated*, edited by Jeremy Adler, Richard Fardon, and Carol Tully, 105–21. London: Institute of Germanic Studies, 2003.

Schößler, Franziska. "Masse, Musik und Narzissismus: Zu den Dramen von Elias und Veza Canetti." *Text und Kritik* 28 (Elias Canetti issue) (2005): 76–91.

Scholz, Hannelore. "'Keine Angst geht verloren, aber ihre Verstecke sind rätselhaft.' Frauen im autobiographischen Wahrnehmungsspektrum von Elias Canetti." In Angelova and Staitschev, *Autobiographie zwischen Fiktion und Wirklichkeit*, 249–68.

Seybert, Gislinde, ed. *Das literarische Paar: Intertextualität der Geschlechterdiskurse: Intertextualität der Geschlechterdiskurse.* Bielefeld: Aisthesis, 2003.

Spiel, Hilde (interview with Robert Scheding). *Gegenwart* 23 (1994): 15–16.

Spörk, Ingrid. "'Ich sammelte Ketten. Ich bekam Ketten. Sie sind mir geblieben . . .' Zu Liebe und Ehe im Werk Veza Canettis." In Spörk and Strohmaier, *Veza Canetti*, 91–120.

Spörk, Ingrid, and Alexandra Strohmaier, eds. *Veza Canetti.* Graz/Vienna: Droschl, 2005.

Stach, Rainer. *Kafka: Die Jahre der Entscheidungen.* Frankfurt am Main: Fischer, 2002.

Steiner, George. "A Note on Günter Grass" (1964). *Language and Silence: Essays 1958–1966.* London: Faber and Faber, 1967.

Stephan, Inge. *Das Schicksal der begabten Frau im Schatten berühmter Männer.* Stuttgart: Kreuz, 1989.

Stieg, Gerald. "Kain und Eva: Eine Replik auf Anna Mitgutsch." *Literatur und Kritik* 339/340 (1999): 36–40.

Theweleit, Klaus. *Buch der Könige: Orpheus und Eurydike.* Basel/Frankfurt am Main: Stroemfeld/Roter Stern, 1988.

Timms, Edward. *Karl Kraus: Apocalyptic Satirist: The Post-War Crisis and the Rise of the Swastika.* New Have: Yale UP, 2005.

Walser, Karin. *Dienstmädchen, Frauenarbeit und Weiblichkeitsbilder um 1900.* Frankfurt am Main: Neue Kritik, 1986.

Warren, John. "Austrian Theatre and the Corporate State." In *Austria in the Thirties: Culture and Politics,* edited by John Warren and Kenneth Segar, 267–91. Riverside, CA: Ariadne, 1991.

Weber, Therese, ed. *Mägde: Lebenserinnerungen an die Dienstbotenzeit bei Bauern.* Vienna: Böhlau, 1985.

Weidle, Barbara. "Ich bin in mir selbst zu Hause." In Weidle and Seeber, *Anna Mahler,* 47–71.

Weidle, Barbara, and Ursula Seeber, eds. *Anna Mahler: Ich bin in mir selbst zu Hause.* Bonn: Weidle, 2004.

Weinzierl, Ulrich. "Ins Gesicht gebrannt: Späte Gerechtigkeit für Veza Canetti." *Frankfurter Allgemeine Zeitung,* 1 June 1990. Reprinted in Spörk and Strohmaier, *Veza Canetti,* 159–60.

Wieprecht-Roth, Stefanie. *"Die Freiheit in der Zeit ist die Überwindung des Todes": Überleben in der Welt und im unsterblichen Werk. Eine Annäherung an Elias Canetti.* Würzburg: Königshausen & Neumann, 2004.

Wierling, Dorothee. *Mädchen für alles: Arbeitsalltag und Lebensgeschichte städtischer Dienstmädchen um die Jahrhundertwende.* Berlin: Dietz, 1987.

Wilson, A. N. *Iris Murdoch as I Knew Her.* London: Hutchinson, 2003.

Winkler, Willi. "Die Kraft und ihre Herrlichkeit." *Süddeutsche Zeitung,* 17/18 April 1999.

Index